Progressive Business Plan for a Microbrewey

Microbrewery
Business Plan
_____ (date)

Business Name: _____

Plan Time Period: 2018 - 2020

Founding Directors:
Name: _____
Name: _____

Contact Information:
Owner: _____
Address: _____
City/State/Zip: _____
Phone: _____
Cell: _____
Fax: _____
Website: _____
Email: _____

Submitted to: _____
Date: _____
Contact Info: _____

This document contains confidential information. It is disclosed to you for informational purposes only. Its contents shall remain the property of _____ (business name) and shall be returned to _____ when requested. This is a business plan and does not imply an offering of securities.

NON-DISCLOSURE AGREEMENT

_____ (Company)., and _____ (Person Name), agrees:

_____ (Company) Corp. may from time to time disclose to _____ (Person Name) certain confidential information or trade secrets generally regarding Business plan and financials of _____ (Company) corp.

_____ (Person Name) agrees that it shall not disclose the information so conveyed, unless in conformity with this agreement. _____ (Person Name) shall limit disclosure to the officers and employees of _____ (Person Name) with a reasonable "need to know" the information and shall protect the same from disclosure with reasonable diligence.

As to all information which _____ (Company) Corp. claims is confidential, _____ (Company) Corp. shall reduce the same to writing prior to disclosure and shall conspicuously mark the same as "confidential," "not to be disclosed" or with other clear indication of its status. If the information which _____ (Company) Corp. is disclosing is not in written form, for example, a machine or device, _____ (Company) Corp. shall be required prior to or at the same time that the disclosure is made to provide written notice of the secrecy claimed by _____ (Company) Corp. _____ (Person Name) agrees upon reasonable notice to return the confidential tangible material provided by it by _____ (Company) Corp. upon reasonable request.

The obligation of non-disclosure shall terminate when if any of the following occurs:
(a) The confidential information becomes known to the public without the fault of _____ (Person Name), or;
(b) The information is disclosed publicly by _____ (Company) Corp., or
(c) a period of 12 months passes from the disclosure, or;
(d) the information loses its status as confidential through no fault of _____ (Person Name).

In any event, the obligation of non-disclosure shall not apply to information which was known to _____ (Person Name) prior to the execution of this agreement.

Dated: _____

_____
_____ (Company) Corp.
_____(Person Name)

Business and Marketing Plan Instructions

1. If you want the digital file for this book, please send proof-of-purchase to probusconsult2@yahoo.com.

2. Complete the Executive Summary section, as your final step, after you have completed the entire plan.

3. Feel free to edit the plan and make it more relevant to your strategic goals, objectives and business vision.

4. We have provided all of the formulas needed to prepare the financial plan. Just plug in the numbers that are based on your particular situation. Excel spreadsheets for the financials are available on the microsoft.com website and www.simplebizplanning.com/forms.htm
    http://office.microsoft.com/en-us/templates/

5. Throughout the plan, we have provided prompts or suggestions as to what values to enter into blank spaces but use your best judgment and then delete the suggested values (?).

6. The plan also includes some separate worksheets for additional assistance in expanding some of the sections, if desired.

7. Additionally, some sections offer multiple choices and the word 'select' appears as a prompt to edit the contents of the plan.

8. Your feedback, referrals and business are always very much appreciated.

Thank you

Nat Chiaffarano, MBA
Progressive Business Consulting, Inc.
Pembroke Pines, FL 33027
ProBusConsult2@yahoo.com

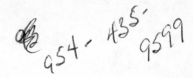 954- 435- 9599

4

Microbrewery Business Plan: Table of Contents

Section	Description	Page
1.0	**Executive Summary**	___
1.1.0	Tactical Objectives	___
1.1.1	Strategic Objectives	___
1.2	Mission Statement	___
1.2.1	Core Values Statement	___
1.3	Vision Statement	___
1.4	Keys to Success	___
2.0	**Company Summary**	___
2.1	Company Ownership	___
2.2	Company Licensing and Liability Protection	___
2.3	Start-up To-do Checklist	___
2.4.0	Company Location	___
2.4.1	Company Facilities	___
2.5.0	Start-up Summary	___
2.5.1	Inventory	___
2.5.2	Supply Sourcing	___
2.6	Start-up Requirements	___
2.7	SBA Loan Key Requirements	___
2.7.1	Other Financing Options	___
3.0	**Products and Services**	___
3.1	Service Descriptions	___
3.1.1	Product Descriptions	___
3.2	Alternate Revenue Streams	___
3.3	Production of Products and Services	___
3.4	Competitive Comparison	___
3.5	Sale Literature	___
3.6	Fulfillment	___
3.7	Technology	___
3.8	Future Products and Services	___
4.0	**Market Analysis Summary**	___
4.1.0	Secondary Market Research	___
4.1.1	Primary Market Research	___
4.2	Market Segmentation	___
4.3	Target Market Segment Strategy	___
4.3.1	Market Needs	___
4.4	Buying Patterns	___
4.5	Market Growth	___

Section	Description	Page
4.6	Service Business Analysis	____
4.7	Barrier to Entry	____
4.8	Competitive Analysis	____
4.9	Market Revenue Projections	____
5.0	**Industry Analysis**	____
5.1	Industry Leaders	____
5.2	Industry Statistics	____
5.3	Industry Trends	____
5.4	Industry Key Terms	____
6.0	**Strategy and Implementation Summary**	____
6.1.0	Promotion Strategy	____
6.1.1	Grand Opening	____
6.1.2	Value Proposition	____
6.1.3	Positioning Statement	____
6.1.4	Distribution Strategy	____
6.2	Competitive Advantage	____
6.2.1	Branding Strategy	____
6.3	Business SWOT Analysis	____
6.4.0	Marketing Strategy	____
6.4.1	Strategic Alliances	____
6.4.2	Monitoring Marketing Results	____
6.4.3	Word-of-Mouth Marketing	____
6.5	Sales Strategy	____
6.5.1	Customer Retention Strategy	____
6.5.2	Sales Forecast	____
6.5.3	Sales Program	____
6.6	Merchandising Strategy	____
6.7	Pricing Strategy	____
6.8	Differentiation Strategies	____
6.9	Milestone Tracking	____
7.0	**Website Plan Summary**	____
7.1	Website Marketing Strategy	____
7.2	Development Requirements	____
7.3	Sample Frequently Asked Questions	____
8.0	**Operations**	____
8.1	Security Measures	____
9.0	**Management Summary**	____
9.1	Owner Personal History	____

Section	Description	Page
9.2	Management Team Gaps	_____
9.2.1	Management Matrix	_____
9.2.2	Outsourcing Matrix	_____
9.3	Employee Requirements	_____
9.4	Job Descriptions	_____
9.4.1	Job Description Format	_____
9.5	Personnel Plan	_____
9.6	Staffing Plan	_____
10.0	**Business Risk Factors**	_____
10.1	Business Risk Reduction Strategies	_____
10.2	Reduce Customer Perceived Risk Strategies	_____
11.0	**Financial Plan**	_____
11.1	Important Assumptions	_____
11.2	Break-even Analysis	_____
11.3	Projected Profit and Loss	_____
11.4	Projected Cash Flow	_____
11.5	Projected Balance Sheet	_____
12.0	**Business Plan Summary**	_____
13.0	**Potential Exit Strategies**	_____
	Appendix	_____
	Helpful Resources	_____

"Progressive Business Plan for a Microbrewery"

1.0 Executive Summary

Industry Overview

Microbreweries are one segment of the larger craft brewing industry, which also includes brewpubs, regional craft breweries and contract brewers. A microbrewery is a brewery which produces a limited amount of beer. In the U.S, the "Brewers Association" use a fixed maximum limit of 15,000 US beer barrels a year to define microbrewery. An American "craft brewery" is a small, independent and traditional brewery. A regional brewery has annual production between 15,000 and 2,000,000 U.S. beer barrels per year. In order to be classified as a "regional craft brewery", a brewery must possess "either an all-malt flagship or have at least 50% of its volume in either all-malt beers or in beers which use adjuncts to enhance rather than lighten flavor. A "brewpub" brews and sells beer on the premises. A brewpub may also be known as a microbrewery if production has a significant distribution beyond the premises - the American Brewers Association use a fixed 75% of production to determine if a company is a microbrewery.

At the end of 2013, the number of breweries in the United States reached the highest level seen in the country since the early 1870s. At the end of December, the Brewers Association counted 2,722 brewing facilities in the US, an increase of almost 400 from the end of 2012.
Source: www.brewersassociation.org/insights/us-brewery-number-climbs-over-2700/
Resources:
http://scholars.unh.edu/cgi/viewcontent.cgi?article=1008&context=honors
http://www.businessinsider.com/american-microbreweries-are-on-the-rise-2014-4

Business Overview

The first step in the process will be to check with the Federal Alcohol and Tobacco Tax and Trade Bureau (TTB.gov) and the particular state liquor or alcohol control board for personal eligibility, brewer license availability and location requirements.

_____ (company name) will handcraft its beers in small ___ (20?) barrel batches under the close personal attention of our brewmaster. The latest brewing equipment and technologies will be seamlessly combined with traditional brewing methods to ensure consistently excellent taste, whether packaged in bottles or draft kegs. The goal of the Company is to become one of the city's most popular microbreweries. _____ (company name) microbrews will be available in bars as well as retail outlets, such as local markets and corner stores. It will also aim to distribute through supermarkets, but it is envisioned that getting shelf space in national supermarkets will be more difficult and more expensive. Our goal is to tap into the growing thirst for new tastes and experiences.

The _____ (company name) will be a microbrewery that will be located in ___ (city), _____ (state). The brewery will occupy ___ (#) square feet of commercial space at _____ (address). This is a new business in the start-up phase. _____ (company name) plans to start production at ____ (3000) barrels and with phased expansion grow to _____ (#) barrels over five years. Initial plans are to produce one product that shall be an amber-style ale. This beer will be sold in kegs to a local distributor for resale to the tri-county draught beer market. In-house sales of beer as well as take-out sales are also planned. Tours and sampling will be offered.

The long-term goals of the _____ (company name) are to slowly add capacity up to the constraints of the site (7500 BBL). A second product is planned once the market has accepted the initial ale offering. This second product will be a lager beer. Specialty and seasonal brews will also be crafted once the business is up and running. These types of beers sell quickly and are usually quite popular. In addition, specialty "house" beers will be brewed and labeled for local taverns.

The Microbrewery will compete on the following basis:
1.   Product variety, including new seasonal selections.
2.   Efficient microbrewery layout and design.
3.   Superior level of service.
4.   Craft beer value.
5.   Wraparound services, including event planning and catering.

We believe that we can become the Microbrewery of choice in the _____ area for the following reasons:
1.   We will develop a training program to create a competent staff, dedicated to continuously improving their skill sets to better assist our customers in making informed purchase decisions.
2.   We will develop a questionnaire to survey changing customer needs and wants, build a customer preference profile and enable customers to express their level of satisfaction.
3.   We will become a one-stop destination for customers in need of beer party planning products and services.
4.   We will offer quality craft beers, using the latest technological advances, at value-based prices with convenient microbrewery hours and access.

In order to succeed, _____ (company name) will have to do the following:
1.   Conduct extensive market research to demonstrate that there is a demand for a Microbrewery with our aforementioned differentiation strategy.
2.   Make superior customer service our number one priority.
3.   Stay abreast of developments in the Microbrewery industry.
4.   Precisely assess and then exceed the expectations of all customers.
5.   Form long-term, trust-based relationships with customers to secure profitable repeat business and referrals.
6.   Develop process efficiencies to achieve and maintain profitability.

Target Market
Our target market is the college educated drinking age residents of _____ (city), with disposable household incomes above \$_____, and who have a preference for celebrating good times with distinctive craft beers.

Mission Statement   (optional)

Our Mission is to address the following customer pain points or unmet needs and wants, which will define the opportunity for our business: _____

In order to satisfy these unmet needs and wants, we will propose the following unique solutions, which will create better value for our customers:

_____

Marketing Strategy

The foundation for this plan is a combination of primary and secondary research, upon which the marketing strategies are built. Discussions and interviews were held with a variety of individuals and other area retail small businesses to develop financial and proforma detail. We consulted census data, county business patterns, and other directories to develop the market potential and competitive situation. Our market strategy will be based on a cost-effective approach to reach this defined target market. The basic approach to promote our craft beers and services will be through establishing relationships with key influencers in the community and then through referral activities, once a significant client base has been established. As a Microbrewery, _____ (company name) will adopt a different marketing strategy than large, mass-market breweries, offering products that compete on the basis of quality and diversity, instead of low price and advertising. The Microbrewery intends to develop an expansive marketing campaign that will effectively brand the Company's premium line of beers. With the help of an aggressive marketing plan, ___ (company name) expects to experience steady growth. ___ (company name) also plans to attract its customers through the use of local newspaper advertisements, circulating flyers, a systematic series of direct mailings, press releases in local newspapers, a website, and online directories. We will also become an active member of the local Chamber of Commerce.

Products and Services

_____ (company name) will develop a highly specialized microbrewery that will produce a number of seasonal and specialized beers such as stouts, pale ales, porters, lagers, and a number of specialized ales/lagers with proprietary formulas developed by the Company's experienced brewmaster. At any given time, the business will have three to four different types of beers in production. The business expects to initially distribute approximately _____ (10,000?) barrels of beer per year.

Critical Risks

Management recognizes there are several internal and external risks inherent in our business concept. Quality, diversity of selection, value pricing and convenience will be key factors in the consumers' decision to utilize our services. Consumers must be willing to accept our one-stop services and products and become repeat and referral customers in order for the microbrewery to meet its sales projections. Building a loyal and trusting relationship with our customers and referral partners is a key component to the success of _____ (company name).

Customer Service

We will take every opportunity to help the customer, regardless of what the revenue might be. We will outshine our competition by doing something "extra" and offering added-value services in a timely manner. We will take a long-term perspective and focus on the client's possible lifetime value to our business. By giving careful consideration to customer responsiveness, _____ (company name) goal will be to meet and exceed every service expectation. Quality service, and quick and informed responsiveness will be the philosophy guiding a customer-centric approach to our microbrewery.

Business Plan Objectives

This business plan serves to detail the direction, vision, and planning necessary to achieve our goal of providing a superior Microbrewery experience. The purpose of this document is to provide a strategic business plan for our company and to support a request for a $ _____, five-year bank loan to purchase equipment and supplies, as part of the financing for a start-up Microbrewery. The plan has been adjusted to reflect the particular strengths and weaknesses of _____ (company name). Actual financial performance will be tracked closely, and the business plan will be adjusted when necessary to ensure that full profit potential and loan repayment is realized on schedule. The plan will also help us to identify and quantify objectives, track and direct growth and create benchmarks for measuring success.

The Company

The business _____ (will be/was) incorporated on _____ (date) in the state of _____, as a _____ (Corporation/LLC), and intends to register for Sub-chapter 'S' status for federal tax purposes. This will effectively shield the owner(s) from personal liability and double taxation.

Business Goals

Our business goal is to continue to develop the _____ (company name) brand name. To do so, we plan to execute on the following:
1.   Offer quality craft beers and customer support.
2.   Focus on quality controls and ongoing operational excellence.
3.   Recruit and train the very best ethical employees.
4.   Create a marketing campaign with a consistent look and message content.

Location

_____ (company name) will be located in the ___ (complex name) on _____ (address) in ___ (city), ___ (state). The ___ (purchased/leased) space is easily accessible and provides ample parking for ___ (#) customers and staff. The location is attractive due to the area demographics, which reflect our middle-class target customer profile.

Competitive Edge

_____ (company name) will compete well in our market by offering competitive prices on an expanded line of quality craft beers, event planning services, knowledgeable and approachable staff, and by using the latest software to manage inventory and enable convenient online ordering. Furthermore, we will maintain an excellent reputation for trustworthiness and integrity with the community we serve.

We will focus the following capabilities to create a competitive advantage:

1. Quality: The brewery, workforce training, marketing materials and brewing ingredients will operate on quality-first principles.
2. Efficiency: The company will create a lean production system due to initial capital constraints and develop the ability to easily adapt to change.
3. Innovation: We will apply creative marketing techniques, original packaging graphics and unique recipes to develop brand recognition.
4. Responsiveness: Our brewery will provide personalized attention and sampling programs to customers to create intimacy and customer loyalty.

The Management Team

_____ (company name) will be led by _____ (owner name) and _____ (co-owner name). ____ (owner name) has a _____ degree from ___ (institution name) and a ____ background within the industry, having spent ____ (#) years with ____ (former employer name or type of business). During this tenure, ___ (he/she) helped grow the business from $_____ in yearly revenue to over $___. ____ (co-owner name) has a ___ background, and while employed by __ was able to increase operating profit by __ percent. These acquired skills, work experiences and educational backgrounds will play a big role in the success of our microbrewery. Additionally, our president, _____ (name), has an extensive knowledge of the _____ area and has identified a niche market retail opportunity to make this venture highly successful, combining his ___ (#) years of work experience in a variety of businesses. _____ (owner name) will manage all aspects of the business and service development to ensure effective customer responsiveness while monitoring day-to-day operations. Qualified and trained clerks personally trained by _____ (owner name) in customer service skills will provide additional support services. Support staff will be added as seasonal or extended hours mandate.

Past Successful Accomplishments

____ (company name) is uniquely qualified to succeed due to the following past successes:
1. **Entrepreneurial Track Record**: The owners and management team have helped to launch numerous successful ventures, including a _____.

2. **Key Milestones Achieved**: The founders have invested $___ to-date to staff the company, build the core technology, acquire starting inventory, test market the _____ (product/service), realize sales of $_____ and launch the website.

Start-up Funding

_____ (owner name) will financially back the new business venture with an initial investment of $_____ and will be the principal owner. Additional funding in the amount of $_____ will be sought from _____, a local commercial bank, with a SBA loan guarantee. This money will be needed to start the company. This loan will provide start-up capital, financing for a selected site lease, remodeling renovations, inventory purchases, pay for permits and licensing, staff training and certification, equipment and working capital to cover expenses during the first year of operation.

Financial Projections

We plan to open for business on ___(date). __ (company name) is forecasted to gross in excess of $___ in sales in its first year of operation, ending ___ (month/ year). Profit margins are forecasted to be at about __ percent. Second year operations will produce a net profit of $__. This will be generated from an investment of $__ in initial capital. It is expected that payback of our total invested capital will be realized in less than __ (#) months of operation. It is further forecasted that cash flow becomes positive from operations in year __ (one?). We project that our net profits will increase from $___ to over $ __ over the next three years.

Financial Profile Summary

Key Indicator	2018	2019	2020
Total Revenue			
Expenses			
Gross Margin			
Operating Income			
Net Income			
EBITDA			

EBITDA = Revenue - Expenses (excluding tax, interest, depreciation and amortization)
EBITDA is essentially net income with interest, taxes, depreciation, and amortization added back to it, and can be used to analyze and compare profitability between companies and industries because it eliminates the effects of financing and accounting decisions.

Gross Margin (%) = (Revenue - Cost of Goods Sold) / Revenue

Net Income = Total revenue - Cost of sales - Other expenses - Tax

Exit Strategy

If the business is very successful, ____ (owner name) may seek to sell the business to a third party for a significant, earnings multiple. Most likely, the Company will hire a qualified business broker to sell the business on behalf of _____ (company name). Based on historical numbers, the business could generate a sales premium of up to __(#) times earnings.

Summary

Through a combination of a proven business model and a strong management team to guide the organization, _____ (company name) will be a long lasting, profitable business. We believe our ability to create future product and service opportunities and growth will only be limited by our imagination and our ability to attract talented people who understand the concept of branding.

1.1.0   Tactical Objectives   (select)

The following tactical objectives will specify quantifiable results and involve activities that can be easily tracked. They will also be realistic, tied to specific marketing strategies and serve as a good benchmark to evaluate our marketing plan success. (Select Choices)

1. Establish strong relationships with local beer distributors in selected sales areas.
2. Maintain a reputation for producing a high-quality craft beer.
3. Establish and maintain ___ (30?) % minimum gross profit margins.
4. Achieve a profitable return on investment within _____ (two?) years.
5. Recruit talented and motivated staff.
6. Capture an increasing share of the commuter traffic passing through_____.
7. Offer our customers superior products, at an affordable price.
8. Create a company whose primary goal is to exceed customer expectations.
9. To develop a cash flow that is capable of paying all salaries, as well as grow the business, by the end of the _____ (first?) year.
10. To be an active networking participant and productive member of the community by _____ (date).
11. Create over __(30?) % of business revenues from repeat customers by ___ (date).
12. Achieve an overall customer satisfaction rate of ____ (98?) % by _____ (date).
13. Get a business website designed, built and operational by _____ (date), which will include an online shopping cart.
14. Achieve total sales revenues of $_____ in _____ (year).
15. Achieve net income more than ___ percent of net sales by the ____ (#) year.
16. Increase overall sales by _____ (20?) percent from prior year through superior service and word-of-mouth referrals.
17. Reduce the cost of new customer acquisition by ___ % to $ ___ by _____ (date).
18. Provide employees with continuing training, benefits and incentives to reduce the employee turnover rate to _____ %.
19. To pursue a growth rate of ____ (20?) % per year for the first ____ (#) years.
20. Enable the owner to draw a salary of $ _____ by the end of year ____ (one?).
21. To reach cash break-even by the end of year ____ (one?).

1.1.1   Strategic Objectives

We will seek to work toward the accomplishment of the following strategic objectives, which relate back to our Mission and Vision Statements:

1. Improve the overall quality of our production capabilities.
2. Make the buyer experience better, faster and more customer friendly.
3. Strengthen personal relationships with customers.
4. Enhance affordability and accessibility.
5. Foster a spirit of innovation.

1.2.0   Mission Statement   (select)

Our Mission Statement is a written statement that spells out our organization's overall goal, provides a sense of direction and acts as a guide to decision making for all levels of management. In developing the following mission statement, we will encourage input from employees, volunteers, and other stakeholders, and publicize it broadly in our website and other marketing materials.

The following are guidelines for preparing our mission statement:
1. Use terms that are understandable to employees.
2. Word our mission to inspire the human spirit, as a person should read the statement and feel good about working for the hotel.
3. Catchy (but not cliché) slogans can help people remember the mission.
4. Keep the mission statement as short as possible.
5. Widely distribute the mission.
6. Communicate the mission to employees regularly.

Source:
http://scholarship.sha.cornell.edu/cgi/viewcontent.cgi?article=1295&context=articles

Our mission is to develop into the best location to buy craft beers in _____ (city), which will be measured by our growth in sales, and in opinions and ratings published in the media. ___ (company name) will strive to provide its quality craft beers in a convenient and cost competitive manner, while providing our customers the finest service available. Our mission is to enhance our customers quality of life by providing the most remarkable experience possible. We strive to discover and empower an artistic approach in all aspects of our craft and to make sure the customer's quality brew creates an impressive experience.

Our mission is to become a recognized regional brewery that provides an outstanding variety of specialized and seasonal beers. Our mission is to not only take advantage of the opportunity to embrace the local area and immerse our business into the local economy, but to also truly embrace it and become part of its fabric.

We will organize our location, hours, products, staffing and staff schedule to create a positive and effective environment in order to achieve our mission and to ensure future growth. Our mission is to realize 100% customer satisfaction and generate long-term profits through referrals and repeat business. Our goal is to set ourselves apart from the competition by making customer satisfaction our number one priority and to provide customer service that is responsive, informed and respectful.

1.2.1   Mantra

We will create a mantra for our organization that is three or four words long. Its purpose will be to help employees truly understand why the organization exists. Our mantra will serve as a framework through which to make decisions about product and business direction. It will boil the key drivers of our company down to a sentence that defines our most important areas of focus and resemble a statement of purpose or significance.
Examples: Quality First / Healthy beverages / Seasonal Flavors
Our Mantra is _____

1.2.2   Core Values Statement

The following Core Values will help to define our organization, guide our behavior, underpin operational activity and shape the strategies we will pursue in the face of various challenges and opportunities:

Being respectful and ethical to our customers and employees.

Building enduring relationships with clients.

Seeking innovation in our brewing industry.

Practicing accountability to our colleagues and stakeholders.

Pursuing continuous improvement as individuals and as a business entity.

Performing tasks on time to satisfy the needs of our internal and external clients.

Taking active part in the organization to meet the objectives and the establishment of continuous and lasting relationships.

Offering professional treatment to our clients, employees, shareholders, and the community.

Continuing pursuit of new technologies for the development of the projects that add value for our clients, employees, shareholders, and the community.

1.3   Vision Statement   (select)

The following Vision Statement will communicate both the purpose and values of our organization. For employees, it will give direction about how they are expected to behave and inspires them to give their best. Shared with customers, it will shape customers' understanding of why they should work with our organization.

_____ (company name) will strive to become one of the most respected and favored Microbreweries in the _____ area. It is our desire to become a landmark business in _____ (city), _____ (state), and become known not only for the quality of our craft beers and services, but also for our community and charity involvement.

_____company name) is dedicated to operating with a constant enthusiasm for learning about the Microbrewery business, being receptive to implementing new ideas, and maintaining a willingness to adapt to changing customer needs and wants. To be an active and vocal member of the community, and to provide continual reinvestment through participation in community activities and financial contributions.

To incorporate the use of more state-of-the-art technologies to create high-quality craft beers, and thereby improve the effectiveness, efficiency and competitiveness of the business. To add a brewpub that will offer an operating brewing operation in full view of dining customers to add even more ambience. To get our craft beers distributed in the entire _____ region.

1.4   Keys to Success

In broad terms, the success factors relate to providing what our clients want and doing what is necessary to be better than our competitors. The following critical success factors are areas in which our organization must excel in order to operate successfully and achieve our objectives:

1. Oversize the chiller and boiler because the productivity gains will offset the cost fairly quickly.
2. Get everything in writing to maintain professional relationships.
3. Save capital by purchasing quality used equipment.
4. Buy the best quality equipment that the business can afford.
5. When selecting a manufacturer, first talk to both brewers and brewery owners to get a full picture of the quality, service and follow-up.
6. When purchasing equipment, make everything negotiable, including payment and down payment terms, and help with installation.
7. Evaluate equipment in terms of quality of construction and ease of operation.
8. The primary focus should be on getting the beer on tap in bars and restaurants to become better known.
9. Look for niche markets not being supplied by the mega brewers such as Anheuser-Busch and Coors. For example, German-style lagers, Belgian-style fruit flavored beers and Irish-style stout are currently being produced by microbreweries.
10. New product and service innovation is seen as the key to attracting and retaining customers.
11. Provide employee stock options to facilitate a healthy company culture and image.
12. Computerized inventory and sales records will allow the company to identify and exploit best-selling products, match volumes and profitability to service levels, anticipate demand, manage cash flows, assist with revenue growth plans, and optimize supplier/distributor relationships.
13. Develop craft beers and services offered specifically for the local area.
14. Securing regular and ongoing customer feedback
15. The offering of good quality products at competitive prices.
16. Providing excellent customer service that will promote customer loyalty.
17. Launch a website to showcase our services and customer testimonials, provide helpful information and facilitate online order placement.
18. Local community involvement and strategic business partnerships.
19. Conduct a targeted and cost-effective marketing campaign that seeks to differentiate our one-stop, convenient services from competitor offerings.
20. Institute a pay-for-performance component to the employee compensation plan.
21. Control costs and manage budgets at all times in accordance with company goals.
22. Institute management processes and controls to insure the consistent replication of operations.
23. Recruit screened employees with a passion for delivering exceptional service.
24. Institute an employee training to insure the best techniques are consistently practiced.
25. Network aggressively within the community, as word of mouth will be our

most powerful advertising asset.

26. Retain clients to generate repeat purchases and initiate referrals.
27. Competitive pricing in conjunction with a differentiated service business model.
28. Stay abreast of technological developments and new product/service offerings.
29. Build our brand awareness, which will drive customers to increase their usage of our services and make referrals.
30. Business planning with the flexibility to make changes based on gaining new insightful perspectives as we proceed.

31. Build trust by circulating to our Code of Ethics and Guarantees.
32. A good reputation is built upon a great selection and knowledgeable staff.
33. It is essential to partner with producers who can offer unique products.
34. Schedule staff trainings with winery people and distributor personnel to improve their suggestive selling knowledge and skills.
35. Must institute management controls to prevent shrinkage or loss of inventory due to employee theft, shoplifting, damage of items while in the microbrewery, administrative errors, and spoilage of perishable goods.
36. Must contact a qualified business attorney familiar with Microbrewery issues to help work through all the various legal and license issues.
37. Make sure the brew has passed the taste test by folks other than your friends before expanding.
38. Check your ingredients and brewing process and think about how to adapt your beer for a larger audience.
39. Study microbrewery success stories, such as Redhook Ale, the Brooklyn Brewery and others.
40. Pick up copies of "The New Brewer," "Brewer's Digest" and "Modern Brewery Age" to study the competition.
41. Assemble your team of dedicated professionals who will work for low or deferred wages at first.
42. Keep the business plan handy and updated as your assumptions change.
43. Check out all of your financing options and line up contingency funding sources.
44. Try to barter for equipment to conserve capital.
45. Strive for 40 percent of your sales from house beer, 50 percent from food and 10 percent from the sale of pub-related logo imprinted merchandise.
46. The skill of the brewmaster is as important as the ingredients and the equipment.
47. Must start by distributing your own product line door-to-door, because the major distributors will not give the product line the start-up attention that it requires.
48. Must use the local media to help build the confidence in retailers to try the product line and help supplement our own sales force.
49. To build credibility, distribute not only your own product line, but also your microbrew competitors and some limited number of fancy European beers.
50. Must design of a professional-looking logo to create a corporate identity.
51. Offer products that compete on the basis of quality and diversity, instead of low price and advertising.
52. As the completion increases, it is more important to differentiate our beer and target a niche underserved market with a distinctive beer, such as a lager. .
53. Focus on the styles and beers we do best, because a successful flagship beer will

allow the microbrewery to take risks in other markets.

54. Advertise that we use local ingredients and donate waste products to farmers as a way to support the local community.

55. Know whether our product is better or cheaper than the alternatives to establish a starting point.

56. Develop interview questions to determine whether a job candidate has the same motivational needs and behavioral attributes that have made others successful in a particular position.

57. Learn to fail quickly and pull the plug to minimize the damage and learn a valuable lesson before moving on.

58. Brands are resorting to innovative packaging as a major marketing tool, such as the use of double vented, wide-mouth cans.

59. In printing labels, use a four-color process and pressure sensitive labels produced at a high density preferably with 150-line screens or higher.

60. Develop a tap handle that is intriguing, unique, descriptive and/or clever in design.

61. Plan ahead for the need to expand your footprint to increase production.

62. Must understand industry regulations and distribution laws.

63. Secure intellectual property rights early on to avoid the risk of having to re-brand the product later and lose name recognition.

64. Need tap room to capitalize on the "honeymoon" period of local interest, and to bring in revenue to stay afloat during their first year.

65. Prepare a 'Master Brewer Employment Agreement' which will include a covenant not to compete and provisions that clearly state that the beer formulas are "trade secrets" and thus the property of the brewery.

66. Consider starting the business using the contract brewing model if you can not afford to do it any other way, as it will allow the start-up company to brew without spending a lot of money on equipment and own physical space, and to focus on developing signature products and brand image.

67. Must master the weekly challenge of sorting out the difference between real consumer taste demands to justify production runs and temporary fads.

68. Consider the advantages of buying new bottling equipment because of the technical support provided by the manufacturer.

69. Develop an in-depth microbrewery industry knowledge and brewmaster skills, keep regulatory compliance a top priority and continually seek to make inroads in the local market.
Resource:
www.brewersassociation.org/government-affairs/ba-position-statements/

70. Make sure to choose a beer style that fills a market gap and will be profitable in your local area.

71. Due to consolidation among beer distributors, self-distribution is a rational option for a new brewery in the right community, but it is limited.

72. Seek to establish knowledge sharing alliances with fellow brewers to better focus on growing the overall craft market.
Source: http://www.entrepreneur.com/article/246098

73. Foster a culture that values collaboration, learning and team spirit.

74.   Invest in the technology, processes and systems to be in the position to grow.
      Source: http://fortune.com/2015/03/03/5-tips-for-launching-your-own-brewery/

75.   Because of license and equipment unexpected acquisition/installation costs and
      delays, open with ample working capital beyond the initial start-up costs.

76.   Because the microbrewery business is a very capital intensive, excess earnings
      need to get poured back (retained) into the business.

77.   Build into the financial plan, adequate funding for a quality tasting room and
      a spacious visitor center.

78.   Post a 'Beer Quiz' to the website that helps to gain insights as to what our
      customers want when purchasing beer.
      Resource:
      www.surveymonkey.com/curiosity/what-kind-beer-people-like/
      https://gotbeer.com/beer-styles

79.   Create ads that speak to the beautiful natural surroundings (pristine water source)
      of the microbrewery.

Note: Beer start-ups, according to the Beer Assoc. of America, typically fail for one of
       two reasons: they're undercapitalized, or they're not making consistent beer.

Resources:
http://money.cnn.com/2015/03/03/smallbusiness/craft-beer-startup-how-to-guide/
https://byo.com/grains/item/1408-start-your-own-brewery
https://www.fundera.com/blog/2015/04/02/the-economics-of-starting-a-brewery/

2.0   Company Summary

_____ (company name) plans to be a microbrewery with a reputation for handcrafted care, time-honored methodology, and the finest natural ingredients from around the world. The company's product lines will be ____ Pilsner and Red Ale.

_____ (company name) will handcraft its beers in small ___ (20?) barrel batches under the close personal attention of our brewmaster. The latest brewing equipment and technologies will be seamlessly combined with traditional brewing methods to ensure consistently excellent taste, whether packaged in bottles or draft kegs.

_____ (company name) intends to expand its distribution to selected metro areas within the state of _____ and to become one of the city's most popular microbreweries. In addition, the company will introduce a new product, a traditional _____ style lager.

_____ (company name) will be a small-scale microbrewery located in ___ (city), _____ (state). It will occupy a one-floor, light-industrial building at _____ (address). _____ (company name) will occupy approximately _____ (#) square feet and faces _____ Street. The brewery will produce up to _____ 3200 barrels of beer per year in its initial design. There are the capacity and space available to expand to ____ (7500) barrels per year. Initial plans are to produce one product that shall be an amber-style ale.

The _____ Company is incorporated in the State of _____ as a sub-chapter S Corporation. The Internal Revenue Service has officially accepted _____'s (company name) election as an S-Corporation as of _____ (date). The corporation is currently in the investigation stage by the State Liquor Control Commission. In addition, application materials have been sent to the Bureau of Alcohol, Tobacco, and Firearms. Their investigation has yet to commence. These two investigations, once complete will result in the issuance of a Brewers License and a Brewers Notice respectively.

Key vendors have been identified and quotes obtained. Cost figures for equipment, inventory, building renovation, and labor have been identified and figured into the business plan. Production costs have been calculated, product pricing has been estimated, and profit potential has been approximated. A tentative lease has been written up, but it is not yet signed.

The legal name of the corporation is __ (company name). The company was incorporated in the State of _____ in ___ (year). The corporation has also registered a DBA or "Doing Business As" under "_____ Brewery". The Internal Revenue Service has issued an Employer Identification Number which is _____, issued _____ (date).

The owner of the company will be investing $ ___ of ____ (his/her) own capital into the company and will also be seeking a loan of $ __ to cover start-up costs and future growth. The owner, _____ , has ___ (#) years of experience in managing _____ (businesses?).

The company plans to use its existing contacts and customer base to generate short-term revenues. Its long-term profitability will rely on focusing on referrals, networking within community organizations and a comprehensive marketing program that includes public relations activities and a structured referral program.

Sales are expected to reach $_____ within the first year and to grow at a conservative rate of _____ (20?) percent during the next two to five years.

Facilities Renovations

The necessary renovations are itemized as follows: Estimate

    Partition of space into functional areas.   _____

    Build storage areas and retail showroom.   _____

    Painting and other general cosmetic repairs   _____

    Install brewing equipment.   _____

    Install computer equipment   _____

    Install refrigeration units.   _____

    Other _____   _____

Total: _____

Hours of Operations

_____ (company name) will open for business on _____ (date) and will maintain the following office business hours:

    Monday through Thursday: _____   (7 AM to 11 PM?)

    Friday: _____

    Saturday: _____

    Sunday: _____

The company will invest in customer relationship management software (CRM) to track real-time sales data and collect customer information, including names, email addresses, key reminder dates and preferences. This information will be used with email, e-newsletter and direct mail campaigns to build personalized fulfillment programs, establish customer loyalty and drive revenue growth.

2.0.1   Test Marketing   (select)

We will use the following methods to help test market our microbrewery products, and make an informed 'go/no-go' business decision before investing larger sums of money:

1.   Solicit justified feedback from microbrew industry experts and other investors.
2.   Track the response rate from free classified ads placed on Craigslist.
3.   Gain insights from a microbrewery in another geographic market.
4.   Build a prototype and use a survey to ask potential buyers for feedback.
5.   Purchase a limited quantity of goods for sale through online sales channels such as Amazon and/or eBay, and festivals, fairs, trade shows and flea markets.
6.   Offer a special beta release or pre-release version of the service to a select group of customers in exchange for feedback.

7. Make an offer through social networking portals like Twitter or Facebook noting that the first people to reply will get access to the new release product.
8. Release the product to a test group at a drastically reduced price to gauge interest for the product and learn how to refine it.
9. Make the discounted sales strategy offer contingent on a response to surveys or questions about the service.
10. Hire or form a market research group to conduct focus groups.
11. Compare the product to others on the market to make sure that something about the new product either improves on an existing product or meets a need better than it can be met by something that's currently available.
12. Use a commissioned sales representative to sample the local market demand and secure future sale dates.
13. Offer the product for sale through an appropriate end user purchasing outlet and price the product as though it were in production, even though each sale may result in a loss.
14. Issue a product press release to appropriate trade publications to gauge response to products.
15. Encourage comments to a Youtube.com video about our business model concept.

2.0.2   Traction (optional)

We will include this section because investors expect to see some traction, both before and after a funding event and investors tend to judge past results as a good indicator of future projections. It will also show that we can manage our operations and develop a business model capable of funding inventory purchases. Traction will be the best form of market research.

Period _____
Product/Service Focus _____
Our Sales to Date: _____
Our Number of Users to Date: _____
Number of Repeat Users _____
Number of Pending Orders: _____
Value of Pending Orders: _____
Reorder Cycle: _____
Key Reference Sites _____
Mailing List Subscriptions _____
Competitions/Awards Won _____
Notable Product Reviews _____
Actual Percent Gross Profit Margin _____
Industry Average: GPM _____
Actual B/(W) Industry Average _____

Note: Percent Gross Profit Margin equals the sales receipts less the cost of goods sold divided by sales receipts multiplied by 100.

2.1   Company Ownership

_____ (company name) is a _____ (Sole-proprietorship /Corporation/ Limited Liability Corporation (LLC)) and is registered to the principal owner, _____ (owner name). The company was formed in _____ (month) of ____ (year). It will be registered as a Subchapter S to avoid double taxation, with ownership allocated as follows: _____ (owner name) ____ % and _____ (owner name) ____ %.

The owner is a _____ (year) graduate of _____ (institution name), in _____ (city, ____ (state), with a _____ degree. He/she _____ has a second degree in _____ and certification as a _____ . He/she also has ____ years of executive experience in the _____ (?) industry as a _____ , performing the following roles: _____.
His/her major accomplishments include: _____

Ownership Breakdown:

Shareholder Name	Responsibilities	Number and Class of Shares	Percent Ownership

The remainder of the issued and outstanding common shares are retained by the Company for ___(future distribution / allocation under the Company's employee stock option plan).

Shareholder Loans

The Company currently has outstanding shareholder loans in the aggregate sum of $_____. The following table sets out the details of the shareholder loans.

Shareholder Name	Loan Amount	Loan Date	Balance Outstanding

Directors

The Company's Board of Directors, which is made up of highly qualified business and industry professionals, will be a valuable asset to the Company and be instrumental to its development. The following persons will make up the Board of Directors of the Company:

Name of Person	Educational Background	Past Industry Experience	Other Companies Served

2.2   Company Licensing & Liability Protection

We will use the services of a local attorney or liquor license consultant to help us with starting our Microbrewery, as these individuals have more experience with the process, and typically have more insight into the people who will be in a position to approve or deny our application for a Brewer's License. They will also help to work through all the various legal issues that will surface, including what kind of entity to use for our business, how to best protect against liability problems, how to meet rules against selling to under age buyers, what rules apply to advertising, and so forth. We will contact an insurance agent to find out how much insurance will cost.
Resource: http://growlermag.com/so-you-want-to-start-your-own-brewery/

After we have established our company from a legal perspective, we will apply for a brewer's license for that company, at the address of the building that we have _____ (purchased/leased). It is our goal to purchase the property as the brewer's license will be attached to the property.

The process of applying for a liquor license varies from state to state. There is typically an Alcoholic Beverage Control Board at the State level, with local approval also needed from the local City Council. We will contact the City Clerk's office in the town where we wish to do business for more information on how to apply for a brewer's license in our area.

The typical coverage for Microbreweries includes property, CGL, liquor liability and crime coverage. Our business will consider the need to acquire the following types of insurances. This will require extensive comparison shopping, through several insurance brokers, listed with our state's insurance department:
1.   Workers' Compensation Insurance,
2.   Business Policy: Property & Liability Insurance
3.   Health insurance.
4.   Commercial Auto Insurance
5.   State Unemployment Insurance
6.   Business Interruption Insurance (Business Income Insurance)
7.   Disability Insurance
8.   Life Insurance
9.   Liquor Liability
10.   Crime Coverage
11.   Equipment Breakdown Coverage
12.   Employment Practices Liability

We will carry business liability and property insurance and any other insurance we deem necessary after receiving counsel from our lawyer and insurance agent. Health insurance and workers' compensation will be provided for our full-time employees as part of their benefit package. We feel that this is mandatory to ensure that they do not leave the company for one that does offer these benefits. Workers' Compensation covers employees in case of harm attributed to the workplace. The Property and Liability Insurance protects the building from theft, fire, natural disasters, and being sued by a third party. Life and Disability Insurance may be required if a bank loan is obtained.

Liquor Liability Insurance covers an insured for damages that the business becomes legally obligated to pay for injury arising from the selling, serving, or furnishing of any alcoholic beverage. As most claims against bars and restaurants are the results of fights, our liquor liability policy will include coverage for assault and battery claims. The policy will also provide our business with skilled, appointed legal counsel that does not reduce coverage and covers our employees as patrons. Finally, we must make all employees aware of the fact that liquor liability insurance will not cover sales that are contrary to law and sales to minors.

Liability Insurance includes protection in the face of day-to-day accidents, unforeseen results of normal business activities, and allegations of abuse or molestation, food poisoning, or exposure to infectious disease.

Property Insurance - Property Insurance should take care of the repairs less whatever deductible you have chosen.

Loss of Income Insurance will replace our income during the time the business is shut-down. Generally, this coverage is written for a fixed amount of monthly income for a fixed number of months.

Product Liability Insurance covers injuries caused by products that are designed, sold or specified by the business.

Resources:

The Hanover's Craft Brewers Advantage total solution covers a brewery's property, autos, employees, and customers as well as risks such as goods in transit, professional liability, employment practices liability, and fidelity & crime. It also enables craft brewers to take advantage of the company's loss control expertise in this industry, including assessments and recommendations for improving their property and theft risks, process flow, disaster preparedness/business continuity plans, storage techniques, and quality control plans. Other highlights of Craft Brewers Advantage include:

1.   Brewers Spoilage, Contamination and Change in Temperature
2.   Property Broadening Endorsement
3.   Transit Broadening Endorsement
4.   Liquor Liability Coverage with a liability limit up to $1 million.
5.   General Liability Broadening Endorsement covers product recall expense.
Source: www.hanover.com/business-insurance-mid-sized-craftbrewers.html

The Coyle Group
                www.thecoylegroup.com/craft-beer-micro-brewery-insurance-new-york/
Diversified Insurance   www.divinsurance.com/commercial-insurance-blog/bid/
                341657/Microbrewery-Insurance-Coverage-Options

To help save on insurance cost and claims, management will do the following:

1. Stress employee safety in our employee handbook.
2. Screen employees with interview questionnaires and will institute pre-employment drug tests and comprehensive background checks.
3. Videotape our equipment and inventory for insurance purposes.
4. Create an operations manual that shares safe techniques.
5. Limit the responsibilities that we choose to accept in our contracts.
6. Consider the financial impact of assuming the exposure ourselves.
7. Establish loss prevention programs to reduce the hazards that cause losses.
8. Consider taking higher deductibles on anything but that which involves liability insurance because of third-party involvement.
9. Stop offering services that require expensive insurance coverage or require signed releases from clients using those services.
10. Improve employee training and initiate training sessions for safety.
11. Require Certificate of Insurance from all subcontractors.
12. Make staff responsible for a portion of any damages they cause.
13 Always check for valid identification to prevent underage customers from purchasing alcohol.
14. Require all microbrewery personnel to attend TIPS [Training for Intervention Procedures] Off Premise program, which addresses the sale of alcohol at grocery stores, microbreweries and package stores to prevent illegal alcohol sales to underage or intoxicated customers.
15. We will investigate the setting-up of a partial self-insurance plan.
16. Convince underwriters that our past low claims are the result of our ongoing safety programs and there is reason to expect our claims will be lower than industry averages in the future.
17. At each renewal, we will develop a service agreement with our broker and get their commitment to our goals, such as a specific reduction in the number of incidents.
18. We will assemble a risk control team, with people from both sides of our business, and broker representatives will serve on the committee as well.
19. When an employee is involved in an accident, we will insist on getting to the root cause of the incident and do everything possible to prevent similar incidents from re-occurring.
20. At renewal, we will consult with our brokers to develop a cost-saving strategy and decide whether to bid out our coverage for competitive quotes or stick with our current carrier.
21. We will set-up a captive insurance program, as a risk management technique, where our business will form its own insurance company subsidiary to finance its retained losses in a formal structure.
22. Review named assets (autos and equipment), drivers and/or key employees identified on policies to make sure these assets and people are still with our company.
23. As a portion of our business changes, that is, closes, operations change, or outsourcing occurs, we will eliminate unnecessary coverage.
24. We will make sure our workforce is correctly classified by our workers' compensation insurer and liability insurer because our premiums are based on the

type of workers used.

25. We will become active in Trade Organizations or Professional Associations, because as a benefit of membership, our business may receive substantial insurance discounts.

26. We will adopt health specific changes to our work place, such as adopting a no smoking policy at our company and allow yoga or weight loss classes to be held in our break room.

27. We will consider a partial reimbursement of health club membership as a benefit.

28. We will find out what employee training will reduce rates and get our employees involved in these programs.

In addition to the insurance included in the lease, the brewery is responsible for certain business insurances. These additional insurances are liability (includes State mandated liquor liability), Workmen's Compensation, and contents insurance. The policy will through the _____ Agency, of _____ (city), ____ (state) at a yearly cost of $____ (6,000).

REGULATIONS

Regulation of microbreweries is done in many ways. The Department of the Treasury through the Bureau of Alcohol, Tobacco, and Firearms regulates and collects Federal excise tax. The State of _____ Liquor Control Commission collects state excise tax. In addition, the state Department of Agriculture inspects and licenses facilities. Local ordinances must be followed as well.

The Alcohol and Tobacco Trade and Tax Bureau ("TTB") not only collects Federal excise taxes on alcohol, tobacco, firearms, and ammunition, but also assures compliance with Federal tobacco permitting and alcohol permitting, labeling, and marketing requirements to protect consumers. The TTB must approve our operations, recipes, beer labels and the like. We will have to send in a Brewer's Notice and a Brewer's Bond and TTB must approve our operations before we begin to make beer for public consumption. TTB may also initiate an on-site inspection of the proposed premises and operations prior to the issuance of our Brewer's Notice. Background checks on directors, officers and significant owners will also be required. This process typically takes 6-12 months to complete.

Resource: http://growlermag.com/so-you-want-to-start-your-own-brewery/

Besides TTB approval, our new brewery will also need to apply for a state wholesaler's license as well as any licenses required by the municipality in which the brewery will operate; including a possible taproom license. Since our micro-brewery intends to construct and operate a taproom where patrons can purchase pints of beer onsite at our brewery, the taproom license must be issued through the local municipality, and not the state government.

Resources:
http://www.ttb.gov/wine/state-ABC.shtml
http://www.ttb.gov/faqs/alcohol_faqs.shtml

Labels

_____ (state) label requirements state that the brewery must adopt Federal Alcohol Administration labeling regulations. The product label must have federal approval. Product samples must be analyzed, and a registration number of approval assigned before the product can be sold in the state. Once the label has federal approval, two samples of 12-ounce bottles must be submitted as well as one set of loose labels. A special provision requires the refund value of the container and the name of the state to be clearly indicated on the label.

Taxes & Deposits

A keg deposit is required upon sale of the keg. The deposit for ___ (state) is $___ (10?). Bottle deposits are $_____ (.10?) per bottle. The state beer tax rate for Michigan is $_____ (6.30?) per 31-gallon barrel. In-state brewers receive a rebate of tax on beer shipped outside of the state. The tax per case of 24 12oz. bottles is $_____ (.4645).

Shipping Requirements

Beer may only be shipped from the brewery to a licensed wholesaler. If beer sales are made out-of-state, then a special seller's license is required. It costs $_____ (1000?). A bond is required of the brewery of either $1000 or 1/2 of the total excise taxes paid in the last calendar year, whichever is greater. Shipping brewers must pay taxes twice monthly. In addition, a monthly report of shipments is required.

Wholesaler Relations

The brewery shall grant each wholesaler with a written agreement and designate a specific sales territory. The brewery may not fix, maintain, or establish the resale price. The wholesaler may not sell outside his sales territory. The brewery may not terminate, cancel, refuse to renew, or discontinue an agreement, except for good cause, and must afford the wholesaler 30 days in which to submit a plan of corrective action to comply with the agreement and an additional 90 days to cure such noncompliance.

Zoning

This project may require contacting the local Planning and Appeals Board to initiate a request to rezone a warehouse from general business to light industrial.

The business will need to acquire the following special licenses, accreditations, certifications and permits:
1.   A Sales Tax License is required through the State Department of Revenue.
2.   Use Tax Registration Certificate
3.   A County and/or City Occupational License.
4.   Business License from State Licensing Agency
5.   Permits from the Fire Department and State Health Department.
6.   Building Code Inspections by the County Building Department.
7.   Brewer's License
8.   Liquor License from the Alcoholic Beverage Control Board.

Resource: http://www.ttb.gov/beer/index.shtml
9.   Sign Permit

Note: In most states, you are legally required to obtain a business license, and a dba certificate. A business license is usually a flat tax assessment and a percentage of your gross income. A dba stands for Doing Business As, and it is the registration of your trade name if you have one. You will be required to register your trade name within 30 days of starting your business. Instead of registering a dba, you can simply form an LLC or Corporation and it will have the same effect, namely register your business name.

Resources:
Workers Compensation Regulations
            http://www.dol.gov/owcp/dfec/regs/compliance/wc.htm#IL
New Hire Registration and Reporting
            www.homeworksolutions.com/new-hire-reporting-information/
State Tax Obligations
            www.sba.gov/content/learn-about-your-state-and-local-tax-obligations
Resource:
www/sba.gov/content/what-state-licenses-and-permits-does-your-business-need

Note: Check with your local County Clerk and state offices or Chamber of Commerce to make sure you follow all legal protocols for setting up and running your business.

Note: State liquor license laws often require the offering of food for sale as a part of the beer business, so consider selling frozen pizzas and burgers for folks to take home and eat with their gourmet beer.

Resources:
Insurance Information Institute   www.iii.org/individuals/business/
National License Directory   www.sba.gov/licenses-and-permits
Independent Insurance Agents & Brokers of America   www.iiaa.org
The Whalen Agency   www.breweryinsurance.com
The Ballard Agency   www.beerinsurance.com
Find Law   http://smallbusiness.findlaw.com/starting-business/starting-business-
            licenses-permits/starting-business-licenses-permits-guide.html
Business Licenses   www.iabusnet.org/business-licenses
Legal Zoom   www.legalzoom.com

2.3   Start-up To-Do Checklist

1.   Describe your business concept and model, with special emphasis on planned multiple revenue streams and services to be offered.
2.   Create Business Plan and Opening Menu of Products and Services.
3.   Determine your startup costs of Microbrewery business, and operating capital and capital budget needs.
4.   Seek and evaluate alternative financing options, including SBA guaranteed loan,

equipment leasing, social networking loan (www.prosper.com) and/or a family loan (www.virginmoney.com).

5. Do a name search: Check with County Clerk Office or Department of Revenue and Secretary of State to see if the proposed name of business is available.

6. Decide on a legal structure for business.
    Common legal structure options include Sole Proprietorship, Partnership, Corporation or Limited Liability Corporation (LLC).

7. Make sure you contact your State Department of Revenue, Secretary of State, and the Internal Revenue Service to secure EIN Number and file appropriate paperwork. Also consider filing for Sub-Chapter S status with the Federal government to avoid the double taxation of business profits.

8. Protect name and logo with trademarks, if plan is to go national.

9. Find a suitable location with proper zoning for a Microbrewery.

10. Research necessary permits and requirements your local government imposes on your type of business. (Refer to: www.business.gov & www.ttb.gov)

11. Call for initial inspections to determine what must be done to satisfy Fire Marshall and Building Inspector requirements.

12. Adjust our budget based on build-out requirements.

13. Negotiate lease or property purchase contract.

14. Obtain a building permit.

15. Obtain Federal Employee Identification Number (FEIN).

16. Obtain State Sales Tax ID/Exempt Certificate.

17. Open a Business Checking Account.

18. Obtain Merchant Credit Card /PayPal Account.

19. Obtain City and County Business Licenses

20. Create a prioritized list for equipment, furniture and décor items.

21. Comparison shop and arrange for appropriate insurance coverage with product liability insurance, public liability insurance, commercial property insurance and worker's compensation insurance.

22. Locate and purchase all necessary equipment and furniture prior to final inspections.

23. Get contractor quotes for required alterations.

24 Manage the alterations process.

25. Obtain information and price quotes from possible supply distributors.

26. Set a tentative opening date.

27. Install 'Coming Soon' sign in front of building and begin word-of-mouth advertising campaign.

28. Document the preparation, project and payment process flows.

29. Create your accounting, purchasing, payroll, marketing, loss prevention, employee screening and other management systems.

30. Start the employee interview process based on established job descriptions and interview criteria.

31. Contact and interview the following service providers: uniform service, security service, trash service, utilities, telephone, credit card processing, bookkeeping, cleaning services, etc.

32. Schedule final inspections for premises.

33. Correct inspection problems and schedule another inspection.
34. Set a Grand Opening date after a month of regular operations to get the bugs out of the processes.
35. Make arrangements for website design.
36. Train staff.
37. Schedule a couple of practice lessons for friends and interested prospects.
38. Be accessible for direct customer feedback.
39. Distribute comment cards and surveys to solicit more constructive feedback.
40. Remain ready and willing to change your business concept and offerings to suit the needs of your actual customer base.

2.3.1   EMPLOYER RESPONSIBILITIES CHECKLIST

1. Apply for your SS-4 Federal Employer Identification Number (EIN) from the Internal Revenue Service. An EIN can be obtained via telephone, mail or online.
2. Register with the State's Department of Labor (DOL) as a new employer. State Employer Registration for Unemployment Insurance, Withholding, and Wage Reporting should be completed and sent to the address that appears on the form. This registration is required of all employers for the purpose of determining whether the applicants are subject to state unemployment insurance taxes.
3. Obtain Workers Compensation and Disability Insurance from an insurer. The insurance company will provide the required certificates that should be displayed.
4. Order Federal Tax Deposit Coupons – Form 8109 – if you didn't order these when you received your EIN. To order, call the IRS at 1-800-829-1040; you will need to give your EIN. You may want to order some blanks sent for immediate use until the pre-printed ones are complete. Also ask for the current Federal Withholding Tax Tables (Circular A) – this will explain how to withhold and remit payroll taxes, and file reports.
5. Order State Withholding Tax Payment Coupons. Also ask for the current Withholding Tax Tables.
6. Have new employees complete an I-9 Employment Eligibility Verification form. You should have all employees complete this form prior to beginning work. Do not send it to Immigration and Naturalization Service – just keep it with other employee records in your files.
7. Have employees complete aW-4 Employees Withholding Allowance Certificate.

2.4.0   Company Location

The microbrewery has decided to locate in ____ (city), in the heart of _____ County. This was a purposeful decision. In _____ County, in ____ (year), _____ (#) jobs were created, representing __ (#) out of every ___ (#) new jobs in the state. In addition, ___% of all foreign money invested in ___ (state) is in ____ County. There are _____ (#) businesses in

_____ County, including ___ (#) of the Fortune 500. The population shift and pursuant demand for goods and services is in full swing in the _____ area.

The business success here is due to the diversity of government services, the availability of land and office space, and the competitive costs to do business. Additionally, _____ College will design tailor-made training programs for existing and newly-created high tech businesses to attract them. There are ____ (#) students currently enrolled in _____ University.

The selection of our microbrewery location will be driven by local zoning restrictions as most places have restrictions that prohibit liquor from being sold near schools, churches, libraries and hospitals. Other communities may also have more Microbreweries than the local population requires, making it difficult to convince the city council to issue an additional license. Conducting detailed research into local regulations with the appropriate government agencies will be a critical step to opening our Microbrewery.

_____ (company name) will be located in the _____ commercial area in ____ (city). The site is one of the densest and _____ (affluent?) markets in the state. Our storefront will be prime retail space in the _____ (northeast?) corner of the ____ Avenue building, facing ___, a main artery for vehicles and city buses coming and going from the complex. The microbrewery is centered within a cluster of ___ (#) commercial _____ (buildings?).

_____ (company name) will be located in the _____ (complex name) in _____ (city), ___ (state). It is situated on a _____ (turnpike/street/avenue) just minutes from _____ (benchmark location), in the neighborhood of _____. It borders a large parking lot which is shared by all the businesses therein. Important considerations relative to practice location are competition, visibility, accessibility, signage, community growth trends, demographics, and drive by traffic patterns. A visible, busy location will make the difference between a business that is stagnant and a business that thrives.

The location has the following advantages: (Select Choices)
1.   It is easy to locate and accessible to a number of major roadways.
2.   Easy access from public transportation.
3.   Ground level access.
4.   Good neighborhood visibility and traffic flow.
5.   Plentiful parking.
6.   Proximity to _____ and _____ income growth areas.
7.   Proximity to businesses in same affinity class with same ideal client profiles.
8.   Reasonable rent.
9.   Conveniently located to customer base.
10.   Proximity to the growing residential community of _____.
11.   Low crime rate with good police and fire protection.
12.   Proximity to a tourist attraction.
13.   Zoning approved for a Microbrewery.
14.   Possesses expansion possibilities.

2.4.1   Company Facilities

_____ (company name) signed a _____ (#) year lease for _____ (#) square foot of space. The cost is very reasonable at $____/sq. foot. We also have the option of expanding into an additional _____ sq. ft. of space and subletting the space. A leasehold improvement allowance of $____ /sq. ft. would be given. Consolidated area maintenance fees would be $___/month initially. _____ (company name) has obtained a _____ (three) month option on this space effective _____ (date), the submission date of this business plan, and has deposited refundable first and last lease payments, plus a $ _____ security deposit with the leasing agent.

The lease is intended to function and operate as a triple net lease, with the brewery responsible for its pro rata portion of real estate taxes, insurance, and operating expenses. The approximate cost of the lease is $_____ per month inclusive.

Notes: Triple Net vs. Gross Lease
In a triple net, the tenant pays rent to the landlord, as well as a pro-rated share of taxes, insurance and maintenance expenses. In the typical triple net lease, the tenant pays a fixed amount of base rent each month as well as an "additional rent" payment which constitutes 1/12 of an estimated amount for taxes, insurance and maintenance expenses This is also called CAM or common area maintenance expenses. At the end of the lease year, the estimated amounts are compared to actual expenses incurred and adjusted depending upon whether the tenant paid too much or too little through its monthly payments. In a "gross" lease, the landlord agrees to pay all expenses which are normally associated with ownership. The tenant pays a fixed amount each month, and nothing more.

The facilities will incorporate the following room parameters into the layout:

		Percentage	Square Footage
1.	Retail Floor Area	_____	_____
2.	Supplies Storage	_____	_____
3.	Product Inventory Storage	_____	_____
4.	Malt Storage Area	_____	_____
5.	Brewhouse	_____	_____
6.	Fermentation area	_____	_____
7.	Walk-in Cooler	_____	_____
8.	Shipping/Receiving Area	_____	_____
9.	Packaging Area	_____	_____
10.	Staff Room	_____	_____
11.	Admin Offices	_____	_____
12.	Tasting Room	_____	_____
13.	Restrooms	_____	_____
Totals:		_____	_____

Tasting Room Design

We will create a welcoming local hotspot that will offer craft beer enthusiasts a place to hang out, sample new craft beers, learn about the brewing process and how to match brews to foods, shoot pool or throw darts, and even see a live performance on the tasting room's stage. We will craft a tasting room to showcase our unique, independent spirit, and signature brews.

Resource:

www.craftbrewingbusiness.com/business-marketing/tasting-room-tips-build-run-brand-brewery-showcase/

The brewhouse area will generate waste water and as such, a trench drain running in front of the brewing vessels will be installed. The floor will be pitched 1/8" - 1/4" to the drain and covered with a suitable covering to stand up to the anticipated high temperature, both acidic and alkaline cleaning solutions. Brewhouse walls and ceilings will be of materials that will withstand a wet environment and not harbor bacterial growth. The brewhouse will be considered a manufacturing area and as such, sufficient lighting will be provided to allow for safe efficient working conditions. We will install a drop down "trouble light" over the brewhouse platform to allow for interior tank inspection. A water house, complete with spray nozzle, will also be provided at the platform for use during the actual brew. The brewhouse will require an input of malted barley (approximately 50 lbs per barrel) per batch and its storage area will be readily accessible yet not exposed to excessive moisture or temperature. All electrical outlets will have moisture resistant covers. The glycol chiller and steam boiler will both generate heat and will require adequate ventilation and make up air. The water filter will occasionally require back flushing and will have access to a drain. The boiler will be located close to the brewhouse to allow for a minimal piping run of steam and condensate. The glycol chiller will primarily supply the fermentation and/or bright tanks and as such, will be installed in close proximity areas.

Basic brewhouse electrical requirements are:
Temperature Control Panel 110v / 60 hz / FLA 2
Brewhouse Control 110v / 60 hz / FLA 2
Hot Liquor Pump 208v / 3 phase / 60 hz / FLA 5
Wort Pump 208 v / 3 phase / 60 hz / FLA 5
CIP Pump 208 v / 3 phase / 60 hz / FLA 5
Glycol Chiller (2HP) 208 v / 3 phase / 60 hz / FLA 17
Steam Boiler 208 v / 3 phase / 60 hz / FLA 10

Basic brewery water: A minimum of 1" line delivering 10.5 GPM @ 40 p.s.i. will be installed. This amount is based on the wort cooling demand. The type of water and the ambient temperature of the water will affect these requirements.

HVAC: Local codes will dictate but the steam boiler will require exterior venting of the combustion gases. The brewkettle will either require a vapor stack vented to the atmosphere or a vapor condenser. The area housing the brewkettle will require a positive pressure.

2.5.0   Start-up Summary

The start-up costs for the Microbrewery will be financed through a combination of an owner investment of $ _____ and a short-term bank loan of $ _____. The total start-up costs for this business are approximately $ _____ and can be broken down in the following major categories:

1.	Land, Building and Improvements	$ _____
2.	Equipment and Installation Expenses	$ _____
3.	Development Expense	$ _____
4.	Office Furniture: Work Tables and Cabinets	$ _____
5.	Initial Product Inventory (200K?)	$ _____
6.	Working Capital (6 months)	$ _____
	For day-to-day operations, including payroll, etc.	
7.	Renovate Retail Space	$ _____
	Includes architect, lighting update, flooring, etc.	
8.	Marketing/Advertising Expenses	$ _____
	Includes sales brochures, direct mail, opening expenses.	
8.	Utility/ (Rent?) Deposits	$ _____
9.	Licenses and Permits	$ _____
10.	Contingency Fund	$ _____
11.	Other (Includes training, legal expenses, etc.)	$ _____

Start-up Costs

Start-up costs include improvements made to the building which are necessary for brewing operations. This includes bringing water, electric, and natural gas into the building to where the brewhouse equipment will be located. In addition, floor drains and waste water handling improvements are necessary. The build-out costs are broken down into a labor component and a supply component.

Initial inventories for one month of brewing are also included in the start-up costs. Malt, hops, yeast, and cleaning supplies are included in this amount. After start-up, inventory costs will be handled on a month-to-month basis.

Basic Use of Funds Sought:

    To acquire brewing equipment, supplies, and inventory
    To reconstruct portions of the building and bring in the necessary utilities.
    To make the building meet local zoning requirements.
    To provide working capital.
    To purchase initial inventory (1-month supply or 60 barrels).

The company will require $_____ in initial cash reserves and additional $_____ in assets. The start-up costs are to be financed by the equity contributions of the owner in the amount of $ _____ , as well as by a ____ (#) year commercial loan in the amount of $ _____. The funds will be repaid through earnings.

These start-up expenses and funding requirements are summarized in the tables below.

2.5.1   Inventory

Inventory:	Supplier	Qty	Unit Cost	Total
Bags and Supplies				
Grocery Products				
Cleaning Supplies				
Office Supplies				
Computer Supplies				
Marketing Materials				
Finished Beer Inventory				
Dry malt extract				
Malted barley				
Yeast				
Hops				
Beer Glassware				
Bottles				
Kegs				
Water Filters				
Sheet Filters				
Misc. Supplies				
Totals:				

Note: An average budget for a production brewery that takes advantage of used start-up equipment will fall between $150,000-$200,000. A third of this could be used to make improvements necessary to the building. For a mature market the price would be more along the lines of $250,000-$350,000 for a draft-only operation. For those willing to invest sweat equity, starting a brewery may be launched for less, but it's best to raise capital because debt often destroys small brewers. Plus finding distributors willing to take on unproven brands can be onerous. Brewpubs can cost a few million dollars, depending on their size.

2.5.2   Supply Sourcing

Basic Supplies

Malt

Malted barley is the primary ingredient by which beer is produced. The malt will be supplied by Briess Malting Company, Chilton, Wisconsin. Briess is one of the national premier maltsters, with the ability to ensure timely delivery and consistent quality of the mal product. Malt one packaged in 501b. bags. Each brew will consume 15 bags. 60 bags will be used weekly at a cost of $900/week, or in other terms, $225 per brew.

Hops

Hops will be bought from John I. Haas and Company, Yakima, Washington. Like Briess maltsters, Haas and Company enjoys the reputation of being a national leader in hop production. The ingredient suppliers were chosen for their known reputations of timely delivery as well as consistent and known quality.

Each brew will use 7.5 lbs. of hops at a cost of $15.00 per brew or $60 per week.

Yeast & Additives

Yeast, beer clarifiers, stabilizers, finings, cleaning supplies, as well as laboratory and technical services will be purchased from J.E. Siebel Sons, Chicago, Illinois.

Cleansing and Sanitation

The proper cleaning and sanitation levels necessary to meet strict health department guidelines will be achieved through the use of Orasan, (previously Huwa-San). Orasan is a new, complex compound of highly concentrated oxygen carriers, stabilizing agents on an acid base, and synergistically acting trace elements. It is superior to chlorine in its ability to kill germs, is completely safe for human and animal consumption, and will not create adverse environmental conditions. The advantages to using Orasan is no unpleasant taste; no odor; disinfects by separation of oxygen; assisted by trace elements; long-term effect; single application for long distance water conduits; not harmful to pipes and installations; water doesn't foam in it; and it is heat resistant and efficacious in hot water. Orasan is supplied by International Connection, Inc., Kewaskum, Wisconsin.

Filters

Sheet filters will be used to filter the fresh beer. From one to two pad filters are used per barrel brewed, resulting in a cost of approximately $0.80 - $1.20 per barrel. This type of filtering is easy to operate, easy to clean and sanitize. It leaves no particulate matter in the beer and is suitable for aseptic filtration. Sheet filters will be obtained from Siebel Company, Chicago, Illinois.

Growlers

GrowlerWerks   **www.growlerwerks.com/**

They have created uKeg, a portable, pressurized growler for transporting craft beer and other beverages. The vacuum insulated uKeg growler has a removable tap and is topped with a patent pending variable regulation pressure cap, powered by food-grade CO_2 cartridges that maintains the internal pressure necessary to keep beer fresh and cold.

Labels

Screen Printed Labels	http://bottleprint.com/
Oak Printing Company	www.oakprintingco.com/
World Label	www.worldlabel.com/Pages/bottle-labels.htm

We will search for and contact several wholesale suppliers for our microbrewery. We will first contact the National Association of Wholesaler-Distributors and ask our contact person if they can supply a list of _____ wholesalers. We will also visit the Tradepub.com website and order some free trade publications on retailing. We will read through the classified ads for potential _____ wholesalers. We will consider the wholesalers that offer the best mix of lowest unit cost of _____ products, the fastest re-order turnaround service, and the best open credit terms. We will meet up with suppliers and inquire if we can avail discounted prices if we buy in bulk.

Initially, ____ (company name) will purchase all of its equipment from _____ and supplies from _____, the _____ (second/third?) largest supplier in _____ (state), because of the discount given for bulk purchases. However, we will also maintain back-up relationships with two smaller suppliers, namely _____ and _____.
These two suppliers have competitive prices on certain products.

Resources:
Kegs: https://thielmann.com/
www.getmybrewery.com/sitemap.htm
www.brewplants.com/eurotech-micro.html
www.dmemart.com/
www.imperialmalt.com
www.beerinfo.com/index.php/pages/brewingequipment.html
www.nealhknapp.com/Microbrewery-Equipment/Beer-Brewing-Supplies.aspx
https://www.probrewer.com/the-probrewer-supplier-directory/
www.ebay.com

Input Products	Description	Source	Back-up	Cost

2.5.3   Supplier Assessments
We will use the following form to compare and evaluate suppliers, because they will play a major role in our procurement strategies and significantly contribute to our profitability.

	Supplier #1	Supplier #2	Compare
Supplier Name			
Website			
Address			
Contacts			
Annual Sales			
Distribution Channels			
Memberships/Certifications			
Quality System			
Positioning			
Pricing Strategy			
Payment Terms			
Discounts			
Delivery Lead-time			
Return Policy			
Rebate Program			
Technical Support			
Core Competencies			

Primary Product	_____
Primary Service	_____
New Products/Services	_____
Innovative Applications/Uses	_____
Competitive Advantage	_____
Capital Intensity	_____
State of Technology	_____
Capacity Utilization	_____
Price Volatility	_____
Vertical Integration	_____
References	_____
Overall Rating	_____

2.5.4   Equipment Leasing

Equipment Leasing will be the smarter solution allowing our microbrewery to upgrade our equipment needs at the end of the term rather than being overly invested in outdated equipment through traditional bank financing and equipment purchase. We also intend to explore the following benefits of leasing some of the required equipment:

1.   Frees Up Capital for other uses.   2.   Tax Benefits
3.   Improves Balance Sheet   4.   Easy to add-on or trade-up
5.   Improves Cash Flow   6.   Preserves Credit Lines
7.   Protects against obsolescence   8.   Application Process Simpler

Our leasing strategy will also be shaped by the following factors:
1.   Estimated useful life of the equipment.
2.   How long our business plans to use the equipment.
3.   What our business intends to do with the equipment at the end of the lease.
4.   The tax situation of our business.
5.   The cash flow of our business.
6.   Our company's specific needs for future growth.

List Any Leases:

Leasing Company	Equipment Description	Monthly Payment	Lease Period	Final Disposition

Resources:

LeaseQ   www.leaseq.com
An online market place that connects businesses, equipment dealers, and leasing companies to make selling and financing equipment fast and easy. The LeaseQ Platform is a free, cloud-based SaaS solution with a suite of on-demand software and data solutions for the equipment leasing industry. Utilizes the Internet to provide business process optimization (BPO) and information services that streamline the purchase and

financing of business equipment across a broad array of vertical industry segments.

Innovative Lease Services   http://www.ilslease.com/equipment-leasing/
This company was founded in 1986 and is headquartered in Carlsbad, California. It is accredited by the Better Business Bureau, a longstanding member of the National Equipment Finance Association and the National Association of Equipment Leasing Brokers and is the official equipment financing partner of Biocom.

2.5.5   Funding Source Matrix

Funds Source	Amount	Interest Rate	Repayment Terms	Use

2.5.6   Distribution or Licensing Agreements (if any)

Note: These are some of the key factors that investors will use to determine if we have a competitive advantage that is not easily copied.

Licensor	License Rights	License Term	Fee or Royalty

2.5.7   Trademarks, Patents and Copyrights (if any)

Our trademark will be virtually our branding for life. Our choice of a name for our microbrewery business is very important. Not only will we brand our business and services forever, but what may be worthless today will become our most valuable asset in the years to come. A trademark search by our Lawyer will be a must, because to be told down the road that we must give up our name because we did not bother to conduct a trademark search would be a devastating blow to our business. It is also essential that the name that we choose suit the expanding product or service offerings that will be coming down the pike. With new craft breweries launching every day, the competition for beer names has become intense. Once we select the beer names and design logos, we will need to file trademark for these as well. (NOTE: If we have our beer names selected at the time we apply for a Federal trademark for the micro-brewery name we can also submit the applications for the beer names at the same time.

Note: These are some of the key factors that investors will use to determine if we have a competitive advantage that is not easily copied.

Resources:
Patents/Trademarks   www.uspto.gov / Copyright   www.copyright.gov
Growler Magazine   http://growlermag.com/so-you-want-to-start-your-own-brewery/

2.5.8 Innovation Strategy   (optional)

____ (company name) will create an innovation strategy that is aligned with not only our firm's core mission and values, but also with our future technology, supplier, and manufacturing strategies. The objective of our innovation strategy will be to create a sustainable competitive advantage. Our education and training systems will be designed to equip our staff with the foundations to learn and develop the broad range of skills needed for innovation in all of its forms, and with the flexibility to upgrade skills and adapt to changing market conditions. To foster an innovative workplace, we will ensure that employment policies facilitate efficient organizational change and encourage the expression of creativity, engage in mutually beneficial strategic alliances and allocate adequate funds for research and development. Our radical innovation strategies include _____ to achieve first mover status. Our incremental innovation strategies will include modifying the following _____ (products/services/processes) to give our customers added value for their money. Resource: https://hbr.org/2015/04/the-5-requirements-of-a-truly-innovative-company

2.5.9 Summary of Sources and Use of Funds

Sources:

Owner's Equity Investment $ _____
Requested Bank Loans $ _____
Total: $ _____

Uses:

Capital Equipment $ _____
Beginning Inventory $ _____
Start-up Costs $ _____
Working Capital $ _____
Total: $ _____

2.5.9.1 Funding to Date   (optional)

To date, _____'s (company name) founders have invested $_____ in _____ (company name), with which we have accomplished the following:
1.   _____ (Designed/Built) the company's website
2.   Developed content, in the form of ____ (#) articles, for the website.
3.   Hired and trained our core staff of __(#) full-time people and ____ (#) part-time people.
4.   Generated brand awareness by driving ____ (#) visitors to our website in a ___(#) month period.

5. Successfully _____ (Developed/Test Marketed) ___ (#) new _____ (products/services), which compete on the basis of _____.
6. _____ (Purchased/Developed) and installed the software needed to _____ (manage _____ operations?)
7. Purchased $ _____ worth of _____ (supplies) to make _____.
8. Purchased $ _____ worth of _____ equipment for _____.

2.6 Start-up Requirements

Start-up Expenses:		Estimates
Legal	_____	
Accountant	_____	300
Accounting Software Package	_____	300
Liquor License	_____	3000
Other State Licenses & Permits	_____	
Microbrewery Set-up	_____	
Employment Agency Fees	_____	
Unforeseen Contingency	_____	3000
Market Research Survey	_____	300
Research & Development	_____	
Office Supplies	_____	300
Sales Brochures	_____	300
Direct Mailing	_____	500
Other Marketing Materials	_____	2000
Logo Design	_____	500
Advertising (2 months)	_____	2000
Consultants	_____	5000
Contractor Fees	_____	
Insurance-Prepaid	_____	
Rent (2 months security)	_____	5000
Rent Deposit	_____	2500
Utility Deposit	_____	1000
DSL Installation/Activation	_____	100
Telecommunications Installation	_____	3000
Telephone Deposit	_____	200
Expensed Equipment	_____	1000
Website Design/Hosting	_____	2000
Computer System	_____	2000
Used Office Equipment/Furniture	_____	2000
Organization Memberships	_____	300
Cleaning Supplies	_____	200
Staff Training	_____	3000
Promotional Signs	_____	2000
Security System	_____	3000

Other   _____
Total Start-up Expenses   _____ **(A)**

Start-up Assets:

Cash Balance Required   _____ (T)   15000
Start-up Equipment   _____ See schedule
Start-up Inventory   _____ See schedule
Other Current Assets   _____
Long-term Assets   _____
Total Assets   _____ **(B)**
Total Requirements   _____ (A+B)

Start-up Funding

Start-up Expenses to Fund   _____ (A)
Start-ups Assets to Fund   _____ (B)
Total Funding Required: _____ **(A+B)**

Assets

Non-cash Assets from Start-up   _____
Cash Requirements from Start-up   _____ (T)
Additional Cash Raised   _____ (S)
Cash Balance on Starting Date   _____ (T+S=U)
Total Assets: _____ **(B)**

Liabilities and Capital

Short-term Liabilities:
Current Borrowing   _____
Unpaid Expenses   _____
Accounts Payable   _____
Interest-free Short-term Loans   _____
Other Short-term Loans   _____
Total Short-term Liabilities   _____ **(Z)**

Long-term Liabilities:
Commercial Bank Loan   _____
Other Long-term Liabilities   _____
Total Long-term Liabilities   _____ **(Y)**
Total Liabilities   _____ **(Z+Y = C)**

Capital

Planned Investment
Owner   _____
Family   _____
Other   _____
Additional Investment Requirement   _____

Total Planned Investment _____ **(F)**

Loss at Start-up (Start-up Expenses) (-)_____ **(A)**
Total Capital (=)_____ **(F+A=D)**
Total Capital and Liabilities _____ **(C+D)**
Total Funding _____ (C+F)

2.6.1 Capital Equipment List

Equipment Type	Model No.	New/ Used	Lifespan	Quantity	Unit Cost	Total Cost
Brewhouses:						
mash tun						
lauter tun						
brew kettle						
whirlpool						
cold water tank						
hot water tank						
wort-collecting tank						
Fermenting Components:						
fermenting/conditioning uni-tanks						
brigh-beer tanks						
control system						
wort cooling & aeration						
steam generator						
cooling unit						
malt-mill						
platform & piping						
beer-filters						
yeast propagation						
stainless-steel fermentation tanks						
Beer tapping tanks						
Brewery tanks & vessels.						
Bottling Equipment						
Filler/Capper PEPA 2/2						
Bottle Rinser						
Bottle Washer						
Labeller						
Bottle Air-Evacuating Devices						
Bottle Inspectors						
Bottle & Crate Conveyors						
Flow & tunnel pasteurizing equip.						

Air Conveyors _____

Wrapping Machines _____

Kegging Equipment:

KEG-Washing _____

KEG-Filling Machines _____

Capping Machines _____

KEG Conveyors _____

KEG Turners _____

Palletizing equipment _____

Vacuum pump Keg-Washers _____

Weighing Devices _____

CIP-Stations _____

Other:

Electrical service panel _____

Water filtration system _____

Steam boiler _____

Glycol chiller _____

Refrigeration Equipment:

Display Coolers _____

Sold Door Freezer _____

Walk-in Cooler _____

Security System _____

Electronic Safe _____

Computer System _____

Fax Machine _____

Copy Machine _____

Video Surveillance System _____

Electronic Cash Register _____

Phone System _____

Answering Machine _____

Broadband Internet Connection _____

TV and DVD Player _____

Office Furniture _____

Accounting Software _____

Microsoft Office Software _____

Operations Management Software _____

Shelving Units _____

Lockers _____

Hand Truck _____

Pallet Jacks _____

Mop Station _____

Marquee Sign _____

Assorted Signs	_____
Telephone headsets	_____
Calculator	_____
Filing & Storage Cabinets	_____
Cabinetry	_____
Credit Card Verification Machine	_____
Pricing Guns	_____
Emergency First Aid Kit	_____
Other	_____
Total Capital Equipment	_____

Note: **Equipment costs dependent on whether purchased new or used or leased.** All items that are assets to be used for more than one year will be considered a long-term asset and will be depreciated using the straight-line method.

Resources:

www.craftbrewingbusiness.com/featured/craft-beer-bottling-equipment-advice/
www.moderntimesbeer.com/2018/12/10/how-much-does-it-cost-to-start-a-brewery/
www.americanbeerequipment.com/
www.epakmachinery.com/
www.brewbids.com/

Capital Equipment Descriptions

Brewhouse

The brewhouse is supplied by _____ (JV Northwest of Wilsonville, Oregon?). The brewhouse will be a 15-barrel turnkey system complete with all tanks, hoses, fittings, controls, and gauges to brew 3120 barrels of ale per year. Each additional fermentation tank adds 780 barrels more production. Expansion can reach 7500 barrels per year with the 15-barrel brewkettle. The initial cost of the brewhouse is $_____ (175,000?).

Barrels

Barrels will be bought from _____ (SABCO Industries, Toledo, Ohio?). Initial plans are to buy ____ (500?) barrels, which will provide a four-week barrel supply when brewing to capacity. Cost per barrel is $_____ (30.00?) for a standard Hoff-Stevens keg. Total barrel cost is $15,000.

Keg Filler

A semi-automatic single valve keg washing, sanitizing, and filling machine will be bought from _____ (I.D. Distributions, Thousand Oaks, California?). It is a complete washer/sterilizing/racking machine complete with detergent and water supply system, include dual compartment tank, stainless steel pumps, heater dosing system, and controls. The machine can fill up to 30 half kegs per hour, therefore it is estimated kegging operations for 60 barrels weekly production will take a minimum of 4 hours, and most likely complete in one working day. The cost of the machine is $14,000.

Laboratory Equipment

The laboratory equipment necessary for proper testing and evaluation of the beer throughout the brewing and fermentation process includes the following items: Microscope, for counting yeast cells, Hydrometer, for measuring specific gravity,

PH meter, accurate to 0.01 of a unit, plus combination electrode suitable for use with wort and fermentation products, and Air tester. These will be purchased from _____ (Cole-Parmer Instrument Company, Niles, Illinois?). Cost for the above, plus any incidental supplies, is approximately $2000.

Resource: http://www.brauhaus-austria.com/pricelist.htm

Water Filtration System

World Water Works' Ideal MBBR-DAF advanced water treatment system provides the perfect solution by combining moving bed biofilm reactor (MBBR) technology and dissolved air flotation (DAF) technology.

http://www.worldwaterworks.com/

2.7.0   SBA Loan Key Requirements

In order to be considered for an SBA loan, we must meet the basic requirements: 1. Must have been turned down for a loan by a bank or other lender to qualify for most SBA Business Loan Programs. 2. Required to submit a guaranty, both personal and business, to qualify for the loans. 3. Must operate for profit; be engaged in, or propose to do business in, the United States or its possessions; 4. Have reasonable owner equity to invest; 5. Use alternative financial resources first including personal assets.

All businesses must meet eligibility criteria to be considered for financing under the SBA's 7(a) Loan Program, including: size; type of business; operating in the U.S. or its possessions; use of available of funds from other sources; use of proceeds; and repayment. The repayment term of an SBA loan is between five and 25 years, depending on the lift of the assets being financed and the cash needs of the business.

Working capital loans (accounts receivable and inventory) should be repaid in five to 10 years. The SBA also has short-term loan guarantee programs with shorter repayment terms.

A Business Owner Cannot Use an SBA Loan:

To purchase real estate where the participant has issued a forward commitment to the developer or where the real estate will be held primarily for investment purposes. To finance floor plan needs. To make payments to owners or to pay delinquent withholding taxes. To pay existing debt, unless it can be shown that the refinancing will benefit the small business and that the need to refinance is not indicative of poor management.

SBA Loan Programs:

Low Doc: www.sba.gov/financing/lendinvest/lowdoc.html

SBA Express   www.sba,gov/financing/lendinvest/sbaexpress.html

Basic 7(a) Loan Guarantee Program

    For businesses unable to obtain loans through standard loan programs. Funds can be used for general business purposes, including working
     capital, leasehold improvements and debt refinancing.
     www.sba.gov/financing/sbaloan/7a.html

Certified Development Company 504 Loan Program
> Used for fixed asset financing such as purchase of real estate or machinery.
> www. Sba.gov/gopher/Local-Information/Certified-Development-Companies/

MicroLoan 7(m) Loan Program
> Provides short-term loans up to $35,000.00 for working capital or purchase of fixtures.
> www.sba.gov/financing/sbaloan/microloans.html

2.7.1 Other Financing Options

1. Grants:

    Health care grants, along with education grants, represent the largest percentage of grant giving in the United States. The federal government, state, county and city governments, as well as private and corporate foundations all award grants. The largest percentage of grants are awarded to non-profit organizations, health care agencies, colleges and universities, local government agencies, tribal institutions, and schools. For profit organizations are generally not eligible for grants unless they are conducting research or creating jobs.

    A. Contact your state licensing office.
    B. Foundation Grants to Individuals: www.fdncenter.org
    C. US Grants   www.grants.gov
    D. Foundation Center   www.foundationcemter.org
    E. The Grantsmanship Center   www.tgci.com
    F. Contact local Chamber of Commerce
    G. The Catalog of Federal Domestic Assistance is a major provider of business grant money.
    H. The Federal Register is a good source to keep current with the continually changing federal grants offered.
    I. FedBizOpps is a resource, as all federal agencies must use FedBizOpps to notify the public about contract opportunities worth over $25,000.
    J. Fundsnet Services   http://www.fundsnetservices.com/
    K. SBA Women Business Center
        www.sba.gov/content/womens-business-center-grant-opportunities

Local Business Grants

Check with local businesses for grant opportunities and eligibility requirements. For example, Bank of America sponsors community grants for businesses that endeavor to improve the community, protect the environment or preserve the neighborhood.

Resource:

www.bankofamerica.com/foundation/index.cfm?template=fd_localgrants

Green Technology Grants

If you install green technology in the business as a way to reduce waste and make the business more energy efficient, you may be eligible for grant funding. Check your state's Economic Development Commission. This grant program was developed as part of the American Recovery and Reinvestment Act.

Resource: www.recovery.gov/Opportunities/Pages/Opportunities.aspx

2.   Friends and Family Lending   www.virginmoney.com
3.   National Business Incubator Association   www.nbia.org/
4.   Women's Business Associations   www.nawbo.org/
5.   Minority Business Development Agency   www.mbda.gov/
6.   Social Networking Loans   www.prosper.com
7.   Peer-to-Peer Programs   www.lendingclub.com
8.   Extended Credit Terms from Suppliers   30/60/90 days.
9.   Community Bank
10. Prepayments from Customers
11. Seller Financing: When purchasing an existing Microbrewery.
12. Business Funding Directory   www.businessfinance.com
13. FinanceNet   www.financenet.gov
14. SBA Financing   www.sbaonline.sba.gov
15. Micro-Loans   www.accionusa.org/
16. Private Investor
17. Use retirement funds to open a business without taxes or penalty. First, establish a C-corporation for the new business. Next, the C-corporation establishes a new retirement plan. Then, the owner's current retirement funds are rolled over into the C-corporation's new plan. And last, the new retirement plan invests in stock of the C-corporation. Warning: Check with your accountant or financial planner. Resource: http://www.benetrends.com/
18. Business Plan Competition Prizes www.nytimes.com/interactive/2009/11/11/business/smallbusiness/Competitions-table.html?ref=smallbusiness
19. Unsecured Business Cash Advance based on future credit card transactions.
20. Kick Starter   www.kickstarter.com
     Resources:
     www.topfermented.com/2012/05/23/how-to-open-a-brewery-using-kickstarter/
     http://beerpulse.com/2012/05/successful-kickstarter-brewery-mystery-brewing-shares-tips/
21. Tech Stars   www.techstars.org
22. Capital Source   www.capitalsource.com
     www.msl.com/index.cfm?event=page.sba504
     Participates in the SBA's 504 loan program. This program is for the purchase of fixed assets such as commercial real estate and machinery and equipment of a capital nature, which are defined as assets that have a minimum useful life of ten years. Proceeds cannot be used for working capital.
23. Commercial Loan Applications   www.c-loans.com/onlineapp/
24. Sharing assets and resources with other businesses.
25. Angel Investors   www.angelcapitaleducation.org
26. The Receivables Exchange   http://receivablesxchange.com/
27. Bootstrap Methods: Personal Savings/Credit Card/Second Mortgages
28. Community-based Crowd-funding   www.profounder.com
                                   www.peerbackers.com
                                   www.fannextdoor.com
                                   www.rockethub.com

www.IndieGogo.com

A funding option designed to link small businesses and entrepreneurs with pools of prospective investors. Crowdfunding lenders are often repaid with goods or services.

29.   On Deck Capital   http://www.ondeckcapital.com/
Created the Short-Term Business Loan (up to $100,000.00) for small businesses to get quick access to capital that fits their cash flow, with convenient daily payments.

30.   LaunchCapital Royalty Lending   http://www.launch-capital.com/
With royalty lending, financing is granted in return for future revenue or company performance, and payback can prove exceedingly expensive if a company flourishes.

31.   Stock Loans   Southern Lending Solutions, Atlanta. GA.
                                  Custom Commercial Finance, Bartlesville, OK
A stock loan is based on the quality of stocks, Treasuries and other kinds of investments in a businessperson's personal portfolio. Possession of the company's stock is transferred to the lender's custodial bank during the loan period.

32.   Lender Compatibility Searcher   www.BoeFly.com

33.   Strategic Investors
Strategic investing is more for a large company that identifies promising technologies, and for whatever reason, that company may not want to build up the research and development department in-house to produce that product, so they buy a percentage of the company with the existing technology.

34.   Bartering   http://www.barternews.com/micro_brewery.htm

35.   Small Business Investment Companies   www.sba.gov/INV

36.   Cash-Value Life Insurance

37.   Employee Stock Option Plans   www.nceo.org

38.   Venture Capitalists   www.nvca.org

39.   Initial Public Offering (IPO)

40.   Meet investors through online sites, including LinkedIn (group discussions), Facebook (BranchOut sorts Facebook connections by profession), and CapLinked (enables search for investment-related professionals by industry and role).

41.   SBA Community Advantage Approved Lenders
                  www.sba.gov/content/community-advantage-approved-lenders

42.   Small Business Lending Specialists
https://www.wellsfargo.com/biz/loans_lines/compare_lines
http://www.bankofamerica.com/small_business/business_financing/
https://online.citibank.com/US/JRS/pands/detail.do?ID=CitiBizOverview
https://www.chase.com/ccp/index.jsp?pg_name=ccpmapp/smallbusiness/home/pa
        ge/bb_business_bBanking_programs

43.   Startup America Partnership   www.s.co/about
Based on a simple premise: young companies that grow create jobs. Once startups apply and become a Startup America Firm, they can access and manage many types of resources through a personalized dashboard.

44.   United States Economic Development Administration   www.eda.gov/

45.   Tax Increment Financing (TIF)

A public financing method that is used for subsidizing redevelopment, infrastructure, and other community-improvement projects. TIF is a method to use future gains in taxes to subsidize current improvements, which are projected to create the conditions for said gains. The completion of a public project often results in an increase in the value of surrounding real estate, which generates additional tax revenue. Tax Increment Financing dedicates tax increments within a certain defined district to finance the debt that is issued to pay for the project. TIF is often designed to channel funding toward improvements in distressed, underdeveloped, or underutilized parts of a jurisdiction where development might otherwise not occur. TIF creates funding for public or private projects by borrowing against the future increase in these property-tax revenues.

46.   Gust   https://gust.com/entrepreneurs

Provides the global platform for the sourcing and management of early-stage investments. Gust enables skilled entrepreneurs to collaborate with the smartest investors by virtually supporting all aspects of the investment relationship, from initial pitch to successful exit.

47.   Lending Club   https://www.lendingclub.com/

48.   Goldman Sachs 10,000 Small Businesses   http://sites.hccs.edu/10ksb/

49.   Earnest Loans   www.meetearnest.com

50.   Biz2Credit   www.biz2credit.com

51.   Funding Circle   www.fundingcircle.com

A peer-to-peer lending service which allows savers to lend money directly to small and medium sized businesses

52.   Quicken Loans   www.quickenloans.com/blog/rise-michigan-microbreweries

Resources: www.sba.gov/category/navigation-structure/starting-managing-business/starting-business/local-resources

http://usgovinfo.about.com/od/moneymatters/a/Finding-Business-Loans-Grants-Incentives-And-Financing.htm

3.0 Products and Services

In this section, we will not only list all of our planned products and services, but also describe how our proposed products and services will be differentiated from those of our competitors and solve a real problem or fill an unmet need in the marketplace.

Assuming that the majority of our product will be consumed in bars that means that the most largely purchased container size will be kegs for the bars to serve our beer. We will sell kegs in bulk at a discounted price to the bars to get a large quantity on the market quickly. As for the home consumption of our product, we will offer bottle sizes of 12oz, 24 oz, and 32 oz. Our product will not be sold in any cans or plastic bottles. This is because it takes away from the status of our beer and makes us look more like a macro brew, low quality and cheaper looking. As for package size, we will offer 6 packs, 12 packs, and 24 packs of all our beers. The most consumed package size is thought to be the 6-packs, so we will reserve most of our shelf space for that. We will only offer the 24 packs at select locations around the _____ area. Kegs and the majority of the 24 packs will be sold from smaller specialty stores or directly from our brewery in ___ (city).

Every microbrewery has its specific products that it produces, meaning specific types of beer. We will focus on having ___ (5?) types of beer available at all times to the public. ____ (company name) intends to develop a highly specialized microbrewery that will produce a number of seasonal and specialized beers such as stouts, pale ales, porters, lagers, and a number of specialized ales/lagers with proprietary formulas developed by the Company's brew master. The business expects to distribute approximately 15,000 barrels of beer per year.

The primary three will be of the following types: a wheat beer, a porter, and brown ale. These three types of beer are some of the most highly consumed from microbrews. The fourth type of beer that we will produce at all times is an experimental light beer which will fill two roles, the first being a low-calorie alternative to heavier beers and the second is following the social trend of light beers being the most consumed. The last type of beer that we will offer will be a seasonal beer. We will have four seasonal beers that will be alternated into and out of circulation as the seasons of the year change. The types of these beers will be as follows: for summer a wizen beer, for spring a berry beer, for fall an IPA, and for winter a stout beer. This will also help increase our market share by giving the consumers more to look forward to throughout the year. Variety packs will also be offered to the consumers throughout the year with two or three of a few different types of beers we offer. Overall, our product line will cover all of the bases in the microbrew industry and will provide us with a very profitable company.

The microbrewery will be open to the public for tours and sampling. The hours of operation will be from 9:00 a.m. to 5:00 p.m. Beer will be offered for sale on the premises as well as take-out. Kegged beer will be sold to _____ Distributors for further sale to retail outlets. Sales will be in half barrels, quarter barrels, cases of bottles, and six-packs.

Beer Name: _____ (Summer Ale, Winter Reserve, etc.)
Malts: _____ (Two-row pale, US Crystal, Munich, White Wheat, Demerara sugar)
Hops: _____ (Magnum, Simcoe, Styrian Golding)
Yeast: _____ (English Ale, Dusseldorf Alt)
Original Gravity: _____ (21.5 Plato)
Alcohol by volume: _____ (10% ?)
Formats: _____ (draft only, 12 oz. bottles, 1/2 kegs, 1/6 kegs, cask-conditioned)
Availability: _____ (released date or available months)
Food Pairings: _____
Price: _____

Beer Name: _____ (Summer Ale, Winter Reserve, etc.)
Malts: _____ (Two-row pale, US Crystal, Munich, White Wheat, Demerara sugar)
Hops: _____ (Magnum, Simcoe, Styrian Golding)
Yeast: _____ (English Ale, Dusseldorf Alt)
Original Gravity: _____ (21.5 Plato)
Alcohol by volume: _____ (10% ?)
Formats: _____ (draft only, 12 oz. bottles, 1/2 kegs, 1/6 kegs, cask-conditioned)
Availability: _____ (released date or available months)
Food Pairings: _____
Price: _____

Beer Name: _____ (Summer Ale, Winter Reserve, etc.)
Malts: _____ (Two-row pale, US Crystal, Munich, White Wheat, Demerara sugar)
Hops: _____ (Magnum, Simcoe, Styrian Golding)
Yeast: _____ (English Ale, Dusseldorf Alt)
Original Gravity: _____ (21.5 Plato)
Alcohol by volume: _____ (10% ?)
Formats: _____ (draft only, 12 oz. bottles, 1/2 kegs, 1/6 kegs, cask-conditioned)
Availability: _____ (released date or available months)
Food Pairings: _____
Price: _____

Services:

Party/Event Planning Services	Private Tasting Parties
Custom Gift Baskets	Delivery Services
Seminars	Consulting
Bar/Tasting Room	Beer Garden
Restaurant	Custom Embroidered Items
Beer to Go	Home delivery
Tours	Internet Access Available

Other Products

Logo Imprinted T-shirts and hats.	Mugs
Glassware	Calendars
Bike Jerseys	Bottle Openers
Coasters	

3.1 Service Descriptions

In creating our service descriptions, we will provide answers to the following types of questions:
1. What does the service do or help the customer to accomplish?
2. Why will people decide to buy it?
3. What makes it unique or a superior value?
4. How expensive or difficult is it to make or copy by a competitor?
5. How much will the service be sold for?

Brewery and beer consulting

We will provide knowledgeable, to the point and reasonably priced consulting to the brewing industry. Given the expertise we have developed over the years, we have experience with all aspects of brewpub and microbrewery projects such as engineering, commercial development, production, quality control, and marketing. We will bring a wealth of knowledge to the table. We will consult restaurants on how-to create a new beer list, price beers, train staff, create marketing materials and programs, improve profitability, etc. For our consulting we both use the vast amount of knowledge and expertise we have in house and can rely upon a number of experts for very specific problems or issues as brewery consultant.

Other brewery related services

Other services that will be provided are as follows:
Water analysis;
Beer analysis (biochemical and organoleptic);
Beer recipe analysis and procedure optimization;
Brewery energy and resources savings programs (planning and implementation);
Beer packaging consulting;
HACCP implementation;
ISO structuring and implementation

Custom Gift Baskets

Gift items will include a limited selection of kitchen wares, cocktail recipe books, beers, cookbooks, picnic items, and bartender accessories. Gift baskets will also be available in the microbrewery and over the internet. Customers will be able to purchase pre-stocked baskets and custom designed baskets, where the customer makes all content selections within a certain price range.

Mobile Bartender Services

We will provide complete bartending services, from the glasses, to the bartenders, to the shape and type of bar itself. The service will be professional, and customizable. It will be designed for the avid party host, the busy professional caterer, and event promoter. We will take care of everything, from the beers, to the glasses, to the people.

Party Planning Services
Includes menu and beer selection, bar supplies, invitations, decorations, budgeting, event staffing, sommelier services, food/beer pairings, specialty drink recipes, etc.

Private Beer Tastings (Check State Rules)
During the Tasting Event, guests will learn about a designated, hops growing region, while sampling and evaluating a variety of beers and cheeses.

Seminars
Seminar participants will learn: proper beer tasting techniques and etiquette, beer terms and common descriptive words, the basics of the brewing process, beer characteristics, beer and food pairings and what makes Rocky Mountain beers unique.

3.1.1 Product Benefits

The benefits of our crafted brews are as follows:
1. Brewed locally means a fresh, quality beer.
2. Retailers will realize high profit margins than on domestic brews.
3. Flexible structures make it easy to adapt to changing customer and supplier needs.
4. Quick reaction to meet distributor's needs.
5. Creation of customer demand that increases inventory turnover.
6. Donation of a portion of the profits to environmental causes.
7. Locals will have access to craft beers with prestigious local image.
8. Commitment to continuous brewing process improvements.

3.2 Alternative Revenue Streams
1. Classified Ads in our Newsletter
2. Vending Machine Sales
3. Product Rentals.
4. Website Banner Ads
4. Content Area Sponsorship Fees
5. Online Survey Report Fees
6. Consulting Services
7. Facilities Sub-leases

3.3 Production of Products and Services

We will use the following methods to locate the best suppliers for our business:
- Attend association trade shows and seminars to spot upcoming trends, realize networking opportunities and compare prices.

Craft Brewers Conference   www.craftbrewersconference.com/

- Subscribe to appropriate trade magazines, journals, newsletters and blogs.

- BeerPulse.com
- BrewPublic.com
- CrushBrew.com
- CraftBrewingBusiness.com
- AmericanCraftBeer.com
- BeerandBrewing.com
- BeerGeekNation.com
- Thedrinkbusiness.com

- Join our trade association to make valuable contacts, get listed in any online directories, and secure training and marketing materials.

Brewers Association **www.beertown.org/**
This is the national association for small brewers.

Brewers Association **www.brewersassociation.org/**
An organization of brewers, for brewers and by brewers. More than 4,465 US brewery members and 46,000 members of the American Homebrewers Association are joined by members of the allied trade, beer distributors, individuals, other associate members and the Brewers Association staff to make up the Brewers Association.

Craft Beer Association **www.Craftbeer.com**
Administered by the Brewers Association (BA), the national organization that represents the interests of small and independent craft brewers in America. Protects and promotes small and independent breweries.

National Beer Wholesalers Association **www.NBWA.org**
Through proactive industry affairs initiatives and effective advocacy before government and the public, NBWA represents beer distributors on issues ranging from taxes to regulation, working to promote the value of the American distribution system.

Association of Packaging and Processing Technologies
  www.pmmi.org/gateway

Chicago Homebrew Alchemists of Suds **www.chaosbrewclub.net/**
A coalition of home-brewers, beer aficionados, and enthusiasts in the Chicago, IL area that strives to cultivate appreciation of the science and culture of beer through education, exploration, and community.

- Attend a Brewery-focused Business Incubator Program
  Rocky Mount Mills Brewery Incubator
  www.rockymountmills.com/rocky-mount-mills-brewery-incubator/

- Ask questions of craft beer makers in other states.

www.connecticutmag.com/Blogs/Table-Hopping/January-2018/The-Microbrewery-Boom-in-Connecticut/
http://blog.mysanantonio.com/food/2018/01/branchline-brewing-company-set-to-debut-as-sas-second-microbrewery/

Resources:
Thomas Register   www.thomasregister.com
National Assoc. of Manufacturers   www.nam.org
LexisNexis   www.lexisnexis.com

3.4   Competitive Comparison

There are only ____ (#) other Microbreweries in the neighborhood. _____ (company name) will differentiate itself from its local competitors by offering a broader range of brewed beverages, maintaining a database of customer preferences and transaction history, offering membership club benefits to qualifying customers, using a monthly newsletter to stay-in-touch with customers and offering an array of innovative services. We will also place a heavy emphasis on the development of a staff training program to meet consumer information demands, while also serving to control operational costs.

We will be the only convenience and fast to-go Microbrewery in the _____ area, with a drive-thru window. We will use occasional surveys to solicit customer feedback and stock items requested by local residents. We will also encourage customers to make special order requests.

_____ (company name) does not have to pay for under-utilized staff. Our flexible employee scheduling procedures and use of part-timers ensure that the microbrewery is never overstaffed during slow times. We will also adopt a pay-for-performance compensation plan, and use referral incentives to generate new business.

We will reinvest major dollars every year in professional and educational materials. We will participate in online webinars to bring clients the finest selection of craft beers and services, and industry trend information. Our prices will be competitive with other breweries that offer far less in the way of benefits, innovative services, and product selection.

3.5   Sales Literature

____ (company name) has developed sales literature that illustrates a professional organization with vision. ____ (company name) plans to constantly refine its marketing mix through a number of different literature packets. These include the following:
- direct mail with introduction letter and product price sheet.
- product information brochures
- press releases
- new product/service information literature
- email marketing campaigns

- website content
- corporate brochures

A copy of our informational brochure is attached in the appendix of this document. This brochure will be available to provide referral sources, leave at seminars, and use for direct mail purposes.

3.6   Fulfillment

The key fulfillment and delivery of services will be provided by our director/owner, and certified microbrewery associates. The real core value is the industry expertise of the founder, and staff experience and company training programs.

3.7   Technology

___(company name) will employ and maintain the latest technology to enhance its office management, inventory management, payment processing, customer profiling and record keeping systems. We will also protect ourselves and society from the dangers of underage drinking with a new biometric fingerprint identification technology that can verify ID in a fraction of the time it takes to "card" customers. This will speed checkout while offering enhanced convenience and liability protection. We will also use a Cash Register POS system to manage our Microbrewery. Each item that gets sold will be deducted from our inventory list. Additionally, tracking items in our microbrewery will easily be managed with handheld inventory devices that integrate with Cash Register system.

Our point of sale system will include a small form factor computer, cash drawer, receipt printer and laser bar code scanner or tabletop scanner. An optional pole display will be easily added, which will inform our customers how much they are paying so they are likely to have the cash out quickly. A laser bar code scanner will aggressively scan bar codes that might be on bags or around bottles and quickly add the item to the invoice. All these devices help to reduce the time it takes to process a customer.

Resources:
Master Brewer's Toolbox   http://interactive.mbaa.com
This CD-Rom replicates processing parameters and helps predict how formulation changes will affect the other variables in the brewing process, including the following:
  Calculates raw materials forward from formulas and formulas backward from raw
     materials.
  Calculates brew house water, wort, volumes and degrees Plato.
  Calculates brew house efficiency, lauter efficiency, and hop utilization.
  Estimates hop utilization, mash RDF, and finished color.
  Estimates strike temperatures and combined cooker and mash mixer temperatures.
  Calculates extract priming.
  Converts weights and volumes to any unit, e.g. English or metric.

Rounds results to any increment, e.g. 0.1 bbl or 25 kg bag.
Calculates the cost per bbl including raw materials, utilities, and losses.
Allows raw material cost units to be different form usage units.

Brewsoft 2   **http://www.brewsoft.net/default.asp**
System features include the following:
1.   Custom Brewing Process Creation
2.   Batch Management
3.   Batch Merging
4.   Recipe Management
5.   Dynamic Recipe Adjustment
6.   Advanced Inventory
7.   Brew Batch Forecasting/Scheduling
8.   Brewery Calendar
9.   Integrated Touch Screen POS System for brewpubs or tasting rooms.
10.   Employee Time Clock Management
11.   Racking Management to enable shrinkage calculations.
12.   Distribution invoicing and account management.
13.   Sales Invoicing
14.   Sampling Log to track line sampling for weights and measures records.
15.   Product Management
16.   US/UK/Metrics Modes and Conversions
17.   QuickBooks Import/Export
18.   Aloha POS Import to export PMIX report.
19.   Customer / Vendor / Distributor Relations Management
20.   Tax Calculations with State Form Designer

Orchestrated Beer   www.orchestratedbeer.com/ondemand-cloud-brewery-software
All-in-one, cloud-based brewery management software for startups and small breweries.

Sap Business One
                http://go.sap.com/product/enterprise-management/business-one.html
The SAP Business One platform can be pre-configured for a Craft Brewery and includes
functionality such as; inventory management, production management, recipe
management, planning & forecasting, sales opportunity management, lab data
management, purchase orders, sales orders, automated accounting, and more.
Resources:
http://www.orchestratedbeer.com/blog/orchestratedbeer-sap-craft-breweries

3.8   Future Products, Services and Promotions

_____ (company name) will continually expand our offering of services based
on industry trends and changing client needs. We will not only solicit feedback via surveys
and comments cards from clients on what they need in the future, but will also work to
develop strong relationships with all of our clients and vendors. We also plan to open

_____ (#) additional locations in the _____ area starting in _____ (year).

We plan to expand our offering of services to include the following:
Note: Must check with state laws regarding the legal right to pursue these services.
1.   Pre-ordering and automatic re-ordering via our website and fax transmissions.
2.   Mobile Bartending Services
4.   A beer and cheese catering program for company sales meetings, staff promotion celebrations, company parties and luncheons. (Check state rules)
5.   Custom designed Gift Baskets for special events and holiday celebrations, available in-microbrewery and via our website.
8.   Home Party Plan Sales
9.   Consulting services
10.   Party/Event Planning Services
11.   Cooking with Beer Classes.
12.   Continuity Program: Beer of the Month Club.
13.   Marketing Consulting to Restaurants (from beverage menus to themed events)
14.   Beer Storage for clients in a controlled-environment space.

Our Future Growth Strategy will focus on the following initiatives:
1.   Increase hours of operation.
2.   Expand the selection of consumptions products, such as party supplies.
3.   Add home delivery service.
6.   Add a drive-through window.
7.   Online sales.
8.   Customized gift baskets.
9.   Wholesaler for other microbreweries
10.   Build On-site Brewpub
11.   Home Brewing Kits
12.   Company Logo Licensing Agreements

Microbrew Beer of the Month Club

The customer will simply choose one of our **"Beer of the Month"** memberships in 6-packs or 12-packs and decide how many months they would like to receive them.
This will be the ideal gift for anyone who appreciates good micro brewed beer.
Join our **"Beer of the Month Club"** and you will get a different 6- pack or 12-pack every month consisting of three delicious microbrew flavors (...two bottles of each flavor for the 6-pack club, or four bottles of each flavor for the 12-pack club). You choose how long you want to join. Memberships range from 2 to 12 months. You can also decide to keep getting Brews "Forever" if you like! You will also receive our monthly **"Beer Newsletter"** full of cool beer facts, stories, interviews with brewers, information about our featured beers, and lots of other cool stuff.

Wholesaling

We will act as a wholesaler for other brands of beer, which will allow the company to offer a wide variety of craft and imported beers to our retailers.

Brewpub
A brewpub for on-premise consumption will be built and properly licensed. This will also serve to promote our catering and beer tasting parties.

Home Brewing Kits
There is a market segment that prefers to make and consume this type of beverage at home. There are already mail-order companies that provide individuals and families with prepared ales, lagers and do-it-yourself home brewing kits. This opportunity will be researched and developed on a trial basis. If successful, it could become a major new source of income without creating the need for additional staff or production space.

Home Brewing Supplies
We plan to expand our carry-out selection of grains, hops, and other supplies for homebrewers.

Beer Hall Facility Rental
We will offer our Beer Hall and Pub as a rental space for special group gatherings.
Example: http://www.saintarnold.com/brewery/rentals.html

Catering
Catering after-hours office parties for special occasions and holidays (even outside of our local area) may become a large part of our future gross sales. At that point, a sales agent would be hired to directly market our products for catered functions.

Licensing
We plan to negotiate with the local college to exclusively produce their school-themed, private-labeled beer. We will sell the beer the company that is handling concessions at the football stadium.

Breakfast/Gourmet Coffee Service
We will expand our hours to offer a limited breakfast menu that focuses on gourmet coffees and homemade granola.
Source: www.nashvillescene.com/bites/archives/2018/10/26/jackalope-brewing-co-
           adding-coffeehouse-inside-taproom

Organize Annual Microbrewery Crawl Tour
We will organize an annual microbrewery crawl that will start at our microbrewery and then head by bus to _____ before ending at _____. Participants will get product samples at each stop and plant tours at each brewery.
Example:
As a result, new beer-oriented tours have added to the buzz, such as the bar and brewery motorbike excursion operated by Vespa Adventures.
Source:
http://www.cnn.com/2018/07/04/asia/vietnam-craft-beer/index.html

Hold Beer Recipe Contest
Our microbrewery will invite home brewers to submit beer recipes to be considered for a special "_____ (name of town) Beer." The winning recipe will be used to make one of the first beers offered in the new tap room.

Hold a Marketing Contest
We will distribute stacks of fill-in-the-blank stories about our brand and ask beer drinkers to furnish their own nouns and adjectives. The aim is to offer a party game in a bar setting - and to keep building a mystery about our brand's story. This will help to get people more involved in, and interacting with our brand.

New Types of Wholesale Accounts
We will work with the following types of businesses to help secure beer and wine licenses, so they can work with our microbrewery to sell more product:
1.   Mobile Food Trucks
2.   Pizza Shops
3.   Coffee Houses
4.   Diners
5.   Sports Bars

New Product Introductions
We will introduce potent Indian pale ales (IPAs) and sour gose -- a tart and salty style of German beer -- to the market.

Localization
Localization (also referred to as "l10n") is the process of adapting a product or content to a specific locale or market. The aim of localization is to give a product the look and feel of having been created specifically for a target market, no matter their language, culture, or location. As a microbrewery we will customize our offerings to local markets or consumer communities that are growing more diverse in terms of ethnicity, wealth, lifestyle, and values. We will roll out different types of product lines, and alternative approaches to pricing, marketing, staffing, and customer service. Localization and the resulting customization will encourage local experimentation, which will be difficult for competitors to track, let alone replicate. When well executed, localization strategies will provide a durable competitive edge. As an example, we will add the nectar of local fruits to our beers.

Example:
The brewers reach for everything from locally made Marou chocolate to Dalat coffee, passion fruit and even divisive durian -- a spiky Asian fruit with a distinct smell.
Source:
http://www.cnn.com/2018/07/04/asia/vietnam-craft-beer/index.html

Resources:
Globalization and Localization Association   www.gala-global.org

GALA is comprised of members worldwide who specialize in localization, translation, internationalization, and globalization. Every day they help companies, non-profit organizations, and governments communicate effectively to global audiences. They do this by making sure the content of their clients' communications is culturally sensitive and presented in languages that their audiences understand.

Art Gallery Sales

We will turn our tasting room into an art gallery and sell the following types of artwork on a consignment basis:

1. Enlargements of our beer labels
2. Composite collections of many different beer labels.
3. People drinking beer at festive events.
3. Hops Farming Scenes
4. Historical beer-making equipment images.

Subscription Box Program

We will develop a subscription program to generate a steady cash flow. We will try to up-sell customers on a monthly or quarterly or semi-annual subscription for oil our craft beers. To improve the chances for customer acceptance of our subscription program, we will do the following:

1. Charge very competitively for our services so the customer realizes a savings for their steady business.
2. Enable hassle-free, automatic monthly Credit Card payments.
3. Do not require a long-term contract or commitment from customers so they are free to terminate the subscription at any time without any hassles or penalties.
4. Use an upfront survey to determine what types of products are more highly desired by specific clients.

Resource:
http://www.digitalbusinessmodelguru.com/
Examples:
http://urbantastebud.com/best-beer-subscription-boxes/

4.0 Market Analysis Summary

Our Market Analysis will serve to accomplish the following goals:
1.   Define the characteristics and needs and wants of the target market.
2.   Serve as a basis for developing sales, marketing and promotional strategies.
3.   Influence the e-commerce website design.

Over the past ten years, regional microbreweries have gained market share of beer sales in the state of _____. A number of regional brands have moved from the specialty market to the supermarket. The numbers have been impressive. At present, regional microbrews represent ____ (10?) % of beer sales in ____ (state). This represents a ___% increase over sales numbers for the year 2000. Most importantly, the increased sales have occurred in the affluent communities in _____'s (state)metro areas.

_____'s (state) population has grown by ____% annually for the past ten years. Most of the growth has been in response to the explosion of hiring in the _____ (high-tech?) industry. The growth has added to the customer base that purchases regional microbrews. Traditionally, microbrews have been favored by young professional men and women in their late twenties and early thirties.

Another growth area that has had an impact on microbrew sales is the dramatic enrollment increase in the state's colleges and universities. Currently, there are ____ (#) college students in the cities of _____, _____ and _____. Microbrews represent ___% of beers sales in the campus communities.

Craft Beer consumption is on the increase in the United States, and customers are trading up. Consumption trends and demographics point to robust specialty beer sales growth for the next 10 years.

Each of our targeted market segment consists of people who either live, work, or vacation in the ___ area. Our target market will be seeking a Microbrewery that will meet their desire for responsive and knowledgeable service, convenient microbrewery hours, a broad selection of new beverage choices, innovative services, all provided from an easy to shop microbrewery. The target audience for our microbrewery will be upscale, well-educated people who are more interested in a distinctive flavor than quantity

Our Microbrewery will be located on the main road through town and is used daily by thousands of commuters between the two local _____ (towns/cities?). The closest Microbrewery in either direction is over ____ (#) miles away.

Forces and trends in the market environment will affect _____ (company name), like all businesses. These include economic, competitive, legal/political, technology, and recordkeeping issues.
>   **Economic Environment**—It is believed that the Microbrewery business is basically
>   recession resistant, as craft beer is seen as an affordable luxury. Positive forces
>   include the generally stable local economy that is searching for a way to return,

flat-lining unemployment, stable wages and low inflation, leading more people and businesses to be willing to purchase beer to forget their problems and find a way to de-stress and celebrate friendships.

Legal/Political Environment—Town of _____ supports the opening of this needed business venture and has issued and approved building permits and licenses to support use of the property.

Technology and Recordkeeping Environment—Use of computerized databases and electronic cash registers will capture and generate accounting/inventory detail. Computer programs will greatly simplify the inventory management, purchasing, financial recordkeeping and tax preparation functions, with which all businesses must comply. We will outsource the accounting tax functions but will maintain the daily financial records in-house.

_____ (company name) has a defined target market of middle and upper-middle class consumers that will be the basis of this business. Effective marketing combined with an optimal product and service offering mix is critical to our success. The owner possesses solid information about the market and knows a great deal about the common attributes of those that are expected to be loyal clients. This information will be leveraged to better understand who we will serve, their specific needs, and how to better communicate with them. The owner strongly believes that as more and more products become commodities that require highly competitive pricing, it will be increasingly important to focus on the development of innovative services, that can be structured, managed and possibly outsourced.

Research indicates that there are three types of beer drinkers:
1. The Beginner
2. The Enthusiast
3. The Beer Geek.

The enthusiasts and the geeks are growing in numbers and spending a little more. A shift has occurred in the entire category toward more beer lovers, which is good because they have very strong loyalty.

Composite profile of the typical craft beer drinker...
1. Lives in a two-person household with a combined income over 75 K.
2. Is a Caucasian who lives in a "cosmopolitan center.
3. Is either a boomer or a millennial.
4. Skews toward active leisure activities.
5. Is a heavy Internet user.
6. Reads a lot of newspapers.
7. Listens to sports on the radio and watches the Golf Channel.
8. More likely to spend time thinking about beer rather than work.
9. More open-minded than most people.
10. Seek out interesting and varied experiences and are intellectually curious.
11. Don't stress about missed deadlines and tend to be happy-go-lucky about life.
12. ore likely to always buy organic.
13. More likely to choose the movie they are going to see at the theater.

The customer base will come from the following major segments:

1. Local population — the city of _____ with a year-round population of ___ (#) is centrally located on the ___ coast of ____ (state).
2. Colleges and Universities --- _____ (city) has several schools within a __(#)-mile radius of _____ (business location) and a seasonal population of _____ (#).
3. Tourism — between hotels, motels, bed & breakfast rooms and inns, there are over ____ (#) rooms available. Last year they were at ____% occupancy.
4. Local businesses — The City of ____ lists over ___ (#) businesses with an average of ___ (#) employees in the _____ area.

Resource:

http://itspurebusiness.wordpress.com/2011/03/14/craft-beer-industry-report-market-research/

4.1   Secondary Market Research

We will research demographic information for the following reasons:

1. To determine which segments of the population, such as Hispanics and the elderly, have been growing and may now be underserved.
2. To determine if there is a sufficient population base in the designated service area to realize the company's business objectives.
3. To consider what products and services to add in the future, given the changing demographic profile and needs of our service area.

We will pay special attention to the following general demographic trends:

1. Population growth has reached a plateau and market share will most likely be increased through innovation and excellent customer service.
2. Because incomes are not growing, and unemployment is high, process efficiencies and sourcing advantages must be developed to keep prices competitive.
3. The rise of non-traditional households, such as single working mothers, means developing more innovative support programs, such as mobile services.
4. As the population shifts toward more young to middle aged adults, ages 30 to 44, and the elderly, aged 65 and older, there will be a greater need for targeted support types of products and services.
5. Because of the aging population, increasing pollution levels and high unemployment, new 'green' ways of dealing with the resulting challenges will need to be developed.

We will collect the demographic statistics for the following zip code(s):

_____

We will use the following sources: www.census.gov, www.zipskinny.com, www.city-data.com, www.demographicsnow.com, www.freedemographics.com, www.ffiec.gov/geocode, www.esri.com/data/esri_data/tapestry and www.claritas.com/claritas/demographics.jsp. This information will be used to decide upon which targeted programs to offer and to make business growth projections.

Resource: www.sbdcnet.org/index.php/demographics.html

Snapshots of consumer data by zip code are also available online:
http://factfinder.census.gov/home/saff/main.html?_lang=en
http://www.esri.com/data/esri_data/tapestry.html
http://www.claritas.com/MyBestSegments/Default.jsp?ID=20

1. **Total Population** _____
2. **Number of Households** _____
3. **Population by Race:** White ____% Black ___%
   Asian Pacific Islander ___% Other ____%
4. **Population by Gender** Male ____% Female ____%
5. **Income Figures:** Median Household Income $_____
   Household Income Under $50K ____%
   Household Income $50K-$100K ____%
   Household Income Over $100K ____%
6. **Housing Figures** Average Home Value - $_____
   Average Rent $_____
7. **Homeownership**: Homeowners % _____
   Renters % _____
8. **Education Achievement** High School Diploma % _____
   College Degree % _____
   Graduate Degree % _____
9. **Stability/Newcomers** Longer than 5 years % _____
10. **Marital Status** ___% Married ___% Divorced ___% Single
    ___% Never Married ___% Widowed ___% Separated
11. **Occupations** ___%Service ___% Sales ___% Management
    ___% Construction ___% Production
    ___% Unemployed ___% Below Poverty Level
12. **Age Distribution** ___%Under 5 years ___%5-9 yrs ___%10-12 yrs
    ___% 13-17 yrs ___%18-years
    ___% 20-29 ___% 30-39 ___% 40-49 ___% 50-59
    ___% 60-69 ___% 70-79 ___% 80+ years
13. **Prior Growth Rate** _____% from _____ (year)
14. **Projected Population Growth Rate** _____%
15. **Employment Trend** _____
16. **Business Failure Rate** _____

Demographic Conclusions

The age, education, and affluence of _____'s (city) diverse population makes it an ideal market for a ____ (microbrewery/brew-pub).

Consumer Reports on Eating Share Trends (CREST) data (cited by Chapdelaine, 1994) reveal that affluent and educated Americans eat out more frequently, are more likely to order beer at restaurants, and are more likely to drink regular (non-light) beer than other consumers.

According to the 1990 census report, _____ (city) is comprised largely of students, professionals, and service industry employees. The University of _____ provides the city with a large pre- and post-graduate student population. The University is also the largest employer in the city with more than ___ (#) employees. _____ (city) is also home to major corporations.

The ___ (year) census reports that almost __% of _____'s (city) employed population hold professional or managerial positions: ____% are clerical or in sales; ____% have blue collar jobs; and ____% are in agriculture. Only ____% of ___ (city) residents are unemployed. The median family income is $_____ with the effective buying income (personal income minus tax and non-tax payments) at $_____ (versus $_____ nationally). $_____ million dollars a year of this buying income is spent in bars and restaurants in the _____ area.

_____'s (city) education level also ranks well above the national average. ___% of the population has a high school diploma and _____% have four or more years of college (compared to 20% nationally). The median age of ____ (city) residents is ____ (compared to the national median of 33.0) and ____% of the population is between the ages of 25 to 44, the target age group of micro and pub-breweries.

According to a recent study by the National Restaurant Association, these demographics are ideal for supporting a _____ (microbrewery/brew-pub). The study (Chapdelaine, 1994) found that higher incomes and higher educational levels were a major factor in determining who orders beer at restaurants. From 1989 to 1993, the percentage of individuals with annual household incomes of $60,000 or more who ordered beers at restaurants rose from 15% to 25%. The study also found that the largest group of beer drinkers (40%) hold some sort of professional or managerial job while only 22% are blue collar workers.

Given these statistics, _____ (city) is sure to attract a growing number of craft brewers. The area's ideal demographics will most likely support multiple _____ (microbreweries/ brew-pubs?). _____'s (company name) goal is to be the one that opens it doors first and sets the high standard for those that will follow.

Other Secondary Market Research Conclusions:
This area will be demographically favorable for our business for the following reasons:

_____

Resources:
www.allbusiness.com/marketing/segmentation-targeting/848-1.html
http://www.sbdcnet.org/industry-links/demographics-links
http://factfinder2.census.gov/faces/nav/jsf/pages/index.xhtml

4.1.1   Primary Market Research

We plan to develop a survey for primary research purposes and mail it to a list of local home magazine subscribers, purchased from the publishers by zip code. We will also post a copy of the survey on our website and encourage visitors to take the survey. We will use the following survey questions to develop an Ideal Customer Profile of our potential client base, so that we can better target our marketing communications. To improve the response rate, we will include an attention-grabbing _____ (discount coupon/ dollar?) as a thank you for taking the time to return the questionnaire.

1.   What is your zip-code?   _____
2.   Are you single, divorced, separated, widowed or married? _____
3.   Are you male or female?   _____
4.   What is your age?   _____
5.   What is your family stage?   _____
6.   What is your approximate household income?   _____
7.   What is your educational level?   _____
8.   What is your profession?   _____
9.   Are you a dual income household?
10.   What are your hobbies/other entertainment forms?   _____
11.   Do you have children? If Yes, what are their ages?   _____
12.   What are your favorite magazines?   _____
13.   What is your favorite local newspaper?   _____
14.   What is your favorite radio station?   _____
15.   What are your favorite television programs?   _____
16.   What are your favorite websites?   _____
17.   What organizations are you a member of?   _____
18.   Does our community have an adequate number of Microbreweries? Yes / No
19.   Does your family currently patronize a local Microbrewery?   Yes / No
20.   Are you satisfied with your current Microbrewery?   Yes / No
21.   How many times on average per month do you visit your Microbrewery? ____
22.   What services do you typically purchase? _____
23.   What products do you typically purchase? _____
24.   On average, how much do you spend on Microbrewery purchases per month? __
25.   What is the name of your currently patronized Microbrewery?
26.   What are their strengths as service providers?
27.   What are their weaknesses or shortcomings?
28.   What would it take for us to earn your Microbrewery business?
29.   What is the best way for us to market our Microbrewery?
30.   Do you live in _____ community?
31.   Do you work or study in _____ community?
32.   Do you think you will be in need of Microbrewery items in the near future?
33.   Would you be interested in joining a Microbrewery Club that would offer special Membership benefits?
34.   Which container size, or package size is purchased/consumed most?
35.   Do you purchase more beer in bars, restaurants or in stores?
36.   Has your beer consumption rate changed in the past few years?

37. Describe your experience with other Microbrewery establishments.
38. Please rank (1 to 17) the importance of the following factors when choosing a Microbrewery:

___ Quality of Product   ___ Brand Selection
___ Reputation   ___ Staff Courtesy/Friendliness
___ Waiting time before service   ___ Staff Professionalism
___ Convenient location   ___ Value
___ Referral/References   ___ Complaint Handling
___ Security Measures   ___ Convenient Layout
___ Microbrewery Cleanliness   ___ In-stock availability
___ Microbrewery Signage   ___ Price
___ Other _____

39. Please prioritize the importance of the following microbrewery activities:

___ Beer Tasting   ___ Spirit Tasting
___ Gift Cards   ___ Sales of Accessories
___ Sales of Books/Magazines/CDs   ___ Apparel Sales

40. What is your usual method of payment?

___ Cash ___ Credit Card ___ Debit Card ___ Check ___ Other _____

41. Do you have any special requirements that need to be addressed?
42. What information would you like to see in our microbrewery newsletter?
43. Which online social groups have you joined? Choose the ones you access.

___ Facebook   ___ MySpace
___ Twitter   ___ LinkedIn
___ Ryze   ___ Ning

44. What types of Microbrewery services would most interest you?
45. What is your general need for a Microbrewery?

Circle Months: J F M A M J J A S O N D (All)

Circle Days: S M T W T F S (All)

Indicate Hours: _____ or (24 hours)

46. Which container size, or package size do you purchase/consume most?

___ 12 ounce bottles ___ 20 ounce bottles ___ other _____

47. Do you purchase more beer in bars, restaurants or in stores? _____
48. Have your beer consumption rates changed in the past few years? __Yes __ No
49. Are you presently drinking more or less beer? _____
50. Are you presently drinking more or less wine? _____
51. Why has your beer consumption rate changes?
52. What is your favorite flavor additive to beer?
53. What is your favorite beer commercial?
54. Where and when did you view your favorite beer commercial?
55. What are your suggestions for realizing a better Microbrewery experience?
56. Are you on our mailing list? Yes/No   If No, can we add you? Yes / No
57. Would you be interested in attending a free seminar on wine/food pairings?
58. Can you supply the name and contact info of person who might be interested in our micro-brewed products and services?

Please note any comments or concerns about Microbreweries in general.

We very much appreciate your participation in this survey. If you provide your name, address and email address, we will sign you up for our e-newsletter, inform you of our survey results, advise you of any new microbrewery opening in your community, and enter you into our monthly drawing for a free _____.

Name   Address

Email   Phone

4.1.2   Voice of the Customer

To develop a better understanding of the changing needs and wants of our Microbrewery customers, we will institute the following ongoing listening practices:

1.   Focus Groups
      Small groups of customers (6 to 8) will be invited to meet with a facilitator to answer open-ended questions about priority of needs and wants, and our company, its products or other given issues. These focus groups will provide useful insight into the decisions and the decision-making process of target consumers.

2.   Individual Interviews
      We will conduct face-to-face personal interviews to understand customer thought processes, selection criteria and entertainment preferences.

3.   Customer Panels
      A small number of customers will be invited to answer open-ended questions on a regular basis.

4.   Customer Tours
      We will invite customers to visit our facilities to discuss how our processes can better serve them.

5.   Visit Customers
      We will observe customers as they actually use our products to uncover the pains and problems they are experiencing during usage.

6.   Trade Show Meetings
      Our trade show booth will be used to hear the concerns of our customers.

7.   Toll-free Numbers
      We will attach our phone number to all products and sales literature to encourage the customer to call with problems or positive feedback.

8.   Customer Surveys
      We will use surveys to obtain opinions on closed-ended questions, testimonials, constructive feedback, and improvement suggestions.

9.   Mystery Shoppers
      We will use mystery shoppers to report on how our employees treat our customers.

10. Salesperson Debriefing
    We will ask our salespeople to report on their customer experiences to obtain insights into what the customer faces, what they want and why they failed to make a sale.
11. Customer Contact Logs
    We will ask our sales personnel to record interesting customer revelations.
12. Customer Serviceperson's Hotline
    We will use this dedicated phone line for service people to report problems.
13. Discussions with competitors.
14. Installation of suggestion boxes to encourage constructive feedback. The suggestion card will have several statements customers are asked to rate in terms of a given scale. There are also several open-ended questions that allow the customer to freely offer constructive criticism or praise. We will work hard to implement reasonable suggestions to improve our service offerings as well as show our commitment to the customer that their suggestions are valued.

4.2 Market Segmentation

Market segmentation is a technique that recognizes that the potential universe of users may be divided into definable sub-groups with different characteristics. Segmentation enables organizations to target messages to the needs and concerns of these subgroups. We will segment the market based on the needs and wants of select customer groups. We will develop a composite customer profile and a value proposition for each of these segments. The purpose for segmenting the market is to allow our marketing/sales program to focus on the subset of prospects that are "most likely" to purchase our microbrewery products and services. If done properly this will help to insure the highest return for our marketing/sales expenditures.

Customer Analysis
Consumers of craft beers in the _____ metro area can be grouped into three categories:

1. **End Consumers**
2. **Retailers**
3. **Distributors**

Our brewery will seek to increase local support and customer loyalty by conducting sampling programs and establishing relationships with end-consumers and retailers. Our company does not intend to rely solely on distributors to increase demand for the product.

Other category classifications include the following:
Aficionados – This group is generally composed of older upper-class males, ages 35 plus. They are professionals and know what good beer tastes like. Because of their age and professional backgrounds, they are secure financially and their family is well

established. Therefore, this group is able to afford quality craft beer, rarely consuming macro-brews. These individuals are passionate about beer and will consume several glasses a week. While they are generally loyal to two or three main brands, aficionados are willing to sample a new microbrew every now and then. These individuals consume beer primarily in the following places: upscale restaurants, sporting events, sophisticated bars/pubs, and country/athletic clubs.

Active Professional – This group is generally composed of contemporary adults both male and female, ranging in age from 25-35. These individuals are rather inexperience when it comes to beer consumption. Individuals in this group most likely have acquired a fair amount of debt, either from college loans or their first home mortgage. Therefore, they do not have the financial security of aficionados. Because active professionals do not have the financial security of aficionados and are busy establishing families, they tend to be more casual drinkers. On average these individuals consume less expensive beer and have fewer than 5 glasses of beer a week, despite appreciating the taste of microbrews. They are not as loyal as aficionados are to brands and are willing to try a new microbrew more frequently. The most commonplaces beer is consumed by these individuals include: trendy bars/pubs, sports bars/pubs, family restaurants, and at home.

Experimental Drinkers – This group is composed of individuals of all legal drinking ages. They generally consume a small quantity of brew thus they have not acquired any real appreciation for beer. This group is the most popular group for females. Because they do not consume beer very often they have little if any loyalty to specific brands. When they do decide to consume beer, however, they are willing to pay for a quality microbrew. The most commonplaces beer is consumed by this group include: trendy bars/pubs, sports bars/pubs, family restaurants, and at home.

_____ (company name) plans to focus on the following market segments:
   Customers in university campus communities.
   Professional men and women aged 25 - 35 living in affluent metro communities.

Marketing and promotional activities will be grassroots based, rather than more expensive mass marketing. We will reach these people through sponsorship of local entertainment and cultural events, advertising in small niche magazines targeted towards young "fashionable" professionals and sponsorship of activity groups.

MARKET SEGMENT
The brewery has targeted the tri-county area surrounding the city of _____ as the main market area for sales. The population demographic of this area is well-suited to beer sales. It is important to note that the microbrewing industry is now in its third decade. It is important to note the failure rate for microbreweries is 1 in 5, whereas for small business start-ups it is 1 in 2. _____ County ranks ___ (#) highest for per capita income. The per capita income for _____ county is $_____ . In addition, _____ county is ranked first in ___ (state) in per capita income. _____ county is ranked as the ___th largest county in the United States with a population of _____ (#), according to the 2000 census.

_____ (company name) is targeting the bar/restaurant draught beer sales market.

The total potential market in units is shown in the following table and chart.
- There are approximately ___ (#) businesses in ___ (city) that could potentially be our customers.
- There are ____ (#) residents in ____ (city), according to the 2010 U.S. Census, with __ (5) % projected growth over the next ten years.
- Visitors were estimated using _____ Chamber of Commerce visitation report. From ___ - ____ (years), an average of ____ (#) people visited the ___ (city/attraction) annually.

Even though the visitor population appears to be the largest the market segment, it is possible that much of our sales could come from local residents and businesses, due to the fact that these people and companies make purchases for the visitors using their services. The local population is extremely important, because they can carry us through the low _____ (visitation/bad weather) months and will determine whether we become an established community destination.

Target Markets:
Drinking Age Residents of the _____ area
People willing to pay a premium for craft beer with a distinctive flavor profile.

Industry Research indicates that the profile of the _____ (company name) customer consists of the following geographic, demographic, psychographic and behavior factors:

1.	Caucasian	90%
2.	Male	70%
3.	Urban	65%
4.	Household Income >50k/year	75%
5.	College Educated	65%
6.	Ages 21 to 50	90%

Our Composite Ideal Customer Profile:
By assembling this composite customer profile, we will know what customer needs and wants our company needs to focus on and how best to reach our target market. We will use the information gathered from our customer research surveys to assemble the following composite customer profile:

Ideal Customer Profile

Who are they?
age _____
gender _____
occupation _____
location: zip codes _____
income level _____
marital status _____

ethnic group   _____

education level   _____

family life cycle   _____

number of household members   _____

household income   _____

homeowner or renter   _____

association memberships   _____

leisure activities   _____

hobbies/interests   _____

core beliefs   _____

Where are they located (zip codes)? _____

Most popular product/service purchased? _____

Lifestyle Preferences?   Trendsetter/Trend follower/Other _____

How often do they buy?   _____

What are most important purchase factors? Price/Brand Name/Quality/Financing/Sales
Convenience/Packaging/Other_____

What is their key buying motivator? _____

How do they buy it?   Cash/Credit/Terms/Other_____

Where do they buy it from (locations)? _____

What problem do they want to solve? _____

What are the key frustrations/pains that
these customers have when buying? _____

What search methods do they use? _____

What is preferred problem solution? _____

Table: Market Analysis

Potential Customers	Growth	Number of Potential Customers 2018	2019	2020
University Communities	10%			
Affluent Metro Communities	10%			
Professionals	10%			
Visitors	10%			
Commuters	10%			
Other	10%			
Totals:	10%			

4.3   Target Market Segment Strategy

Our target marketing strategy will involve identifying a group of customers to which to direct our microbrewery products and services. Our strategy will be the result of intently listening to and understanding customer needs, representing customers' needs to those responsible for product production and service delivery, and giving them what they want. In developing our targeted customer messages, we will strive to understand things like: where they work, worship, party and play, where they shop and go to school, how they spend their leisure time, what organizations they belong to, and where they volunteer their time. We will use research, surveys and observation to uncover this wealth of information to get our product details and brand name in front of our customers when they are most receptive to receiving our messaging.

Target Market Worksheet   (optional)

Note: Use this worksheet to explore potential target markets for your products/services.

Product Benefits: Actual factor (cost effectiveness, design, performance, etc.) or perceived factor (image, popularity, reputation, etc.) that satisfies what a customer needs or wants. An advantage or value that the product will offer its buyer.

Products Features: One of the distinguishing characteristics of a product or service that helps boost its appeal to potential buyers. A characteristic of a product that describes its appearance, its components, and its capabilities. Typical features include size and color.

Product or Service	Product/ Service Benefits	Product/ Service Features	Potential Target Markets

American microbreweries will distribute through wholesalers in traditional three tier systems, then act as their own distributor and sell to retailers. Selling includes tap rooms, restaurants, or even off premise sales.

The target market profile consists of _____ (city) residents who are educated, between the ages of 21 and 38. successful professionals, with disposable income, and who are regular consumers of alcoholic beverages. According to a 2012 article in Medialife Magazine, microbrewery and brewpub customers tend to be more affluent and well-educated than the average beer drinker -- 40 percent of microbrew drinkers earn $100,000 a year or more. Most of the consumers in this category rely on assistance in selecting beers. Consequently, they tend to reward the most capable merchants with loyalty and word-of-mouth advertising.

Other potential segments (geographic, demographic, preferences):
1.   **Bulk Volume (Private and Business):**
     Much of this business needs to be cultivated through opportunistic networking, and diligent follow-ups of in-microbrewery inquiries and leads.
2.   **Direct Deliverables** (Outside immediate microbrewery neighborhood):
     Viable only as the microbrewery earns its way into a position in which it can invest in vehicle delivery operations and line up target customers that would sustain such an operation.
3.   **Intra-state shipments:**
     Contingent on expansion following the successful implementation of this business plan. This business would develop through direct-mail catalog marketing, and an

Internet sales operation.

We will focus on the following well-defined target market segments and emphasize our good value, high quality, unique and varied selections, and great service.

Target Professional Women
This segment is comprised of women in the age range of 25 to 50. They are married, have a household income >$100,000, own at least one home, and are socially active. They are members of at least one club or organization. They have high disposable or discretionary income and are considered the family decision-makers.

Target University/College Students
We will target the students of local colleges and universities, because this group has a very well-known proclivity to party. In fact, the selling and promoting beer at colleges has become a big business. We will seek the rights to sponsor and promote local college sports teams, such as conference basketball, baseball and soccer tournaments. A drinking responsibly message will always be an important part of our marketing campaign.
Source:
www.craftbrewingbusiness.com/business-marketing/more-and-more-beer-marketing-
       dollars-are-going-to-college-sports-sponsorships/

Target Adult Amateur Athletes
We will sponsor amateur athletic programs, such as the 'Adult Hockey Association' and 'National Adult Basketball Association'.
Directory:
https://www.workinsports.com/wisemployers.asp?catid=7
https://www.nscsports.org/basketball-leagues
http://www.pageyouthcenter.org/Default.aspx?tabid=1731210

Target Community Influencers
We will target community influencers because they possess the trust of the community to make beer recommendations. These are the people that are seen amongst friends, family and colleagues as the 'craft beer guy or gal'. We will try to reach influencers at tastings, festivals and on-site promotions.

We will use the following techniques to target community influencers:
1.   Give them adequate samples so that they may pass samples onto their friends.
2.   Support their passions and charitable causes, such as 'green' businesses.
3.   Conduct regular brewery production line and sampling tours.
4.   Actively seek out and listen to their branding and beer making advice.

Target Millennials (ages 21 to 34)
Millennials are reaching out to social networks and observing behaviors of their friends to look for new, novel, authentic experience. Millennials don't look exclusively to their friends for spirit information, but they do want an accurate, authoritative portrayal of a beverage experience they are hoping to enjoy. As marketers, we will provide useful

information to potential clients via social networking sites. In fact, JWT data from March 2017 suggests that millennial travelers are more likely to grab their smartphones to access their social networks, Yelp reviews or foursquare users to garner real-time suggestions and find local information while on the go. We will provide these types of "concierge-like" services to reach millennials. And to gain the initial trust of these customers, we will join conversations, participate in forums and comment on wine bogs, already in progress, rather than interrupt them to start and control conversations of our own. This group sees craft beer as an affordable luxury and a trade-off for bigger purchases they won't now make. Burger and Pizza chains are now selling craft beers from a select group of local breweries. To appeal to more millennials with aspirational ads, we will focus on music-themed marketing, with the music of contemporary artists like Justin Timberlake. According to drinker demographics compiled by the Brewers Association, young women (21-34) now over-index on craft beer, accounting for 15 percent of total craft volume, and Millennials continue to account for a majority of weekly craft beer drinkers.

Target Professionals
Our target market will be 25 to 45 professionals who drink both beer and wine and can appreciate the difference between a Bud and a microbrew. They seek to communicate a successful and distinctive image to their friends and may have an interest in our event planning services. They also have a tendency to seek out new experiences and enjoy specialty brews that can be uniquely tasty, fun, convenient, and value-priced.

Target Aging Baby Boomers
Since people age 50 and older have more discretionary money, they are more prone to take advantage of new products and services and believe in the status-conferring and health benefits associated with craft beer consumption.

Target Seniors
Seniors with mobility problems will appreciate the convenience of our drive-thru window and open floor plan. We will offer them discounts. We also plan to visit local assisted living facilities and independent living centers to learn how we can better accommodate the needs and wants of seniors.

Target Local Ethnic Groups
Ongoing demographic trends suggest that, in the coming decades, programs will be serving a population of people which is increasingly diverse in economic resources, racial and ethnic background, and family structure. Our plan is to reach out to consumers of various ethnic backgrounds, especially Hispanics, who comprise nearly 13 percent of the country's total population. In addition to embarking on an aggressive media campaign of advertising with ethnic newspapers and radio stations, we will set up programs to actively recruit bilingual employees and make our microbrewery more accessible via signage printed in various languages based on the microbrewery's community. We will accurately translate our marketing materials into other languages. We will enlist the support of our bilingual employees to assist in reaching the ethnic people in our surrounding area through a referral program. We will join the nearest _____ (predominate ethnic group) Chamber of Commerce and partner with _____ (Hispanic/Chinese/Other?)

Advocacy Agencies. We will also develop programs that reflect cultural influences and brand preferences.

Target the Gay People Niche
We will target the local gay market with an appropriate product label name, such as 'Queen', and through ads and stories run in local gay newspapers and magazines and through our support of social and fund-raising events to which gays would normally be attracted. Concurrently, we will make sales calls on local gay bars and restaurants. Then, once we have some distribution in the city, we will capitalize on the fact that many of the managers and staff of mainstream establishments are gay and will help us move our microbrew into non-gay venues. We will sponsor cultural events that will not only attract an exclusively gay crowd, but also aid in our mainstream push.

Target Professionals
We will focus on catering to a more professional type of clientele. We will begin by building an upscale inventory that will appeal to these customers. We will get more exclusive beers on our shelves in anticipation of popular demand. To capture this upscale customer group, we will train our staff to answer questions about various beers – which beers are highly rated, or which go best with a particular kind of food.

Target Restaurant Delivery Companies
Example:
Crying Eagle Brewing Co. came up with a special beer for a partnership it formed with Waitr, a restaurant on-demand platform that connects local restaurants to consumers. Waitr has more than 2,500 restaurant partners and hundreds of thousands of users in more than 100 cities. And now, it has this specialty beer to offer that will now be available in the restaurants it is working with.
Source:
www.craftbrewingbusiness.com/featured/13-best-craft-beer-marketing-ideas-of-2017/

Helpful Resources:
U.S. census Bureau Statistics   www.census.gov
U.S. Dept. of Labor/Bureau of Labor Statistics   www.bls.gov/data/home.htm
National Hispanic Medical Association

4.3.1   Market Needs

The proliferation of microbreweries derives in part from the desire of people to break away from the smothering homogeneity of popular, national culture, and reestablish connections with local communities, settings, and economies.
We plan to pay more attention to the opportunities of geographic extensions through direct shipments of beer throughout our state, and within our county with our own delivery service. We plan to market over the Internet to the _____ (#) actual and potential customers on our mailing list. As a goal, our company will seek to capture of piece of the apparently substantial demand for direct shipment sales.

Local and visiting customers desire high quality, beverages that will appeal to their aesthetics. In addition, they desire a pleasant shopping experience that allows them to learn about and purchase the pure, natural beverage items they want in a comfortable, friendly, hassle-free environment.

4.4 Buying Patterns

A Buying Pattern is the typical manner in which /buyers consumers purchase goods or services or firms place their purchase orders in terms of amount, frequency, timing, etc. In determining buying patterns, we will need to understand the following:
- Why consumers make the purchases that they make?
- What factors influence consumer purchases?
- The changing factors in our society.

Consumption rates over the past five years have been steadily growing. In 2005, growth rates were: "10% on the macro brewery side and 9% on the microbrew side" according to beerinsights.com. Light beers have taken over the market showing the largest jump in this industry. With all of the low-calorie diets overtaking the nation, people are exercising moderation or are going with the alternative of consuming low calorie light beer and still consuming the same amount. If people do exercise moderation they are opting for consuming fewer beers of higher quality, which is one of the major reasons that the microbrewery industry has been steadily increasing in recent years. There are also more bars or social settings for people go to, which is good for microbreweries, because 60% of our sales are from the bars or pubs. Another large reason as to why consumption rates have increased slightly is because there have been rumors that beer can help reduce the chance for prostate cancer in males. Overall, the microbrew industry is expanding and becoming more of a prevalent entity in the area of beer consumption mainly because people are changing their drinking habits, demanding more distinctive flavors and freshness, and there are more areas for our product to be consumed at in today's social setting. Furthermore, in this era of legal restrictions on alcohol consumption and the rise of the health-conscious consumer, people are looking to drink less, but drink better. Given this incredible growth, it is not surprising that restaurant sales for beer have been increasing in the 1990s. In fact, a recent study published by the National Restaurant Association (Chapdelaine, 1994) states that the number of restaurant patrons drinking beer with food is increasing, despite a decline in overall alcohol consumption. Specifically, the Restaurant Association study found that the beers being ordered are expensive, premium-quality craft-brewed beers. According to the National Restaurant Association (Chapdelaine, 1994), consumers will not only order, but also tend to be willing to pay more for menu items that they perceive to be new, popular, or of premium quality. The heightened demand for this product can be explained by the fact that micro-brewed beer meets all three of these criteria:

Locally produced, hand-crafted beers are still a novelty in many areas.

A 1993 Roper Starch Worldwide Study (cited by Chapdelaine, 1994) found that half of all adult consumers believe that locally brewed beer is "in."

According to the National Restaurant Association (Chapdelaine, 1994), locally brewed beer is perceived as fresher and of higher quality.

According to the IBS, "the boom is happening for micro and specialty brewers and it may be a decade or two before it begins to level off." (Edgar, 1994). Beer is the most popular alcoholic beverage in America. Americans drink approximately 23 gallons of beer per year.

Unlike traditional beer drinkers. microbrew drinkers rarely are loyal to just one brand of beer. Instead, they are always looking for the next new thing. Because microbrew drinkers seek out new and interesting brews, it will be essential to use a striking name, and label logo, and continue to experiment with new recipes that can produce new distinctive flavors to continue to attract attention.

Demand is driven by consumer preferences in alcohol consumption and demographic trends. The profitability of individual companies depends on effective sales operations and maintaining low operating costs. Large companies have advantages in exclusive distribution rights in large markets. Small operations can compete effectively by distributing rare and expensive products.

In most cases, clients make the purchase decision on the basis of the following criteria:
1.   Referrals and relationship with other customers.
2.   Personality and expected relationship with the microbrewery personnel.
3.   Internet-based information gathering.
4.   Label graphics
5.   Local convenience and freshness.

People have the following reasons for drinking, (in their order of importance):
1.   To be sociable   2.   Enjoyment of a meal.
3.   Relax.   4.   Feel Good.
5.   Less shy/inhibited.   6.   Forget worries.

Males are the most frequent customers of microbreweries, but it is increasingly important to be female friendly. Microbrewery purchases are driven by occasion type, with purchases directed at enjoying good times at a special social occasion. Consequently, the microbrewery must project a good times image.

According to 1995 industry statistics from the Miller Brewing Company, beer consumption increases during the summer months.

Season	Percent Consumed
Winter	19.90%
Spring	28.10%
Summer	30.10%
Fall	21.90%

_____ (company name) will gear its offerings, marketing, and pricing policies to establish a loyal client base. Our value-based pricing, easy microbrewery access, preferred membership programs, home-based to-go services and basic quality products will be welcomed in _____ (city) and contribute to our success.

4.5   Market Growth

We will assess the following general factors that affect market growth:

Current Assessment

1. Interest Rates
2. Government Regulations
3. Perceived Environment Impact
4. Consumer Confidence Level
5. Population Growth Rate
6. Unemployment Rate
7. Political Stability
8. Currency Exchange Rate
9. Innovation Rate
10. Home Sales
11. Overall Economic Health

Total U.S. beer sales increased in 2008 -- though just under 0.5% by volume, estimates industry newsletter Beer Marketer's Insights. Sales of craft beer, the industry's fastest-growing segment, rose 6% by volume, and dollar sales jumped 10.5% to $6.3 billion, according to the Brewers Association.

Beer is taking market share away from distilled spirits, and craft beer in particular is looking like an affordable luxury.

Forecasters see crafts carving out a 15 per cent market share by 2020.

The growing demand for microbrews stems from drinkers themselves, who are asking for fresher, tastier beer that's made closer to home, by locally owned companies.
Drivers of this growth include a bigger demand for variety and localization, or locally sourced products, and increased sophistication about what we eat and drink.

There are four major reasons restaurants are gravitating to a broader craft beer platform:
    It offers high margins which leads to increased sales and profitability.
    It attracts an ideal customer who is willing to spend a little more on affordable
        luxuries.
    It attracts Millennials, who have a long road of drinking ahead of them.
    It drives high guest satisfaction and customer loyalty/repeat guests.

While microbreweries are not real competition for the major breweries, they do claim approximately 4 percent of the market share. In response to this, most major brewers have begun their own microbrewery lines, spun off from the brand name beers.

American Demographics projects the number of U.S. households will grow by 15% to 115 million by the year 2018. These busy households will require a greater range of convenience-driven microbrewery products and services.

We believe there is a market for our products and services in ___ (city) and that the market has potential for growth. _____ County's population in the year 2000 was ____ and is expected to grow at a rate of ___ (5) % over the next ten years. ___ (city) is dedicated to remaining a travel destination "hot spot" without losing its "small town" feel. Because of its unique appeal it is likely to attract many vacationers and settlers for years to come. Our business will grow as customers become familiar with our unrivaled product selection and home-based entertaining services.

Overall, the environment appears very positive for the ____ (company name). The forces driving market demand, mainly economic, are strong, with industry growth healthy and new residents moving into the area resulting in a greater demand for our stress-relieving products and services.

The general industry analysis shows that _____ (city) is expected to experience _____ (double digit?) population, housing and commercial business growth. This suggests that as more families continue to move into the _____ area, there will be an increasing demand for quality beverage services, and this makes it a prime location for a Microbrewery that is willing to think outside-of-the-box. Trends show that ____ (city), ___ (state) can be a very profitable place to start a microbrewery because of the fact that with so many other similar companies in the area the consumers actually have an appreciation for this craft beer and will acknowledge the product.

4.6.0 Service Business Analysis

Demographics, consumer tastes, and personal income drive demand. The profitability of individual microbreweries can vary. Large companies have advantages in purchasing, finance, and marketing. Small companies can offer superior quality and/or service.

Craft beer in particular is looking like an affordable luxury. Craft brewers produce beer in tiny quantities, and they're known for an ever-increasing array of exotic ingredients, such as chocolate, coffee or berries. Craft brewing, led by companies such as California's Sierra Nevada Brewing Co. and Oregon's Deschutes Brewery Inc., accounts for only 4% of total industry volume, but the beers provide distributors and retailers with high profit margins. At least part of the growing consumer demand stems from drinkers willing to pay a few dollars extra for beer that's often made close to home.

The demand for Microbreweries is increasing for the following reasons:
1.   Alcoholic beverages are seen as an affordable luxury during recessionary times.
2.   The number of drinking age Americans is increasing almost three times as fast as the rest of the population.
3.   More consumers and brewers are looking favorably upon experimentation.
4.   More stores are carrying wide selections of craft beers.

5.   People enjoy the social aspects of brewpubs and tasting rooms.
6.   Craft Beer in cans is making it more portable.
7.   More consumers are seeking to buy locally to support their local economy.

Successful microbreweries offer convenience, freshness, distinctive flavors, reasonable pricing strategies and have a staff that is friendly and approachable. They understand that they are the originating point for good times and are very supportive of customers who require help with selection recommendations and party planning advice.

4.7   Barriers to Entry   (select)

_____ (company name) will benefit from the following combination of barriers to entry, which cumulatively present a moderate degree of entry difficulty or obstacles in the path of other Microbrewery businesses wanting to enter our market.

1.	Business Experience.	2.	Community Networking
3.	Referral Program	4.	People Skills
5.	Marketing Skills	6.	Supplier Relationships
7.	Operations Management	8.	Cash Flow Management
9.	Website Design	10.	Start-up Capital Investment
11.	License Availability	12.	Owner Background Check
13.	Patents	14.	Technical Expertise
15.	Trademarks	16.	Exclusive Distributors
17.	Restrictive Licensing		

4.7.1   Porter's Five Forces Analysis

We will use Porter's five forces analysis as a framework for the industry analysis and business strategy development. It will be used to derive the five forces which determine the competitive intensity and therefore attractiveness of our market. Attractiveness in this context refers to the overall industry profitability.

Competitors The degree of rivalry is moderate in this segment, but less when compared to the overall domestic beer category. Major competitors include:

_____

Substitutes   The threat of substitutes are high for this industry. These include other microbreweries, DIY home brewers and national breweries. Additionally, wine and spirits recently have been taking market share from the overall beer industry. Craft beer drinkers also enjoy trying new products, prices are comparable, and switching costs are low.

Buyer Power Buyer power is high in this business, as Distributors possess substantial power. Their bargaining power is high due to the concentration of distributors, availability of national and regional craft beers, and the state's mandated three-tier distribution system. Retailers also have a large amount of power, as they are highly concentrated, have low switching costs, high availability of information, and an assortment of craft beers to choose from. There is a possibility for brand loyalty, and craft beers allow retailers to generate higher revenues. End-consumers tend to purchase in lower volume, have low switching costs, and a large number of craft beers to choose from. End-consumers are less concerned with the higher price, and they are less loyal than domestic brand customers.

Supplier Power   Supplier power is high in this industry. Ingredients can be obtained from a limited number of vendors. Volume is important to suppliers, and it can be difficult for small brewers to compete with domestic brands placing large orders. There are few differentiating characteristics and substitutes for supplies such as malt, hops and glass bottles. A high level of operational efficiency for managing supplies needs to be achieved.

Internal Rivalry   There is high growth in the craft beer segment. Switching costs are very low and the competition is highly diversified, with greater product differences than domestic brewers. While there is high brand loyalty, it is less than the domestic industry. Fixed storage costs can be high for regional brewers with intermittent overcapacity, due to higher beer consumption in the summer months.

Threat of New Entrants   Relatively moderate in this segment. The business model can be easily copied, but the initial investment is significant. Because craft breweries are distinguished by unique taste profiles, economies of scale are less crucial to achieving profitability. Substantial differences exist between brands, unlike the domestic beer industry. An initial capital investment in equipment is required to enter the industry, and access to distribution can be very competitive, especially when smaller brewers must compete for space with larger brewers. Competitor's retaliation is expected to be fairly low, due to the differentiation of products, but domestic brewers are attempting to enter the craft beer industry. Other entry barriers include the industry learning curve, getting tap and shelf space, as well as forming beneficial relationships with distributors and suppliers.

Conclusions: _____ (company name) is in a competitive field and has to move fast to retain its competitive advantage. The key success factors are to develop operational efficiencies, create innovative flavor profiles and cost-effective marketing campaigns and practice customer service excellence.

4.8   Competitive Analysis

Competitor analysis in marketing and strategic management is an assessment of the strengths and weaknesses of current and potential competitors. This analysis will provide both an offensive and defensive strategic context through which to identify our business opportunities and threats. We will carry out continual competitive analysis to ensure our market is not being eroded by developments in other firms. This analysis needs to be matched with the target segment needs to ensure that our products and services continue to provide better value than the competitors. The competitive analysis needs to be able to show very clearly why our products and services are preferred in some market segments to other offerings and to be able to offer reasonable proof of that assertion.

Competitor	What We Can Do and They Can't	What They Can Do and We Can't

The largest competitive advantage for the microbrewery is the demographic population shift to _ County, coupled with the rise of the __ (city) area as a retail and dining magnet. The ____ area boasts some of the area's finest eating and drinking establishments with more of the same coming into the area. ___(company name) will be highly visible with its product in most area bars and nightclubs, as well as in retail stores. The sheer uniqueness of the business coupled with the great superiority of the product quality and flavor all contribute towards a winning formula for success. On either coast of the United States brewpubs and microbreweries are growing and succeeding at a rapid clip due to demands of the public, which is looking for superior flavor, high quality, and moderate price.

Competition to a large degree depends on location, as companies take a stake in a territory that engenders best in-class sales prospects. Relationships are cultivated with better customers, both individual and wholesale, who may qualify for discounts based on volume purchases. Prices in the ____ (city) marketplace are not subject to much variance, as retailers seek to protect their margins against distributor costs that are virtually the same for all. Distributors, however, reward volume, and high-volume retailers have the capability to build a competitive advantage. Special pricing on a limited number of products is something only a high-volume business could afford to do.

Other competitive factors include breadth and depth of available stock, product knowledge, customer service, expense management, marketing programs, employee training and productivity, management of detailed customer information in databases, merchandising display design, 24/7 online hours of operation, incoming and outgoing delivery efficiencies, product gift packaging, customer loyalty programs, out-of-area competition, pricing, and branded reputation.

There are other direct marketers and major advertisers that can deliver into our territory, But we expect our local delivery service will be faster and more responsive than these bigger players. Internet storefronts are emerging competitors and may be more of a longer-term issue, since the industry is in the process of testing and adapting to changing conditions in search of an online business model that works. We intend to develop our own website and grow with website economics that make this a self-funding outlet for sales and service.

Non-local microbreweries that are in commuter paths of our neighborhood residents are also competitors, which will make us ever aware of the importance of cultivating personal relationships with our neighborhood residents, so we can develop a long-term loyal customer base.

We will conduct good market intelligence for the following reasons:
1.   To forecast competitors' strategies.
2.   To predict competitor likely reactions to our own strategies.
3.   To consider how competitors' behavior can be influenced in our own favor.

Overall competition in the area is _____ (weak/moderate/strong).
Competitive analysis conducted by the company owners has shown that there are _____ (# or no other?) Microbreweries currently offering the same combination of products and services in the _____ (city) area. However, the existing competitors offer only a limited range of traditional products. In fact, of these, _____ (# or none) of the competitors offered a range of brands and services comparable with what _____ (company name) plans to offer to its customers.

Self-assessment

Competitive Rating Assessment:	**1 = Weak ....5 = Strong**		
	Our Company	Prime Competitor	Compare
Our Location	_____	_____	_____
Our Facilities	_____	_____	_____
Our Services and Amenities	_____	_____	_____
Our Management Skills	_____	_____	_____
Our Training Programs	_____	_____	_____
Our Research & Development	_____	_____	_____
Our Company Culture	_____	_____	_____
Our Business Model	_____	_____	_____
Overall Rating	_____	_____	_____

Rationale: _____

The following Microbreweries are considered direct competitors in _____ (city):

Competitor	Address	Market Share	Primary Focus	Secondary Prod/Svcs	Strengths	Weaknesses

Indirect Competitors include the following:

_____
_____

Alternative Competitive Matrix

Competitor Name:	Us	_____	_____	_____
Location:		_____	_____	_____
Location Distance (miles)		_____	_____	_____
Website		_____	_____	_____

Comparison Items:

Sales Revenue	_____
Growth Rate	_____

Buying Power _____

Product Focus _____

Product Range _____

Membership Programs _____

Profitability _____

Market Share _____

Brand Names _____

Specialty _____

Services _____

Capitalization _____

Target Markets _____

Delivery Area _____

Open Days _____

Operating Hours _____

Operating Policies _____

Delivery Time _____

Payment Options _____

Other Financing _____

Pricing Strategy _____

Price Level L/M/H _____

Economies of Scale _____

Discounts _____

Yrs in Business _____

Reputation _____

Customer Loyalty _____

Reliability _____

Quality _____

Marketing Strategy _____

Marketing Goals _____

Innovate Strategy _____

Methods of Promotion _____

Alliances _____

Brochure/Catalog _____

Website _____

Sales Revenues _____

No. of Staff _____

Competitive Advantage _____

Credit Policies _____

Comments _____

We will use the following sources of information to conduct our competition analysis:

1.   Competitor company websites.
2.   Mystery shopper visits.
3.   Annual Reports   (www.annual reports.com)
4.   Thomas Net   (www.thomasnet.com)

5. Trade Journals and Associations
6. Local Chamber of Commerce
7. Sales representative interviews
8. Research & Development may come across new patents.
9. Market research surveys can give feedback on the customer's perspective
10. Monitoring services will track a company or industry you select for news.
     Resources: www.portfolionews.com   www.Office.com
                    news.google.com   www.google.com/alerts
11. Hoover's   www.hoovers.com
12. www.zapdata.com   (Dun and Bradstreet) You can buy one-off lists here.
13. www.infousa.com   (The largest, and they resell to many other vendors)
14. www.onesource.com   (By subscription, they pull information from many sources)
15. www.capitaliq.com   (Standard and Poors).
16. Obtain industry specific information from First Research (www.firstresearch.com) or IBISWorld, although both are by subscription only, although you may be able to buy just one report.
17. Get industry financial ratios and industry norms from RMA (www.rmahq.com) or by using ProfitCents.com software.
18. Company newsletters
19. Industry and Market Research Consultants
20. Local Suppliers and Distributors
21. Customer interviews regarding competitors.
22. Analyze competitors' ads for their target audience, market position, product features, benefits, prices, etc.
23. Attend speeches or presentations made by representatives of your competitors.
24. View competitor's trade show display from a potential customer's point of view.
25. Search computer databases (available at many public libraries).
26. Review competitor Yellow Book Ads.
27. www.bls.gov/cex/ (site provides information on consumer expenditures nationally, regionally, and by selected metropolitan areas).
28. www.sizeup.com
29. Business Statistics and Financial Ratios   www.bizstats.com

4.9 Market Revenue Projection

For each of our chosen target markets, we will estimate our market share in number of customers, and based on consumer behavior, how often do they buy per year? What is the average dollar amount of each purchase? We will then multiply these three numbers to project sales volume for each target market.

Target Market	Number of Customers	No. of Purchases per Year	Average Dollar Amount per Purchase	Total Sales Volume
	A x	B x	C =	D

Using the target market number identified in this section, and the local demographics, we have made the following assessments regarding market opportunity and revenue potential in our area:

Potential Revenue Opportunity =

	_____	Local No. of Households (>60k Income)
(x)	_____	Expected ____% Market Share
(=)	_____	Number of likely local customers
(x) $	_____	Average annual fee dollar amount
(=) $	_____	Annual Revenue Opportunity.

or

	No. of Clients Per Day	(x)	Avg. Sale	(=)	Daily Income
Services	_____		_____		_____
Product Sales	_____		_____		_____
Other	_____		_____		_____
Total:					_____
Annualized:				(x)	300
Annual Revenue Potential:					_____

Recap:

Month Products	Jan Feb Mar Apr May Jun Jul Aug Sep Oct Nov Dec	Total

Gross Sales:	_____
(-) Returns	_____
Net Sales	_____

Revenue Assumptions:

1. The sources of information for our revenue projection are:

    _____

2. If the total market demand for our product/service = 100%, our projected sales volume represents ____% of this total market.

3. The following factors might lower our revenue projections:

    _____

5.0   Industry Analysis

SIC Code 5813
NAICS Code 722410

Although the microbrewery industry is very competitive, the lifestyle changes created by modern living continue to fuel its steady growth. There are more than 2000 malt beverage brands produced in the United States, six times the number of brands produced a decade ago. U.S. and international brewers continue to produce a tremendous array of beer styles with solid niche markets continuing to develop for industry members of every size. The predicated growth trend is very positive both in short and long-term projections. Craft brewers are anticipating the stability of a stronger and wiser craft-brewing industry that is already taking shape and will continue to strengthen in the coming years. The quality of the average brewpub and the average microbrew on the shelf is continually improving.

Currently there are more than 1,600 microbreweries in operation in the United States alone. The number of home brewers is unknown, but brewers of both home brew and microbreweries cite the same reasons for their existence. The taste, body and overall flavor of micro-rewed beer is designed to exceed that of the major brands. The majority of microbreweries produce ales and lagers, generally more robust than regular beer. The craft brewing industry grew by 7.2 percent in volume in 2009 and 10.3 percent in dollars. That is up from 5.9 percent in volume and 10.1 percent in dollars in 2008. Microbreweries claim approximately three percent of the total market for beer sales.

Small local breweries are not a new idea. Before the days of refrigeration, most towns and villages had a brewery, as beer could not be transported before it went bad. After refrigerated transport became possible, most local breweries were closed down in favor of the larger, more consistent brewers such as Miller and Anheiser Busch. In 2008, InBev, a Belgian company, bought out Anheuser-Busch and has been gobbling up other beer companies along the way, such Corona, Hoegaarden, Shock-top and Beck.

5.1   Industry Leaders

We plan to study the best practices of industry leaders and adapt certain selected practices to our business model concept. Best practices are those methods or techniques resulting in increased customer satisfaction when incorporated into the operation.

Resources:
http://www.blogaboutbeer.com/50-beers-from-50-states-in-50-days/
http://americancraftbeer.com/Serious-Top-50-Beers

North American Breweries   **www.nabreweries.com**
Headquartered in Rochester, New York was formed in 2009 by KPS Capital Partners, LP, a private equity fund. The company owns and operates five U.S. breweries and six retail

locations in New York, Vermont, California, Oregon and Washington. The Genesee Brewery, based in Rochester, New York, makes and sells the historic line of Genesee beers, Dundee Ales & Lagers, the Original Honey Brown Lager and Seagram's Escapes. The Washington, California, and Oregon breweries handcraft Pyramid beer, including its famous Hefeweizen, Apricot Ale and Thunderhead I.P.A. Magic Hat is headquartered in Vermont and makes and sells a variety of craft beers including the popular #9. It also regularly features seasonal beers in its rotating series of Variety Packs. North American Breweries was acquired in October 2018 by FIFCO, a Costarican based producer of alcoholic and non-alcoholic beverages as well as other food products for a sum estimated around $400 million.

The Boston Beer Company

It is the US's largest microbrewer. The company produces some 30 seasonal and year-round varieties of craft-brewed beers at its Cincinnati and Boston breweries. Annually, it sells more than 2 million barrels of lager (such as its flagship Samuel Adams Boston Lager), ales (other Samuel Adams brands), HardCore brand cider, and Twisted Tea malt beverages. The company distributes its brews primarily in the US, but they are also sold in Canada, Mexico, the Caribbean, Europe, Israel, and the Pacific Rim. The beers were originally contract brewed by the Pittsburgh Brewing Company and others, though today, over 95% of its beer is brewed in its own breweries located in Boston, Cincinnati and Pennsylvania.

Sierra Nevada Brewing Company

Established in 1980, it is the second largest craft brewery in America and is located in Chico, CA. Producing over 723,000 barrels of beer annually, the most popular brew is their pale ale. The company has a wide range of seasonal brews, porters, stouts and special releases. Sierra Nevada decided to differentiate its offerings by producing a craft beer with a consistently rich and full-bodied flavor profile. To avoid selling beers with an inconsistent taste, THEY committed from the beginning to not selling their product until they knew they could replicate the same flavor in each and every batch. To accomplish this, they set up a small quality lab in the brewery to test ingredients and brews.

Craft Brewers Alliance

Markets and sells the beers of The Redhook Ale Brewery (Seattle), Widmer Brothers Brewing Company (Portland, Oregon), Kona Brewing Company (Kona, Hawaii), and Goose Island Beer Company (Chicago). The Alliance, which is headquartered in Portland, offers approximately 30 craft beers that are available regionally and nationally. Its brands include Longhammer IPA, Wider Hefeweizen, Longboard Island Lager, and Oatmeal Stout. The company's beers are distributed nationally though a partnership with beverage giant Anheuser-Busch, which also owns about 36% of Craft Brewers Alliance.

Pyramid Breweries

Makes and sells small-batch, craft beers and ales (both year-round and seasonal; many of them wheat beers) under the Pyramid and MacTarnahan's brand names. It is a leader in the fruit beer category, especially apricots. Its breweries are located Seattle, Portland,

Oregon, Berkeley, California. In addition to making beer, the company serves it as well. It operates five alehouse restaurants, one each in Portland and Seattle, as well as in Walnut Creek, Berkeley, and Sacramento, California. In 2008 Pyramid was acquired by craft brewer, Magic Hat.

Stoudt's Brewing Company

Pennsylvania's oldest microbrewery. Part of an entertainment complex that includes the Black Angus Restaurant & Pub, Eddie's Breads, and the Black Angus Antiques Mall. The company's most well-known beer brands are Stoudts American Pale Ale and Fat Dog Stout. Its beers are distributed in restaurants, retail outlets, and taverns in 10 adjacent states, as well as Washington DC, Georgia, and California. The brewery plays host each year to several beer festivals and also offers its banquet facilities for weddings and other gatherings. Offering festivals, antiques, steaks, bread, and beer, the enterprise was founded as Stoudt's Kountry Kitchen by Ed Stoudt in 1962.

Horizon Beverage Co.

Distributes the beer and malt liquor beverages brewed by Anheuser-Busch to retail outlets in the East Bay area of Oakland. Imported brands offered by the company include Tsingtao, and Corona, Pacifico, and Negra Modelo. The company also distributes microbrewery products from Craft Brewers Alliance, such as Samuel Adams, Sierra Nevada, Shiner, and Pete's. It also offers retailer services such as beer industry news, beer market data, category management, and package art and logos.

Magic Hat   www.magichat.net/

Known for its uniquely delicious beers and what might be called quirky branding, Magic Hat began in 1994 in Burlington, Vermont. Since its launch, the little brewpub that could has grown into one of the top craft beer producers in the country. They have gone from making kegs for a few Burlington bars to being the number 10 craft brand in the country. People have really flocked to their beer, and they become really devoted to it when they do. The company's reputation for good beer is well known and the numbers show it: its flagship ale, simply known as "#9" is the third best-selling pale ale in the country-even with a deliberately limited distribution strategy. Magic Hat is available in many locations across 28 states. Magic Hat's beer naming and packaging reinforces their brand and popularity. Some ale names include Lucky Kat, Circus Boy, Wacko-a summer seasonal ale, Roxy Rolles-a fall offering, and a soon-to-be-released winter seasonal called "Howl in the Winter," a black-as-night winter lager. A special bonus is included on the underside of each bottle cap with conversation-inspiring phrases. In Magic Hat's *Vision and Values Statement*, the company stresses its focus on innovation, stating that "...ideas cannot be limited by current perception." In 2008, Magic Hat further grew its business by acquiring Seattle-based Pyramid Breweries. Most recently, the brewery has expanded distribution to Texas, Florida, and Southern California, yet 73 percent of its year-to-date growth occurred within existing territories.
Resource:
www.legalzoom.com/articles/microbreweries-that-found-macro-success

BridgePort Brewing   www.bridgeportbrew.com/

Coming off its 25th anniversary which included a community celebration in its their Portland neighborhood known as "The Pearl District," BridgePort Brewery is known for great beer and great causes. In support of local efforts to protect the great blue heron by naming it Portland's official city bird, BridgePort Brewery launched Blue Heron Pale Ale in 1987. BridgePort Brewing Company has gone from producing 600 barrels of beer a year to more than 45,000 barrels annually. As one of the top specialty brewers in Oregon with distribution in 18 states, the brewery has won various awards including the Gold Medal at the 2005 Brewing Industry International Awards. The brewery has managed to combine a love of beer and good causes while it continues to grow. Beyond the recent community block party that included Audubon Society fundraising, there was a live bird demonstration and Audubon Society of Portland Membership drive. Ranked number 33 in the Brewers Association's Top 50 Craft Brewing Companies, BridgePort's brews will likely keep growing and giving.

Throwback Brewery
This company makes a point of not sourcing hops and malts from across the country or Europe but instead from more local sources. They are able to connect with a consumer base that tends to look for more local flavors.

Brooklyn Brewery
Source:
http://nonabrooklyn.com/lessons-from-the-future-the-story-of-brooklyn-
    brewery%E2%80%99s-long-road-to-success/#.VXsNPbMtdmE

Sun King Brewery   **www.sunkingbrewing.com**
This Indianapolis-based microbrewery uses a fleet of Mercedes Benz Sprinters (3500 High Roof Cargo Vans) to make their craft beers available at special events to build their clientele. They serve their brews at more than 400 events and festivals annually, and they also use the same vehicles to deliver to about 700 commercial accounts, including restaurants and liquor stores. All of their vehicles are up-fitted with refrigeration, a full graphics wrap, and a six-tap draft system with a custom stainless-steel drip tray on the side. The vehicles have become great marketing and promotional tools.
Resources:
Sprinter Build & eQuip Tool   www.MBVans.com/shopping=tools/build-and-equip
                                www.mbsprinterusa.com/shopping=tools/build-and-equip

5.2   Key Industry Statistics

The American craft beer market grew five percent in 2017, reaching 12.7 percent of the entire U.S. beer market, according to the Brewers Association. Retail dollar sales of craft increased eight percent, up to $26.0 billion USD, and now account for more than 23 percent of the $111.4 billion USD U.S. beer market.

Nowhere is the change more evident than in Asheville. With a tenth brewery now open, the North Carolina town has more microbreweries per capita than any other American city. Asheville also hosts five beer-focused festivals (Brewgrass, Oktoberfest, Baseball and Beers, BeerCity BrewFest, and Winter Warmer).

Thirty-four U.S. states have self-distribution rights that allow microbreweries producing less than 10,000 barrels to distribute their beer and permit brewpubs to sell beer outside their establishments. The national average is 27.8 cents tax per gallon of beer.

Imported and specialty beer sales in the U.S. have been growing at 8-10% every year in the 1980's to a market share of over 20,000,000 Bbls., while the total beer market in the country has remained essentially flat.

Americans drink approximately 23 gallons of beer per year. With 46 microbrew outlets, Portland, OR has more breweries and brewpubs per capita than any other city in the United States. Thirty percent of the craft category is sold via draft.

The number of all types of U.S. breweries grew 19 percent in 2014, with 3,464 breweries now operating, according to BA data released in March. All but 46 of those are craft breweries. U.S. craft brewers produced 22.2 million barrels of beer in 2014, an 18 percent increase in volume over 2013, the association's data show. In fact, craft beer has posted double-digit production growth for seven out of the last nine years.

About 94% of U.S. breweries make less than 15,000 barrels of beer a year and the majority don't even distribute outside of their state.

Researchers at Mintel have come out with the following list of craft beer drinker demographic stats:
1.   Consumers who were of legal drinking age in 2012 are most likely to report increased consumption of beer (14 percent), which includes 7 percent of respondents who are drinking more craft beer in 2013 compared to 2012.
2.   Discovery of new beers is popular with 93 percent of imported beer drinkers, 88 percent of domestic fans and 84 percent of craft beer consumers.
3.   Craft beers have found a way to appeal to 49 percent of Millennials and 40 percent of Gen Xers, but just 29 percent of Baby Boomers and 22 percent of Swing Generation/World War II.
4.   Hispanic consumers also turn to craft beer with 38 percent indicating that they consume craft beer at any time.
5.   Eighty-four percent of craft beer consumers like to choose their beer depending on the season.
6.   Liquor or package stores are the preferred outlet for craft beer purchases.
7.   Seventy-three percent of craft beer drinkers say that they usually know what brand of beer they are going to buy before they go to the store.
8.   One-third of craft and imported beer consumers ask sales associates for advice and information when buying beer.

9.   Forty-five percent of craft beer drinkers indicate that they would try more craft beers if they knew more about them.

10.   Beer drinkers aged 36 to 47 are slightly less likely than consumers aged 21 to 35 to show a preference for the taste of craft beer.

11.   Members of Generation X are more likely than their younger counterparts to indicate that imported beer and craft beer are a similar value.

Resources:
http://www.cnbc.com/id/101435252
http://money.cnn.com/2015/03/03/smallbusiness/craft-beer-startup-how-to-guide/

5.3   Industry Trends

We will determine the trends that are impacting our consumers and indicate ways in which our customers' needs are changing and any relevant social, technical or other changes that will impact our target market. Keeping up with trends and reports will help management to carve a niche for our business, stay ahead of the competition and deliver products that our customers need and want.

1.   Large commercial breweries have introduced new brands intended to compete in the same market as microbrewery, but when this strategy failed, they invested in microbreweries; or in many cases bought them outright.

2.   A demand for diversity has led to the greater geographic dispersion of microbreweries.

3.   There continues to be a slow conversion of beer drinkers to craft beer.

4.   Most microbreweries put the bulk of their effort into darker ales, more akin to European beers, than into the light lagers that characterize the American industry giants.

5.   Craft brewers are expanding their market share by riding the organic food and "buy local" trends.

6.   Some states are promoting the brewing industry by allowing onsite consumption of beer made on the premises of a microbrewery, similar to onsite consumption allowed at wineries.

7.   The take-home market is becoming increasingly important across the board for alcohol sales owing to factors such as the recession and stricter drinking and driving laws in the country. Therefore, it is invaluable to be able to offer the public draught beer for sale in bottle stores, as well as the opportunity to collect a keg and take it home with the necessary equipment needed to pour the beer at home.

8.   Brewers continuing to innovate with beer styles and ingredients.

9.   Brewpubs as a category are holding up fairly well in the economy for beer sales, but only 37% of brewpubs showed beer sales growth in 2009.

10.   Fewer brewpubs were transitioning to packaging breweries in 2009.

11.   There were 5 times as many openings than closings in 2009.

12   Six microbreweries became regional craft breweries in 2008.

13. Microbreweries are experiencing greater beer distributor interest and expansion of distribution range.
14. Consumers continue to favor new products, new tastes and new packages.
15. Distilled spirits and wine continue to take market share away from beer.
16. Typically, beer consumers are very brand name loyal.
17. There is a growing interest in specialty beers, handcrafted microbrews and premium spirits.
18. Products made by independent producers are fashionable and attract customers willing to spend extra money for premium products.
19. Overall the online market for wine and beer generally has continued to show a great deal of strength.
20. Consumers are staying home more, and this has proven to a plus for beer retailers, as shoppers spend more for home consumption than in restaurants, because there is bigger value for the consumer in purchasing product for home consumption.
21. Many stores are continuing to cross merchandise party goods, snack foods and assorted bar accessories to encourage incremental sales.
22. States are also doing more extensive background checks before issuing liquor licenses to individuals.
23. Major brews are facing increased competition from craft beer sales made in supermarkets, on the Internet and through catalogues
24. The new microbreweries and pub breweries are competing in the specialty and imported beer market and are able to command a premium price for their products.
25. Microbreweries are forming 'distribution alliances' with big breweries.
26. India pale ales (IPA), though a bitter brew, with its roots in Britain, has become a runaway American sensation.
27. Brewers have gone gaga for hops, crafting increasingly bitter brews bursting with flavors of citrus, pine resin, tropical fruits, mango and more.
28. There is a growing appreciation for the sour beer category.
29. More seasonal or limited-edition beers are being produced.
30. More and more women are getting into the beer industry and are also becoming beer writers, bloggers, and beer sommeliers.
31. People now want from their beer, the same thing they want from their food; local sources and larger-than-life flavors.
32. Brewers are going far beyond tradition flavor profiles to attract attention and win new customers. In addition to unusual fruits flavors, we are seeing honey, smoke and other natural additives that are creating entirely new categories of beers.
33. Wine-sized beer bottles, for example, are becoming popular in South America and in the United States.
34. Beer makers are licensing popular brand names to generate excitement and becoming the official beer brands of certain public companies.
35. A lot of smaller breweries are recognizing the advantages of partnering with larger regional breweries, and those regional craft breweries are recognizing the dynamism that small local breweries can have in small, local markets.
36. Low-alcohol session beers are growing in popularity.
37. Craft breweries are looking more like restaurants and bars with fancy tasting

rooms.

38.   Small breweries are concerned about competing with companies like AB Inbev and SABMiller, both of which have been acquiring smaller, independent brewers.

39.   Sour beers are gaining in popularity, as well as experimental brewing techniques like barrel-aged beer.
Source:
http://thefederalist.com/2018/02/09/tales-of-the-american-craft-beer-renaissance/

40.   Breweries have begun launching new product lines to test-drive beer styles, break free from the same old, mine brewing's past, and explore newfangled techniques and ingredients.
Source: www.bonappetit.com/drinks/beer/article/brewery-spinoffs

41.   Craft breweries are beginning to compete with each other on price.

42.   More Distributors want microbreweries to spend money marketing and provide sales support, or they won't handle the beer.

43.   Direct sales to consumers is the model for new breweries because brewpubs are able to preserve margins and enable direct feedback.
Source: https://www.entrepreneur.com/article/246098

44.   More microbreweries are checking their state laws and pursing the knowledge to be able to self-distribute their products, if permitted.
Resource:
www.brewersassociation.org/government-affairs/laws/self-distribution-laws/
https://www.orchestratedbeer.com/blog/beer-distribution

45.   More brands are selling their craft beers in cans because cans pack easier, chill faster, and are a more effective light and oxygen barrier, which preserve the beer's freshness and integrity.

5.4   Industry Key Terms

We will use the following term definitions to help our company to understand and speak the language of our industry.
Resource: http://www.fattymattybrewing.com/homebrew_dictionary/

Ales
Ales are brewed with "top-fermenting" yeasts at close to room temperatures, 50-70F (10-21C). Ales encompass the broadest range of beer styles including bitters, pale ales, porters, stouts, barley beers, trappist, lambic, and alt. The British Isles are famous for their ales and it is a popular style with homebrewers and micro-breweries.
Beer
The basic ingredients of beer are: Water, a starch, such as malted barley, which can be converted to alcohol, a brewer's yeast to produce the fermentation, and a flavoring agent, such as hops. Since beer is composed mostly of water, the mineral composition in water plays a key role in producing beer. Different regions are better suited to making certain types of beer. The grain is usually barley or wheat, but sometimes corn and rice are used as well. Fruit, herbs, and spices may also be used for special styles. In the distant past, the terms "beer" and "ale" meant different things. "Ale" was originally made without using

hops, while "beer" did use hops. Since virtually all commercial products now use hops, the term "beer" now encompasses two broad categories: ales and lagers.

Beer Marketing Company (Contract Brewers)

A company that puts its own label on beer that is brewed for them by a Brewpub, Microbrewery, or Large Brewer. (Sometimes called a "contract brewer", but more correctly described as a "contract brewee".) These companies develop a recipe and then "buy" excess capacity at a large brewery to have their beer made for them. They, then, market and distribute the finished product.

Brewhouse

Consists of the brewing vessels such as mash / lauter tun, brewkettle, whirlpool, hot liquor tank, and in some cases, cold liquor tank. This is the area in which the actual brewing takes place. An average brew will take about six hours to complete and this area is the most highly visible area to customers.

Brew-On-Premise

A brewery that provides the facilities for people to come in and brew their own beer. Some "BOPs" also brew their own beer for sale like a microbrewery, and some operate restaurants like brewpubs.

Brewpub

A pub or restaurant that brews beer on the premises. Many brewpubs cater to our craving for uniqueness by providing one-of-a-kind social settings, commonly decorated with local historical photos, maps, and other artifacts of a place's personality. Brewpubs are able to save traditional expenses on the bottle, cap, carton, which work out to about 50% of the cost of bottled beer. Brewpub start-up systems are typically a seven-barrel system which is sufficient for small to medium-sized, retail only brewpubs which seat up to 125 people. Brewpubs larger than 125 seats or which plan to wholesale their product to other outlets will probably need a ten-barrel system or more. Startup budgets for this type of operation will require a minimum of $250,000-$300,000

Bunghole

A hole drilled into a barrel, cask, or keg for the purpose of accessing the liquid inside. The use of bungholes dates back to ancient times and persists to this day. Most typically, bungholes are used to access goods like beer and beer, although technically any sort of container of liquid could be tapped to create a bunghole.

Craft Beer

An American term which is also common in Canada and New Zealand and generally refers to beer that is brewed using traditional methods, without adjuncts such as rice or corn, and with an eye to what's distinctive and flavorful rather than mass appeal. Craft brewery describes an approach to brewing, which in principle may be carried out on any scale. Most microbreweries are also craft breweries; however, "craft" beer can certainly also be a product of a large brewery, and there are many such products coming to market as a result of increased consumer interest in traditional beer.

Cask ale ("real ale.")

It's unfiltered, unpasteurized, and contains live yeast. But what it's best known for is the fact that it's not traditionally carbonated like other beer. The carbonation is actually an effect of the pumping the ale into a glass. The hand pump of the cask is known as a beer engine: it's a ½ pint airtight piston chamber. The spout attached to the end has tiny adjustable holes that agitate the beer and give it more of a head – however this usually takes flavor away. True cask ale lovers prefer less head and carbonation, and more flavor.

Distributors

Maintain the beer in a climate-controlled warehouse, freeing the brewery from additional operational costs. Provide the necessary infrastructure to help small scale brewers to gain substantial market reach.

Handcrafted Beer (also known as craft beers)

Beers that have been made in a microbrewery or a craft brewery. Handcrafted beers don't usually have preservatives in them.

Hops

A climbing plant related to hemp, and there are both males and females. The females are the ones that are planted commercially because only the females produce the flower cones used in brewing. Once harvested, those flower cones are called hops. The importance of the hop flowers to the art of brewing comes from their utility as both a bittering agent and a contributor of aroma, as well as being a natural preservative adept at warding off bacterial spoilage.

India Pale Ale (IPA)

A hoppy bitter beer high in alcohol

Irish Reds

A slightly hoppy beer with toasted characteristics.

Kegerator

A device used in the home to contain kegs of draft beer, and a kegerator tap is the attachment that dispenses the beer. Kegerators are either kegs housed in converted refrigerators, or special refrigerators originally manufactured to serve as kegerators. The kegerator tap handle is typically found on the door or on the top of a kegerator so that the beer can remain chilled inside and dispensed without opening any doors to access the keg.

Kegerator Tap

A beer spigot, working in conjunction with carbon dioxide gas (CO_2) and sometimes nitrogen gas (N_2. The beer in the keg is pressurized with these gases so that it is forced into the kegerator tap and is drawn into the dispenser when the kegerator tap handle is engaged. More CO_2 is used for beers that should be highly carbonated, and more N_2 is used for beers that have a smoother, creamier taste. Beer in a pressurized keg will remain fresh for up to eight weeks.

Labeorphilist

A collector of beer bottles.

Large Brewery

A brewery that produces more than 1,000,000 barrels or hectolitres of beer annually.

Lagers

Lagers are brewed with "bottom-fermenting" yeasts at much colder temperatures, 35-50F (2-10C) over long periods of time (months). This is called "lagering". Lagers include bocks, doppelbocks, Munich- and Vienna-style, Märzen/Oktoberfest, and the famous pilsners. Pilsner beer originated in the town of Pilsen, now in the Czech Republic and was the first non-cloudy beer. Most popular beers produced by the large North American breweries were originally of the pilsner style. These have diverged a great deal from the original style and succeed now by the force of the mass-marketing prowess of the brewers rather than any remarkable qualities of the beers themselves.

Microbrewery

A small brewery with a limited production capacity which, of necessity, produces labor intensive hand-crafted beers. A beer maker with limited capacity whose products are typically distributed within a restricted geographic region.

Nanobrewery

The general consensus is that breweries operating systems no larger than 7 barrels are considered nano. And many are far smaller than that; 1-2 barrel systems, operated on evenings and weekends by people who maintain non-brewing day jobs. A microbrewery that produces less than 125 gallons per batch. These breweries are predictably cheaper to start than larger ones and allow passionate homebrewers to share their own recipes with the public.

Pico-brewer

Describes brewers so small that distribution is limited to pubs and bars in their immediate area.

Regional Brewery

A brewery in the United States or Canada that produces between 15,000 and 1,000,000 barrels or hectolitres of beer annually and packages *all* of its beer for sale off the premises.

Regional Craft Brewery

An independent regional brewery who has either an all malt flagship or has at least 50 percent of its volume in either all malt beers or in beers which use adjuncts to enhance rather than lighten flavor.

Self-Distribution

The ability of a manufacturing brewery to make direct sales and deliveries to retailers. Must check individual state laws regarding the right to self-distribute beer. Resource: www.brewersassociation.org/government-affairs/laws/self-distribution-laws/

Stouts

A darker beer with a creamy texture on the tongue

Tasting Room

A room in a brewery where the public can buy a pint or two of the latest ales. Must make certain that this room does not violate zoning regulations.

Three-tier system

The brewery makes the beer and then sells it to a distributor, which then sells the beer to retailers. Typically, smaller breweries benefit the most from the three-tier system because they don't have the means to get into the marketplace.

Wort

A brewing term that oftentimes refers to unfermented beer. The literal definition of wort is the liquid extracted from the mashing process. However, as brewers often use the word, wort is the end product of your mash, malt extracts, adjuncts, and hops after completing a sanitizing boil.

5.5 Industry Growth Strategy

Initiative	Tactics	
Build Awareness	Advertising	
Expand Distribution	Incentives	Discounts

	Sales Reps	
Build Buying Rate	Frequent Buyer Cards	Bulk Purchase Discounts
Build Penetration	Broad Advertising	Sampling Programs
	High-value incentives	
Build Extended Usage	New Usage Ideas	
Increase Loyalty	Frequent Buyer Cards	Rebates
	Volume Discounts	Product Improvements
Strengthen In-store	Demonstrations	
Merchandising	Signage	Display Housekeeping
	Point-of-Purchase Displays	Financial Incentives
Improve Product Quality	Reduce defect rate	Add Features
	Improve Reliability	Enhance Customer Service
Decease Product Costs features	Increase production efficiency	Eliminate unnecessary
	Negotiate lower supplier costs	Utilize cheaper materials
	Realize economies of scale	Master learning curve
Introduce New Brand	Awareness	Consistency
Attract Competitor Clients	Incentive offers	Product Comparisons
	High value trail promotion	
Enter a New Market	Sampling	Incentives
	Build awareness	New application ideas
Increase Referrals	Incentives	Refer-a-friend Programs
Reposition the Brand	Packaging	Pricing
	Endorsements	Partnerships
New Distribution Channel	Online marketing	
Increase Pricing	Better image and selection.	
Strengthen Brand	Customer brand involvement	
Accelerate R & D	Develop new product development processes.	
Modular Components	Assemble into a variety of configurations	
Platform Design	Shared by a variety of products and services.	
Operations Flexibility	Reduce set-up time and costs.	
New Services	Training	Installations
	Retrofitting	Technical Support
	On-site Testing	Educational Seminars
	Field Consulting	Marketing Consulting
	Operations Consulting	Design Consulting

5.5.1 Growth Strategy

We will adopt the following growth strategies to achieve sustainable growth:
1. Schedule free informational craft beer seminars and tastings to generate a consistent string of inquiries and leads.
2. Develop annuity products from the sales of articles, beer books, audiotapes, workbooks, software, speeches, etc.
3. Develop a Virtual Practice Arrangement through flexible subcontractor or partner

relationships.

4. Form a corporation to hire employees.
5. Raise fees to control growth and improve profitability and re-investment.
6. Enable employee telecommuting to reduce overhead expenses.
7. Utilize sales reps to open new territories.
8. Use penetration pricing tactics to enter new markets.
9. Develop new types of customized public relations programs directed at niche market segments.
10. Develop an annual rebate program to encourage client consolidation of vendors.
11. Improve Product Quality by improving reliability and client service.
12. Decease Product Costs by increasing base program standardization.
13. Introduce New Branded Image to foster awareness and remembrance.
14. Use incentives, sampling and comparisons to attract competitor clients
15. Increase Referrals with a structured referral program.
16. Form alliances to reposition the brand
17. Use online affiliated websites as a new distribution channel.
18. Increase pricing to convey a better image
19. Accelerate R & D to develop new products and services.

6.0 Strategy and Implementation Summary

The first step in the strategic development plan will be to introduce the _____ (company name) product line into the selected areas. New sales representatives will be assigned to the _____ (city) tri-county area and the _____ area. The retail marketing focus will be on specialty stores that carry regional microbrews. _____ (company name) will promote sales by reducing wholesale prices _____% for the first three months of sales.

_____ (company name) products will be distributed in the _____ (city) tri-county area by _____ (distribution company name).

_____'s (company name) new product, a traditional _____ (German Marzen?) style lager, will be unique enough in taste and processing to be attractive to any business that serves beers to customers. The added advantage is that the lager has no competitors.

The closest Microbrewery is a _____ (#) minute _____ (walk/ride?) from our location. To sustain this advantage, we will negotiate with the landlord so that our leasing agreement ensures no other liquor distributor can move into the same property complex.

Location is critical to attract the traffic and customer profile required to generate planned sales volumes. The business is highly territorial. We have mapped the location of every retail Microbrewery in _____ (city), and we have been working with executives of _____ (real estate company name) to determine the best possible location for the microbrewery. _____ (#) target areas were identified. Among the target areas investigated, _____ (area name) has been identified as our most promising business opportunity.

Exclusivity within _____ (complex/community name) is a significant competitive edge. It gives _____ (company name) geographic and protected domain as the most convenient source of fine craft beers for over _____ (#) current residents.

Our sales strategy is based on serving our niche markets better than the competition and leveraging our competitive advantages. These advantages include superior attention to understanding and satisfying customer needs and wants, creating a one-stop 'good times' solution, and value pricing. The objectives of our marketing strategy will be to recruit new customers, retain existing customers, get good customers to spend more and return more frequently. Establishing a loyal customer base is very important because such core customers will not only generate the most lifetime sales, but also valuable referrals.

We will generate word-of-mouth buzz through direct-mail campaigns, exceeding customer expectations, developing a Web site, getting involved in community events with local businesses, and donating our services at charity functions in exchange for press release coverage. Our sales strategy will seek to convert potential and first-time customers into long-term relationships and referral agents. The combination of our competitive advantages, targeted marketing campaign and networking activities, will enable _____ (company name) to continue increasing our market share.

6.1.0   Promotion Strategy

Promotion strategies will be focused to our target market segment. Given the importance of word-of-mouth/referrals among the area residents, we shall strive to efficiently service all our customers to gain their business regularly, which is the recipe for our long-term success. We shall focus on direct resident marketing, publicity, beer seminars, and advertising as proposed. Our promotion strategy will focus on generating referrals from existing clients, demonstrating our community involvement, generating volume sales of selected beers, encouraging trial of new beers and upgrading customers to new varietals.

We are planning on making many different types of beers, but we need to have all of them evenly distributed throughout the bars and pubs in the _____ area to get full coverage for our product. Creating light-up signs for the bars/pubs will remind people what our product tasted like and may get them to purchase more in the bar or from a microbrewery for consumption in their homes. Getting as much exposure as possible at the bars and pubs is key to getting our product a reputable name.

From this we will have television advertisements on channels such as: ESPN, CBS, NBC, FOX, and UPN. Marketing on these channels will cover all of the middle-aged people who watch the most popular TV shows, the local news, and sports which is what our target market has an interest in. Billboards will be placed along all major freeways passing through downtown _____ (city) to entice people coming home from work to stop at the local grocery or bar and pick up some of our product.

Our promotional strategies will also make use of the following tools:
- **Advertising**
  - Yearly anniversary parties to celebrate the success of each year.
  - Yellow Pages ads in the book and online.
  - Flyers promoting special promotion events and tastings.
  - Doorknob hangers, if not prohibited by neighborhood associations.
  - Storefront banners to promote a themed promotional event.
  - Bags with microbrewery name, logo and address.

- **Local Marketing / Public Relations**
  - Client raffle for gift certificates or discount coupons
  - Participation in local civic groups.
  - Press release coverage of our sponsoring of events at the local community center for families and residents.
  - Article submissions to magazines describing a party planning checklist.
  - Sales Brochure to convey our program specialties to prospective customers.
  - Seminar presentations to local civic groups, explaining the historical origins of various brews.
  - Giveaway of free recipe booklets with microbrewery contact information.

o Celebration of local ethnic holidays such as Cinco de Mayo.

- **Local Media**
    - o Direct Mail - We will send quarterly postcards and annual direct mailings to residents with a ___ (10?) mile radius of our microbrewery. It will contain an explanation of the benefits of our mobile services.
    - o Radio Campaign - We will make "live on the air" presentations of our trial service coupons to the disk jockeys, hoping to get the promotions broadcasted to the listening audience. We will also make our expertise available for talk radio programs.
    - o Newspaper Campaign - Placing several ads in local community newspapers to launch our initial campaign. We will include a trial coupon.
    - o Website – We will collect email addresses for a monthly newsletter.
    - o Cable TV advertising on local community-based shows focused on food, drink and entertaining.

6.1.1   Grand Opening

Our Grand Opening celebration will be a very important promotion opportunity to create word-of-mouth advertising results. Note: There may be local restrictions on advertising the sale of alcohol. If no restrictions prohibit it, we will advertise the date of our grand opening in local newspapers and on local radio. It is generally a good idea to provide the community with a reason to visit our Microbrewery, such as offering free beer and cheese sampling.

In preparation for the Grand Opening, postcards promoting the Grand Opening will be sent to friends, neighbors, co-workers, home-brewers, the Company's professional team, and to households in the area. These postcards will be redeemable at the Grand Opening for a discount on a Beer Sampler Set. Flyers will also be printed up and posted around area campuses. To reach a good portion of the target market while integrating with the community, the Company anticipates donating part of the Grand Opening proceeds to _____ public radio, in return for two weeks of advertisement time.

The Grand Opening will be an Opening Weekend rather than just a single day. The opening will span a Friday, Saturday, and Sunday. The Thursday before the opening, the brew-pub will sponsor a media event targeting radio, newspapers, and TV in and around _____ (city). Two weeks prior to the Media Event, management plans to send Media Kits containing fact sheets, bios, industry background and the history of brewing in ___ (city). The kits will also contain coasters or T-shirts with the Company logo, press releases, sidebar copy, and tables and graphs related to the industry. The media will be invited to schedule times to come in and receive a full brewery tour and complimentary tasting with the Brewmaster.

We will do the following things to make the open house a successful event:
1.   Enlist local business support to contribute a large number of door prizes.

2. Use a sign-in sheet to create an email/mailing list.
3. Sponsor a beer tasting competition.
4. Schedule appearance by local celebrities.
5. Create a festive atmosphere with balloons, beverages and music.
6. Get the local radio station to broadcast live from the event and handout fun gifts.
7. Offer an application fee waiver.
8. Giveaway our logo imprinted T-shirts as a contest prize.
9. Allow potential customers to view your facility and ask questions.
10. Print promotional flyers and pay a few kids to distribute them locally.
11. Arrange for face painting, storytelling, clowns, and snacks for everyone.
12. Arrange for local politician to do the official opening ceremony so all the local newspapers came to take pictures and do a feature story.
13. Arrange that people can tour our facility on the open day in order to see our facilities, collect sales brochures and find out more about our services.
14. Allocate staff members to perform specific duties, handout business cards and sales brochures and instruct them to deal with any questions or queries.
16. Organize a drawing with everyone writing their name and phone numbers on the back of business cards and give a voucher as a prize to start a marketing list.
17. Hand out free samples of products and coupons. (if state approved)

6.1.2   Value Proposition

Our value proposition will summarize why a consumer should buy our craft beers. We will enable quick access to our broad line of quality products and innovative services, out of our conveniently located and clean microbrewery in the _____ (city) area. Our value proposition will convince prospects that our microbrewery will add more value and better solve their need for a convenient, one-of-a-kind brewery. We will use this value proposition statement to target customers who will benefit most from consuming our unique brews. These are college students and baby boomers looking to socialize and create special 'good time' memories. Our value proposition will be concise and appeal to the customer's strongest decision-making drivers, which are a time-efficient and guided purchase experience, product quality and selection, and quality of personal relationships. Our customers will weigh the following factors when considering the value of our products: body, complexity, crispness, freshness, how strong or weak the hops are, how strong the presence of the malt is, the feel of the beer in their mouth and the intensity of the roast.

Recap of Our Value Proposition:
Trust – We are known as a trusted business partner with strong customer and vendor endorsements. We have earned a reputation for quality, integrity, and delivery of successful event solutions.
Quality – We offer master brewing experience and extensive professional backgrounds in _____ at competitive rates.
Experience – Our ability to bring people with years of _____ experience with deep technical knowledge is at the core of our success.

True Vendor Partnerships – Our true vendor partnerships enable us to offer the resources of much larger organizations with greater flexibility.

Customer Satisfaction and Commitment to Success – Through partnering with our customers and delivering quality solutions, we have been able to achieve an impressive degree of repeat and referral business. Since _____ (year), more than _____% of our business activity is generated by existing customers. Our philosophy is that "our customer's satisfaction is our success." Our success will be measured in terms of our customer's satisfaction survey scores and testimonials.

6.1.3   Positioning Statement

We will create a positioning statement for our company that describes what distinguishes our business from the competition. We will keep it simple, memorable and snappy. We will test our positioning statement to make certain that it appeals to our target audience. We will continue to refine it until it speaks directly to our targeted customer wants, needs and aspirations. We will use our positioning statement in every written communication to customers. This will ensure that our message is consistent and comes across loud and clear. We will create quality image marketing materials that communicate our positioning.

Our positioning strategy will be the result of conducting in-depth consumer market research to find out what benefits consumers want and how our craft beers and services can meet those needs. Due to the increase in two-income families, many service-oriented professions are leaning toward differentiating themselves on the basis of convenience and unique flavor profile. This is also what we intend to do. For instance, we plan to have extended, "people" hours on various days of the week and offer a website ordering feature, a delivery service, and a beer and cheese catering service (if state laws permit).

We also plan to develop specialized services that will enable us to pursue a niche focus on specific interest-based programs, such as a restaurant consulting service. These objectives will position us at the _____ (mid-level/high-end) of the market and will allow the company to realize a healthy profit margin in relation to its low-end, discount rivals and achieve long-term growth.

Market Positioning Recap

Price: The strategy is to offer competitive prices that are lower that the market leader, yet set to indicate value and worth.

Quality: The craft beer quality will have to be very good as the finished product results will be showcased in highly visible situations.

Service: Highly individualized and customized service will be the key to success in this type of business. Personal attention to the customers will result in higher sales and word of mouth advertising.

6.1.4   Unique Selling Proposition (USP)

Our unique selling proposition will answer the question why a customer should choose to do business with our company versus any and every other option available to them in the marketplace. Our USP will be a description of a unique important benefit that our microbrewery offers to customers, so that price is no longer the key to our sales.

Our USP will include the following:
Who our target audience is: _____
What we will do for them: _____
What qualities, skills, talents, traits do we possess that others do not: _____
What are the benefits we provide that no one else offers: _____
Why that is different from what others are offering: _____
Why that solution matters to our target audience: _____
Resource: http://fizzle.co/sparkline/unique-selling-proposition

Some USP Options:
1. Lowest Prices Everyday
2. The Best Quality
3. The Only Place to Get It
4. Customer Friendliness
5. Broadest Selection
6. State-of-the-Art
7. Always on-time

6.1.5   Distribution Strategy

We will start with self-distribution for the first few years to gain good product representation and placement, and then turn the distribution over to a beer wholesaler as sales and demand for their beers increase.

Before selecting a distributor, we will do the following:
1. Make certain the chosen distributor can grow with our business.
2. Obtain price sheets from each wholesaler so we know which distributors carry the various brands in the market.
3. Talk to retailers to gain insight into which distributor they prefer dealing with.
4. Ask questions about service, product knowledge, enthusiasm, etc., of the salespeople.
5. Ascertain which distributor understands and sells craft beers the best.
6. Visit retail accounts and festivals to find out which distributor has the more meaningful presence, has the most draft handles and best shelf positioning for craft beers.
7. Talk with other craft brewers in that market to get their opinions on distributor pros and cons.
8. Get our attorney to draft a written distribution agreement.

As a microbrewery, _____ (company name) will distribute through a wholesaler in a traditional three-tier system. We will also act as our own distributor (wholesaler) and sell to retailers and/or directly to the consumer through a tap room, attached restaurant, or off-premise sales.

Our products will be offered everywhere. At nearly every grocery and convenience store, and all of the bars or pubs that are servicing our target market around the _____ metro area, we will dispatch our sales team. We will want to get more shelf space in the stores around the upscale and highly traveled areas such as some of the biggest stores in the _____ area, along with many easily accessible stores which show to be most profitable.

1. **Order by Phone**
   Customers can contact us 24 hours a day, 7days a week at _____.
   Our Customer Service Representatives will be available to assist customers Monday through Friday from ___ a.m. to ____ p.m. EST.
2. **Order by Fax**
   Customers may fax their orders to _____ anytime.
   They must provide: Account number, Billing and shipping address, Purchase order number, if applicable, Name and telephone number, Product number/description, Unit of measure and quantity ordered and Applicable sales promotion source codes.
3. **Order Online**
   Customers can order online at www._____.com.Once the account is activated, customers will be able to place orders, browse the catalog, check stock availability and pricing, check order status and view both order and patient history.
4. **In-person**
   All customers can be serviced in person at our facilities Monday through Friday from ___ a.m. to ____ p.m. EST.
.5. **Order by EDI (Electronic Data Interchange)**
   Wholesale customers can enter the order once directly into our dealer management system and it is transmitted to us. We will provide customers with electronic notification of expected ship-date, prices, tracking numbers, order status and distribution center from which the order will be shipped. Orders may be reviewed right from the dealer management system.

We plan to pursue the following distribution channels: (select)
1. Our own tap room or brewpub _____
2. Independent retail outlets such as grocery stores, _____
3. Chain store retail outlets, such as national convenience stores, _____
4. Wholesale outlets _____
5. Independent distributors _____
6. Independent commissioned sales reps _____
7. In-house sales reps _____
8. Direct mail using own catalog or flyers _____
9. Catalog broker agreement _____
10. In-house telemarketing _____
11. Contracted telemarketing call center _____
12. Cybermarketing via own website _____
13. Online sales via amazon, eBay, etc. _____

14.   TV and Cable Direct Marketing _____

15.   TV Home Shopping Channels _____

Note: American microbreweries typically distribute through a wholesaler in a traditional three-tier system, others act as their own distributor (wholesaler) and sell to retailers and/or directly to the consumer through a tap room, attached restaurant, or off-premise sales.

Resource:
Liberation Distribution   www.LibDib.com
The first technology company to offer a three-tier compliant web-based platform to sell wholesale alcohol. Their technology enables craft breweries to start selling to restaurants and retailers across the country (in California and New York). LibDib is a licensed distributor with a technology platform that efficiently connects brands directly with buyers, and the only distributor to provide legal market access to any licensed maker. Over 1,500 active resellers are on the platform and restaurants, specialty stores and large chains in both states are purchasing craft products from LibDib.
Resource:
www.craftbrewingbusiness.com/news/web-based-beer-distribution-one-year-later-four-breweries-share-their-experience-growing-via-libdib/

6.1.6   Sales Rep Plan

We will use sales reps to sell to local restaurants, _____, taverns and sports bars. Our Reps will personally visit these establishments, giving samples of the products and educating owners on our distinctive beer characteristics to create a pull or demand in the marketplace.

1.   In-house or Independent   _____
2.   Salaried or Commissioned   _____
3.   Salary or Commission Rate   _____
4.   Salary Plus Commission Rate   _____
5.   Special Performance Incentives _____
6.   Negotiating Parameters   Price Breaks/Added Services/
                                          _____
7.   Performance Evaluation Criteria No. of New Customers/Sales Volume/
                                          _____
8.   Number of Reps   _____
9.   Sales Territory Determinants   Geography/Demographics/
                                          _____
10.   Sales Territories Covered   _____
11.   Training Program Overview   _____
12.   Training Program Cost   _____
13.   Sales Kit Contents   _____
14.   Primary Target Market   Restaurants and Bars

15.   Secondary Target Market   _____

Rep Name   Compensation Plan   Assigned Territory
_____
_____

We will locate sales reps using the following techniques:
1.   Place classified ads in trade magazines that serve the professional crafters.
2.   Seek other owner recommendations.
3.   Ask the managers of shops carrying handcrafted beer, the names of reps showing products to them.
4.   Attend trade shows where the reps are showing product lines.

6.2   Competitive Advantages

A **competitive advantage** is the thing that differentiates a business from its competitors. It is what separates our business from everyone else. It answers the questions: "Why do customers buy from us versus a competitor?", and "What do we offer customers that is unique?". We will make certain to include our key competitive advantages into our marketing materials. We will use the following competitive advantages to set us apart from our competitors. The distinctive competitive advantages which _____ (company name) brings to the marketplace are as follows:
(Note: Select only those you can support)

1.   Our beers are the highest quality and include only the finest natural ingredients.
2.   Carefully selected for their distinctive flavor profile, the beers are classically fermented and cold lagered for a smooth, bold taste.
3.   We use fine North American two row barley malt in addition to imported Belgian specialty malts, generally regarded as among the finest malts in the world.
4.   We use hops from the Pacific Northwest in our ales, and use imported German hops to give our lagers their distinctive taste.
5.   Our beers are stored in small 20-barrel batches under the close personal attention of our brewers.
6.   The latest brewing equipment and technologies are seamlessly combined with traditional brewing methods to ensure consistently excellent taste, whether packaged in bottles or draft kegs.
7.   Our craft brews offer an increasing array of exotic ingredients, like saffron, honey, dark chocolate, bergamot oranges and black cherries.
8.   We run seasonal promotions.
9.   We closely monitor consumption trends to determine which products to list and de-list.
10.   We will initiate a Supplier Scorecard Program to provide suppliers with objective and timely feedback to realize continuous improvement in supplier related activities.

11. Easy access to customer records, purchasing history and information about all the beers helps our sales force to provide customers with the personalized information they need to shop with confidence.

12. Our business operations will be backed by a full team of managers and owners that will each devote their time and efforts into one specialized area of the business. This specialization will increase the effectiveness of each of the aspects of our business through cost-effective micro-management.

13. Our owners/managers we will be able to maintain a direct relationship with our customers.

13. Our involvement with the community and our presence and availability within the microbrewery on a regular basis will give our customers the opportunity to give direct feedback.

14. Location: _____ (company name) is located on _____, a main road that enables us to take advantage of walk-by and drive-by-traffic. The closest competitor is ____ (#) miles into the town of _____.

15. We also have adequate parking to make shopping at our microbrewery convenient for drivers.

16. Our website will enable online ordering and pre-ordering, and the issuance of reminder notices for automatic purchases.

17. We will offer discounts and other incentives for referrals

18. We have the technological and professional staffing capabilities to provide our customers with the highest possible level of personalized service.

19. We have an ethnically diverse and multilingual staff, which is critical for a service-oriented business.

20. We developed a specialized training program for the staff, so they will be proficient at administering our service programs.

21. Our superior customer service, delivered through our trained staff, sets us apart and provides our competitive advantage

22. We have an inventory management system that reduces out-of-stock situations and assures that needed items are in stock.

23. We regularly conduct focus groups to understand changing customer expectations.

24. We utilize reliable equipment with back-up alternatives.

25. We hire and train our employees to be responsive and empathetic to customer needs.

26. We will develop a reputation for using our expertise to maintain a 'well-edited selection' that embodies the concept of reasonable value.

6.2.1   Branding Strategy

Our branding strategy involves what we do to shape what the customer immediately thinks our business offers and stands for. The purpose of our branding strategy is to show customers what we stand for and reduce customer perceived purchase risk and improve our profit margins by allowing us to charge a premium for our microbrewery products and services. We will distil the essence of our microbrewery to a few words that describe what we want to be known for, such as taste, quality, price, etc. We will use these few words as a benchmark for our brand. They will become our touchstone when we are creating our logo, packaging, website, business cards, etc.

We will invest $_____ every year in maintaining our brand name image, which will differentiate our microbrewery business from other companies. The amount of money spent on creating and maintaining a brand name will not convey any specific information about our products, but it will convey, indirectly, that we are in this market for the long haul, that we have a reputation to protect, and that we will interact repeatedly with our customers. In this sense, the amount of money spent on maintaining our brand name will signal to consumers that we will provide products and services of consistent quality.

Our branding strategy will contain the following key ingredients:
1.   Convey a passion and a self-deprecating humor for our products.
2.   Our beers will have catchy product names with consistent logos, colors and other eye-catching graphic design elements in our product labels to create a unique identity and improve visibility.
3.   A promise to make our customers better-educated drinkers about our backstory, processes and ingredients.
4.   The use of social media and video storytelling to communicate the above differentiation strategies and empower consumers to spread the message.
5.   Securing direct feedback at tasting events.
6.   The entering of our beers into domestic and international tasting competitions to secure differentiating awards and recognition.
7.   We will focus on a product line consisting of high-quality German-style brews, complemented with the company's signature _____ (sweet potato?) beer.

Resources:
www.craftbrewingbusiness.com/featured/2018-craft-beer-branding-trends-an-aesthetic-
        state-of-the-union-for-beer-packaging/
http://gykantler.com/how-to-become-a-successful-craft-brewery-in-2014-and-beyond/
http://www.koreatimes.co.kr/www/news/biz/2018/04/342_94162.html

We will use the following ways to build trust and establish our personal brand:
1.   Build a consistently published blog and e-newsletter with informational content.
2.   Create comprehensive social media profiles.
3.   Contribute articles to related online publications.
4.   Earn Career Certifications.
5.   Remain readily accessible.
6.   Find your voice and use it to be relatable on the human level.
7.   Create a persona that combines who you are and who you want to be.
8.   Stick with the niche in which you can offer the greatest value.

Resources:
https://www.abetterlemonadestand.com/branding-guide/

Our key to marketing success will be to effectively manage the building of our brand platform in the market place, which will consist of the following elements:

Brand Vision - our envisioned future of the brand is to be the national source for craft beer with a distinctive flavor profile.

Brand Attributes - Partners, problem solvers, responsive, niche market driven, flexible and easy to work with.

Brand Essence - the shared soul of the brand, the spark of which is present in every experience a customer has with our products, will be "Unique", Accommodating" and "Fresh." This will be the core of our organization, driving the type of people we hire and the type of behavior we expect.

Brand Image - the outside world's overall perception of our organization will be that we are craft beer pros who are alleviating the complications of stale tasting beer.

Brand Promise - our concise statement of what we do, why we do it, and why customers should do business with us will be, "To create a more uniquely flavorful beer drinking experience"

We will use the following methodologies to implement our branding strategy:

1. Develop processes, systems and quality assurance procedures to assure the consistent adherence to our quality standards and mission statement objectives.
2. Develop business processes to consistently deliver upon our value proposition.
3. Develop training programs to assure the consistent professionalism and responsiveness of our employees.
4. Develop marketing communications with consistent, reinforcing message content.
5. Incorporate testimonials into our marketing materials that support our promises.
6. Develop marketing communications with a consistent presentation style. (Logo design, company colors, slogan, labels, packaging, stationery, etc.)
7. Exceed our brand promises to achieve consistent customer loyalty.
8. Use surveys, focus groups and interviews to consistently monitor what our brand means to our customers.
9. Consistently match our brand values or performance benchmarks to our customer requirements.
10. Focus on the maintenance of a consistent number of key brand values that are tied to our company strengths.
11. Continuously research industry trends in our markets to stay relevant to customer needs and wants.
12. Attach a logo-imprinted product label and business card to all products, marketing communications and invoices.
13. Develop a memorable and meaningful tagline that captures the essence of our brand.
14. Prepare a one-page company overview and make it a key component of our sales presentation folder.
15. Hire and train employees to put the interests of customers first.
16. Develop a professional website that is updated with fresh content on a regular basis.
17. Use our blog to circulate content that establishes our niche expertise and opens a

two-way dialogue with our customers.

18.   Attractive and tasteful uniforms will also help our staff's morale. The branding will become complete with the addition of our corporate logo, or other trim or accessories which echo the style and theme of our establishment.

19.   Create an effective slogan with the following attributes:
      a.   Appeals to customers' emotions.
      b.   Shows off how our service benefits customers by highlighting our customer service or care.
      c.   Has 8 words or less and is memorable
      d.   Can be grasped quickly by our audience.
      e.   Reflects our business' personality and character.
      f.   Shows sign of originality.

20.   Create a Proof Book that contains before and after photos, testimonial letters, our mission statement, copies of industry certifications and our code of ethics.

21.   Make effective use of trade show exhibitions and email newsletters to help brand our image.

The communications strategy we will use to build our brand platform will include the following items:

Website - featuring product line information, research, testimonials, cost benefit analysis, frequently asked questions, and ordering information. This website will be used as a tool for both our sales team and our customers.

Presentations, brochures and mailers geared to the facility level (ideally, distributed by the corporate sales office as part of an initiative to penetrate new markets) explaining the benefits of our product line as part of a comprehensive plan to attract a new customer segment.

Presentations and brochures geared to the corporate account decision maker explaining the benefits of our program in terms of positive outcomes, reduced waste from stale dated beer, and reduced risk of negative survey events.

A presentation and recruiting brochure geared to prospective sales people that emphasizes the benefits of joining our organization.

Training materials that help every employee deliver our brand message in a consistent manner.

6.2.2   Brand Positioning Statement

We will use the following brand positioning statement to summarize what our brand means to our targeted market:

To _____ (target market)
_____ (company name) is the brand of _____ (product/service frame of reference) that enables the customer to _____ (primary performance benefit) because _____ (company name) _____ (products/services) _____ (are made with/offer/provide) the best _____ (key attributes)

6.3   Business SWOT Analysis

Definition: SWOT Analysis is a powerful technique for understanding our Strengths and Weaknesses, and for looking at the Opportunities and Threats faced.

Strategy: We will use this SWOT Analysis to uncover exploitable opportunities and carve a sustainable niche in our market. And by understanding the weaknesses of our business, we can manage and eliminate threats that would otherwise catch us by surprise. By using the SWOT framework, we will be able to craft a strategy that distinguishes our business from our competitors, so that we can compete successfully in the market.

Example:
http://hkdevkota.blogspot.com/2012/12/coopers-brewery-analysis-report.html

Strengths   (select)
What Microbrewery products and services are we best at providing?
What unique resources can we draw upon?

1. Our location is in the heart of an upscale neighborhood and is in close proximity to a popular _____ with ample parking facilities.
2. The facility has been established as a Microbrewery for ___ years.
3. The nearest competition is __ miles and has a minimal inventory of convenience goods.
4. Our facility has been extensively renovated, with many upgrades.
5. Our microbrewery has the ability to change inventory with special occasion requirements.
6. Seasoned executive management professionals, sophisticated in business knowledge, experienced in the beer and spirits trade.
7. Strong networking relationships with many different organizations, including _____.
8. Excellent staff are experienced, highly trained and customer attentive.
9. Wide diversity of product/service offerings.
10. High customer loyalty.
11. The proven ability to establish excellent personalized client service.
12. Strong relationships with suppliers, that offer flexibility and respond to special customer requirements.
13. Good referral relationships.
14. Client loyalty developed through a solid reputation with repeat clients.
15. Our company has a focused target market of _____ (college students?).
16. A sales staff with beer and spirit education credentials.
17. Craft brewers well connected to customers and communities.
18. Craft beer seen as a great value.
19. Use of packaging redesign to attract new buyers.
20. Reasonable pricing.
21. Premium quality image.
22. Quality beverage made with natural ingredients created in traditional ways.

23. _____

Weaknesses

In what areas could we improve?

Where do we have fewer resources than others?

1. Lack of developmental capital to complete Phase I start-up.
2. New comer to the area.
3. Lack of marketing experience.
4. The struggle to build brand equity.
5. A limited marketing budget to develop brand awareness.
6. Finding dependable and people-oriented staff.
7. We need to develop the information systems that will improve our productivity and inventory management.
8. Don't know the needs and wants of the local population.
9. The owner must deal with the retail experience learning curve.
10. Challenges caused by the seasonal nature of the business.
11. Management expertise gaps.
12. Inadequate monitoring of competitor strategies, reviews and responses.
13. _____

Opportunities

What opportunities are there for new and/or improved services?

What trends could we take advantage of?

1. Seasonal changes in inventory.
2. Could take market share away from existing competitors.
3. Greater need for mobile home services by time starved dual income families.
4. Growing market with a significant percentage of the target market still not aware that _____ (company name) exists.
5. The ability to develop many long-term customer relationships.
6. Expanding the range of product/service packaged offerings.
7. Greater use of direct advertising to promote our services.
8. Establish referral relationships with local businesses serving the same target market segment.
9. Networking with non-profit organizations.
10. The aging population will need and expect a greater range of __ services.
11. Increased public awareness of the importance of 'green' matters.
12. Strategic alliances offering sources for referrals and joint marketing activities to extend our reach.
13. _____ (supplier name) is offering co-op advertising.
14. A competitor has overextended itself financially and is facing bankruptcy.
15. _____

Threats

What trends or competitor actions could hurt us?

What threats do our weaknesses expose us to?
1. Another microbrewery could move into this area.
2. Further declines in the economic forecast.
3. Inflation affecting operations for gas, labor, and other operating costs.
4. Keeping trained efficient staff and key personnel from moving on or starting their own business venture.
5. Imitation competition from similar indirect service providers.
6. Price differentiation is a significant competition factor.
7. The government could enact legislation that could affect reimbursements.
8. We need to do a better job of assessing the strengths and weaknesses of all our competitors.
9. Sales of craft beers by mass discounters.
10. The health-conscious market is expanding.
11. Must manage bad publicity caused by underage drinking and binge drinking.
12. Susceptibility to an acquisition.
13. _____

Recap:
We will use the following strengths to capitalize on recognized opportunities:
1. _____
2. _____

We will take the following actions to turn our weaknesses into strengths and prepare to defend against known threats.
1. _____
2. _____

6.4.0   Marketing Strategy

_____ (company name) will market their products through two different avenues. The first will focus on the sales of kegged beer to draught accounts throughout the ___ area. The marketing in this area involves the use of Point-of-Sale (POS) materials such as posters, table tents, tap handles, buttons, tee-shirts, etc. In the initial product roll-out, extensive use of our distributor's experience and account knowledge will be made.

Area bars and restaurants will be provided POS materials appropriate to their ability to sell the product. Tap handles will also be provided. Tap handles cost approximately $10 each. Posters and table tents range in price based on quantities ordered. These will be procured through a local printer.

The second marketing thrust will be for sales of bottled beer through retail outlets. Once again, POS materials are necessary, although with differing needs. Posters and shelf markers, as well as posters and vinyl stickers will be used. These will also be procured through a local printer.

Our marketing campaign will feature vivid descriptions of flavors, aromas, pouring techniques and food pairings

Our Marketing strategy will focus on the following:
1. Developing a reputation for great selection, an appealing microbrewery environment, value pricing, mobile services, and exceptional customer service.
2. Developing strong relationships with our suppliers to help insure best discount deals and best supplier services obtainable.
3. Keeping the staff focused, satisfied and motivated in their roles, to help keep our productivity and customer service at the highest obtainable levels.
4. Maintaining the visibility of our microbrewery through regular advertising to our target community.
5. Reaching out to potential wholesale clients, businesses and community organizations, with commissioned independent sales reps.
6. Doing activities that can stimulate additional business: beer tastings, matching beers with food, sharing interesting and educational beer knowledge, publishing a newsletter, offering customer service through a website, free local deliveries, automatic and reminder ordering services and mobile party services.
7. Extending our market penetration beyond the physical boundaries of the microbrewery location through direct catalog sales, outside sales reps and a website.

_____ (company name) intends to actively seek out and attract new customers, whose needs go beyond the need for convenience sales. Our online website will the primary focus of this incentive program. This service will be an interactive feature that will act as a database of our broad product selection and will primarily be focused on our craft beers and high-end products. The goals for this service will be for it to serve as a compilation of our product selection, in which a user will be able to categorize our entire inventory in several different ways and then be able to view individual product descriptions and suggestions. The service is intended to make our customers more comfortable with our product lines. It will provide a way for our customers to survey the attributes of our beers so that they may be able to make an informed purchase decision, as the novice beer drinker may be deterred from purchasing beer due to a lack of knowledge on the intricacies of a specific product. This system seeks to create consumer demand through consumer education. The staff will also be able to access this database in the microbrewery to help serve the needs of the individual consumer.

Another unique service offered through our website is a pre-order form found on our website or available over the phone, which will enable the customer to prearrange a package customized to suit their private medium to large scale function. We will facilitate this target market by offering a preorder program where individuals can call or go online and have a package pre-arranged for them so that pick-up may be quick and easy. These customers may include but are not limited to the organizers of community parties, private club parties, weddings and company functions.

In phase one of our marketing plan, we will gain exposure to our target markets through the use of discounts and grand opening promotional tactics. We will be taking a very aggressive marketing stance in the first year of business in hopes of gaining customer loyalty. In our subsequent years, we will focus less resources on advertising as a whole. But, we do plan to budget for advertising promotions on a continual and season specific basis.

We will start our business with our known personal referral contacts and then continue our campaign to develop recognition among other groups. We will develop and maintain a database of our contacts in the field. We will work to maintain and exploit our existing relationships throughout the start-up process and then use our marketing tools to communicate with other potential referral sources.

The marketing strategy will create awareness, interest and appeal from our target market. Its ultimate purpose is to encourage repeat purchases and get customers to refer friends and professional contacts. To get referrals we will provide incentives and excellent service and build relationships with clients by caring about what the customer needs and wants. Our marketing strategy will revolve around two different types of media, flyers and a website. These two tools will be used to make customers aware of our broad range of product and service offerings. One focus of our marketing strategy will be to drive customers to our website for information about our programs.

Ongoing advertising strategies to ensure long-term success are to advertise through local media outlets like public radio, join the ___ (city) Convention and Visitors Bureau, place brochures with coupons in all area hotels, send flyers with coupons advertising lunch specials to businesses in ____ (city) and advertise in alternative media.
A combination of local media and event marketing will be utilized. _____ (company name) will create an identity-oriented marketing strategy with executions particularly in the local media. Our marketing strategy will utilize prime time radio spots, print ads, press releases, yellow page ads, flyers, and newsletter distribution. We will make effective use of direct response advertising and include coupons in all print ads.

We will use comment cards, newsletter sign-up forms and surveys to collect customer email addresses and feed our client relationship management (CRM) software system. This system will automatically send out, on a predetermined schedule, follow-up materials, such as article reprints, seminar invitations, email messages, surveys and e-newsletters. We will offset some of our advertising costs by asking our suppliers and other local merchants to place ads in our newsletter.

Current Situation

We will study the current marketing situation on a weekly basis to analyze trends and identify sources of business growth. As onsite owners, we will be on hand daily to insure customer service. Our services include products of the highest quality and a prompt response to feedback from customers. Our extensive and detailed financial statements, produced monthly, will enable us to stay competitive and exploit presented opportunities.

Marketing Budget

Our marketing budget will be a flexible $_____ per quarter. The marketing budget can be allocated in any way that best suits the time of year.

Marketing budget per quarter:

Newspaper Ads	$_____	Radio advertisement	$_____
Web Page	$_____	Customer contest	$_____
Direct Mail	$_____	Sales Brochure	$_____
Trade Shows	$_____	Seminars	$_____
Superpages	$_____	Google Adwords	$_____
Giveaways	$_____	Vehicle Signs	$_____
Business Cards	$_____	Flyers	$_____
Labels/Stickers	$_____	Videos/DVDs	$_____
Samples	$_____	Newsletter	$_____
Bandit Signs	$_____	Email Campaigns	$_____
Sales Reps Comm.	$_____	Restaurant Placemats	$_____
Press Releases	$_____	Billboards	$_____
Movie Theater Ads	$_____	Fund Raisers	$_____
Infomercials	$_____	Speeches	$_____
Postcards	$_____	Proof Books	$_____
Social Networking	$_____	Charitable Donations	$_____
Yellow Pages	$_____	Other	$_____
Total:			$_____

Our objective in setting a marketing budget has been to keep it between _____ (5?) and _____ (7?) percent of our estimated annual gross sales.

Marketing Mix

New customers will primarily come from word-of-mouth and our referral program. The overall market approach involves creating brand awareness through targeted advertising, public relations, co-marketing efforts with select alliance partners, direct mail, email campaigns (with constant contact.com), seminars and a website.

Video Marketing

We will link to our website a series of YouTube.com based video clips that talk about our range of microbrewery products and services and demonstrate our expertise with certain ales and lagers. We will create business marketing videos that are both entertaining and informational and improve our search engine rankings. For each video, we will be sure to include our business keyword in the title and at least once in the description section.

Video business marketing is growing significantly in popularity because customers want to see the firm's facility or a product or service in action. Having a video incorporated into a web site or Facebook page can lead to increased views and sales. In fact, Google Business Views are very popular right now. Google Business View is a 360-degree panoramic virtual tour added to a Google Business Page and Google Maps. It increases Search Engine Optimization (SEO) dramatically.

Resource:
https://www.google.com/maps/about/partners/businessview/

The video will include:
- **Client testimonials** - We will let our best customers become our instant sales force because people will believe what others say about us more readily than what we say about ourselves.
- **Product Demonstrations** - We will train and pre-sell our potential clients on our most popular products and services just by talking about and showing them. Often, our potential clients don't know the full range and depth of our products and services because we haven't taken the adequate time to show and tell them.
- **Include Business Website Address**
- **Video tour of our facility.**
- **Post commercial created for Cable TV or DVD sales presentation.**
- **Owner Interview:** Explanation of mission statement and unique selling proposition.
- **Record Frequently Asked Questions Session** - We will answer questions that we often get and anticipate objections we might get and give great reasons to convince potential clients that we are the best Microbrewery in the area.
- **Include a Call to Action** - We have the experience and the know-how to supply your next family or business event, so call us, right now, and let's get started.
- **Seminar** - Include a portion of a seminar on how restaurants can better market their craft beer selection.
- **Comment on industry trends and product news** - We will appear more in-tune and knowledgeable in our market if we can talk about what's happening in our industry and marketplace.

Resources: www.businessvideomarketing.tv
               www.hotpluto.com
               www.hubspot.com/video-marketing-kit
               www.youtube.com/user/mybusinessstory

Analytics Report
http://support.google.com/youtube/bin/static.py?hl=en&topic=1728599&guide=1
     714169&page=guide.cs

Note: Refer to Video Marketing Tips in rear marketing worksheets section.

Example:
http://www.youtube.com/watch?v=tFY-4MyAo6Q

Top 11 places where we will share our marketing videos online:
YouTube   **www.youtube.com**
This very popular website allows you to log-in and leave comments and ratings on the videos. You can also save your favorite videos and allows you to tag posted videos. This makes it easier for your videos to come up in search engines.
Google Video   **http://video.google.com/**
A video hosting site. Google Video is not just focused on sharing videos online, but this is also a market place where you can buy the videos you find on this site using Google search engine.
Yahoo! Video   **http://video.yahoo.com/**

Uploading and sharing videos is possible with Yahoo Video!. You can find several types of videos on their site and you can also post comments and ratings for the videos.

Revver   **http://www.revver.com/**
This website lets you earn money through ads on your videos and you will have a 50/50 profit split with the website. Another great deal with Revver is that your fans who posted your videos on their site can also earn money.

Blip.tv   **http://blip.tv/**
Allows viewers to stream and download the videos posted on their website. You can also use Creative Commons licenses on your videos posted on the website. This allows you to decide if your videos should be attributed, restricted for commercial use and be used under specific terms.

Vimeo   **http://www.vimeo.com/**
This website is family safe and focuses on sharing private videos. The interface of the website is similar to some social networking sites that allow you to customize your profile page with photos from Flickr and embeddable player. This site allows users to socialize through their videos.

Metacafe   **http://www.metacafe.com/**
This video sharing site is community based. You can upload short-form videos and share it to the other users of the website. Metacafe has its own system called VideoRank that ranks videos according to the viewer reactions and features the most popular among the viewers.

ClipShack   **http://www.clipshack.com/**
Like most video sharing websites, you can post comments on the videos and even tag some as your favorite. You can also share the videos on other websites through the html code from ClipShack and even sending it through your email.

Veoh   **http://www.veoh.com/**
You can rent or sell your videos and keep the 70% of the sales price. You can upload a range of different video formats on Veoh and there is no limit on the size and length of the file. However, when your video is over 45 minutes it has to be downloaded before the viewer can watch it.

Jumpcut   **http://download.cnet.com/JumpCut/3000-18515_4-10546353.html**
Jumpcut allows its users to upload videos using their mobile phones. You will have to attach the video captured from your mobile phone to an email. It has its own movie making wizard that helps you familiarize with the interface of the site.

DailyMotion   **www.dailymotion.com**
As one of the leading sites for sharing videos, Dailymotion attracts over 114 million unique monthly visitors (source: comScore, May 2018) 1.2 billion videos views worldwide (source: internal). Offers the best content from users, independent content creators and premium partners. Using the most advanced technology for both users and content creators, provides high-quality and HD video in a fast, easy-to-use online service that also automatically filters infringing material as notified by content owners.
Offering 32 localized versions, their mission is to provide the best possible entertainment experience for users and the best marketing opportunities for advertisers, while respecting content protection.

Business Cards

Our business card will include our company logo, complete contact information, name and title, association logos, slogan or markets serviced, licenses and certifications. The center of our bi-fold card will contain a listing of the brands and services we offer. We will give out multiple business cards to friends, family members, and to each customer, upon the completion of the service. We will also distribute business cards in the following ways:

1. Attached to invoices, surveys, flyers and door hangers.
2. Included in customer product packages.
3. We will leave a stack of business cards in a Lucite holder with the local Chamber of Commerce and any other businesses offering free counter placement.

We will use fold-over cards because they will enable us to list all of our services and complete contact instructions on the inside of the card. We will also give magnetic business cards to new clients for posting on the refrigerator door.

We will place the following referral discount message on the back of our business cards:
   - Our business is very dependent upon referrals. If you have associates who could benefit from our quality services, please write your name at the bottom of this card and give it to them. When your friend presents this card upon their first visit, he or she will be entitled to 10% off discount. And, on your next invoice, you will also get a 10% discount as a thank you for your referral.

Resource: www.vistaprint.com

Direct Mail Package

To build name recognition and to announce the opening of our Microbrewery, we will offer a mail package consisting of a tri-fold brochure containing a discount coupon to welcome our new customers. We plan to make a mailing to local subscribers of Gourmet Food and beverage themed magazines. From those identified local customers, we shall ask them to complete a survey and describe their perception of the microbrewery, and any specific products or services they would like to see added. Those customers returning completed surveys would receive a premium (giveaway) gift.

Beer Events and Trade Shows

We will exhibit at as many local craft beer events and trade shows per year as possible. These include Beer Festivals, County Fairs, open exhibits in shopping malls, business spot-lights with our local Chamber of Commerce, and more. The objective is to get our company name and service out to as many people as possible. When exhibiting at a trade show, we will put our best foot forward and represent ourselves as professionals. We will be open, enthusiastic, informative and courteous. We will exhibit our products and services with sales brochures, logo-imprinted giveaways, sample beers to taste, a photo book for people to browse through and a computer to run our video presentation through.

We will get a branded table cloth and a banner that can be used with our branded tent and branded jockey box cover and we will distribute cool swag like stickers, bottle openers and custom buttons. We will create an event kit, which will contain everything that we need to setup a proper event, from black duct tape to zip ties to extra swag, banners and tablecloths.

We will use a 'free drawing' for a gift basket prize and a sign-in sheet to collect names and email addresses. We will also develop a questionnaire or survey that helps us to assemble an ideal customer profile and qualify the leads we receive. We will train our booth attendants to answer all type of questions and to handle objections. We will also seek to present educational seminars at the show to gain increased publicity, and name and expertise recognition. Most importantly, we will develop and implement a follow-up program to stay-in-touch with prospects.

Resources: www.tsnn.com   www.expocentral.com
              www.acshomeshow.com/   www.EventsInAmerica.com

Note: The Great American Beer Festival (GABF) is a three-day annual event hosted by the Brewers Association. Over 100 beer judges from the United States and abroad evaluate beer in the associated competition, ultimately judging 3,300 beers entered by almost 500 domestic breweries.   http://www.greatamericanbeerfestival.com/
Brewers Guild Festival…State events   www.sandiegobrewersguild.org/
Brewers Association World Beer Cup   www.worldbeercup.org/

We will assign an employee to working local beer events every weekend so that we may get as many people as possible to sample our craft beers. We will find these events by consulting the following sources:

1.   Beer Advocate   www.BeerAdvocate.com
2.   Local Brewers Guild Website
      www.brewersassociation.org/pages/government-affairs/guilds/find-a-guild
      Examples: http://ohiocraftbeer.org/
                   http://www.brewerydb.com/guild/vDxSPd
                   http://www.ohiobeerguide.com/
3.   American Craft Beer Week
      http://www.craftbeer.com/news-and-events/american-craft-beer-week/acbw-news

Note: Brewers Guilds are organizations that promote the overall advancement of breweries and the brewing industry. They are typically funded via dues or tax money and represent a general geographic area, like a state or region.

New Homeowners

We will reach out to new movers in our immediate neighborhood. Marketing to new movers will help bring in more long-term customers. And, because new movers are five times more likely to become loyal, this marketing program, will generate new, fresh customers who are likely to turn in to the regular customers. The value of a new loyal customer will be significant, as a new loyal customer who comes in ___ (#) times a month can be worth up to $_____ a year for standard services. Furthermore, many studies suggest that new movers typically stay in their new homes for an average of 5.6 years. We will also participate in local Welcome Wagon activities for new residents and assemble a mailing list to distribute sales literature from county courthouse records and

Realtor supplied information. We will use a postcard mailing to promote a special get-acquainted offer to new residents.

We will adhere the following routine when marketing to new local homeowners:
1.   Send out a friendly welcome letter / flyer / brochure welcoming each new family to the community along with information on our pest control services.
2.   Include a gift certificate or a new client discount coupon / certificate to entice the new family to try our service, risk free with no obligation.
3.   Send out a new client discount or offer an initial free evaluation.
4.   Send out a postcard with a discount or coupon.

Resources:
Welcome Wagon   www.WelcomeWagon.com
Welcome Mat Services   www.WelcomeMatServices.com
Welcomemat Services uses specialized, patent-pending technology to store and log customer demographics for use by the local companies it supports.

Networking
Networking will be a key to success because referrals and alliances formed can help to improve our community image and keep our practice growing. We will strive to build long-term mutually beneficial relationships with our networking contacts and join the following types of organizations:
1.   We will form a LeTip Chapter to exchange business leads.
2.   We will join the local BNI.com referral exchange group.
3.   We will join the Chamber of Commerce to further corporate relationships.
4.   We will join the Rotary Club, Lions Club, Kiwanis Club, Church Groups, etc.
5.   We will do volunteer work for American Heart Assoc. and Habitat for Humanity.
6.   We will become an affiliated member of the local board of Realtors.
7.   We will form Business & Beer networking groups.
        Ex: http://craftbeerguy.com/tag/networking-event/

Charitable Organizations
We will use the following ways to help the charitable organization to meet their fundraising goals, while seizing the opportunity to promote our jewelry line:
1.   Offer one of our gift baskets at their auction with contact information.
2.   Offer members of chosen charity a special discount when they shop our business.
3.   Set up a display or sponsor a brewery tour for the charity members.
4.   Offer to help charity raise funds by selling a special beer brand. For each sale the members sell to their family and friends, we agree to donate a percentage to their organization.
5   Advertise our business in their organization newsletter or bulletin.
6.   Create a custom beer brand designed for the charity featuring their special colors or logo. They could use this limited brand for charitable fundraising.
7.   Donate a portion of our beer sales to a charity, who will, in turn, allow us to advertise that we support their cause in press releases.

We will use our metropolitan _____ (city) Chamber of Commerce to target prospective business contacts. We will mail letters to each prospect describing our craft beer products and services. We will follow-up with phone calls.

Newsletter

We will develop a one-page newsletter to be emailed to online subscribers via our website and handed out to customers to take home with them as they visit the microbrewery. The monthly newsletter will be used to build our brand and update clients on special promotions. The newsletter will be produced in-house and for the cost of paper and computer time. We will include the following types of information:

1. Our involvement with charitable events.
2. New Service/Product Introductions/Releases
3. Featured employee/customer of the month.
4. New beer industry technologies.
5. Customer/celebrity endorsements/testimonials.
6. Classified ads from local sponsors and suppliers.
7. Announcements / Upcoming beer tasting/seminar events.
8. Tap room specials

We will adhere to the following newsletter writing guidelines:
1. We will provide content that is of real value to our subscribers.
2. We will provide solutions to our subscriber's problems or questions.
3. We will communicate regularly on a weekly basis.
4. We will create HTML Messages that look professional and allow us to track how many people click on our links and/or open our emails.
5. We will not pitch our business opportunity in our Ezine very often.
6. We will focus our marketing dollars on building our Ezine subscriber list.
7. We will focus on relationship building and not the conveying of a sales message.
8. We will vary our message format with videos, articles, checklists, quotes, pictures and charts.
9. We will recommend occasionally affiliate products in some of our messages to help cover our marketing costs.
10. We will consistently follow the above steps to build a database of qualified prospects and customers.

Example:
http://archive.constantcontact.com/fs054/1103406220517/archive/1103573898876.html
Resource: http://www.yourmicrobrewery.com/your-microbrewery-tips/

Example: Our newsletter, *The Beer Bulletin*, includes features and articles on beers from around the world, our beer reviews, beer tasting information, coupon savings and more! Published _____ (four?) times a year, you can have this publication mailed or emailed directly to your home or business. Please provide us with your contact information so we can send you *The Beer Bulletin* from _____ (company name).
Source: http://www.craftbeer.com/about/craftbeer-com-newsletter-sign-up
Resources: Microsoft Publisher   www.aweber.com

Vehicle Signs

We will place magnetic and vinyl signs on our vehicles and include our company name, phone number, company slogan and website address, if possible. We will create a cost-effective moving billboard with high-quality, high-resolution vehicle wraps. We will wrap a portion of the vehicle or van to deliver excellent marketing exposure.
Resource: http://www.fastsigns.com/

Design Tips:
1. Avoid mixing letter styles and too many different letter sizes.
2. Use the easiest to recognize form of your logo.
3. The standard background is white.
4. Do not use a background color that is the same as or close to your vehicle color.
5. Choose colors that complement your logo colors.
6. Avoid the use too many colors.
7. Use dark letter colors on a light background or the reverse.
8. Use easy to read block letters in caps and lower case.
9. Limit content to your business name, slogan, logo, phone number and website-address.
10. Include your license number if required by law.
11. Magnetic signs are ideal for door panels (material comes on 24" wide rolls).
12. Graphic vehicle window wraps allow the driver to still see out.
13. Keep your message short so people driving by can read it at a glance.
14. Do not use all capital letters.
15. Be sure to include your business name, phone number, slogan and web address.

Vehicle Wraps

Vehicle wrapping will be one of our preferred marketing methods. According to company research, wrapped vehicles have more impact than billboards, create a positive image for the company and prompt the public to remember the words and images featured in the company's branding. Vehicle wrapping is also an inexpensive marketing strategy. A typical truck wrap costs about $2,500 and is a one-time payment for an ad that spans the life of a truck's lease.

Moving Billboard

Additionally, our van, painted with the company's logo, will cruise ___ (city)-area streets roughly four out of seven nights a week, carting pedestrians home at no charge. It will be a free shuttle service for pedestrians. Passengers will get pre-recorded information and sales literature about our brewery's countless special events, along with a list of other public-transportation options.

Advertising Wearables

We will give all preferred club members an eye-catching T-shirt or sweatshirt with our company name and logo printed across the garment to wear about town. T-shirts will be printed up with "coming soon on the front and _____ Company logo on the back. These will be sold at cost to friends, co-workers, neighbors, and supporters. We will also give them away as a thank you for customer referral activities. We will ask all employees to wear our logo-imprinted shirts.

Resource: www.logosoftwear.com/

Stage Events

We will stage events to become known in our community and to educate our customers about the beer lifestyle. This is essential to attracting referrals. We will schedule regular events, such as seminar talks, demonstrations, catered open house events, beer cooking classes, beer making seminars and fundraisers in our microbrewery. We will offer seminars through organizations to promote the health benefits of drinking in moderation. We will use event registration forms, our website and an event sign-in sheet to collect the names and email addresses of all attendees. This database will be used to feed our automatic customer relationship follow-up program and newsletter service. Our objective is to help our customers to feel confident about selecting the perfect bottle of beer. Through beer education seminars and beer tastings, we will provide an opportunity for our customers to learn first-hand about beer production techniques. Our beer classes will be given on the following types of topics:

1.   How to Enhance Your Beer Drinking Enjoyment
2.   How to Pair Beers with Foods

_____ (company name) will also be promoting several special events throughout the year such as beer tastings, seasonal food festivals, brewer's lunches, etc. We will offer one monthly charity tank where non-profit clubs and organizations (like sports teams, travel clubs, home-brewers clubs) could keep a specified percentage of the revenue earned on a specific tank of beer during an evening. They would be encouraged to bring in as many customers as possible to help support their cause. This would boost business on slow nights and introduce more people to the brewpub. Other promotional campaigns include sponsoring one men's and one women's softball team by providing them with uniforms bearing the _____ (company name) logo in return for their business and support; and sponsoring a bar dart league and a dart team to compete in the _____ Dart Association.

Example:

We will team up with our suppliers and local farmers to host chefs for a day of beer and food pairings along with behind-the-scenes tours of each manufacturing facility. This event will give credence to the fact that taste and flavor have always been essential features of beer, but now more than ever these components are being assessed against the new canvas of food. Chefs will be tasked to create innovative food pairings featuring locally fresh ingredients and our signature beers.

Sales Brochures

The sales brochure will enable us to make a solid first impression when pursing business from commercial accounts. Our sales brochure will include the following contents and become a key part of our sales presentation folder and direct mail package:

- Contact Information	- Microbrewery Description
- Customer Testimonials	- Brands/Services/Benefits

- Competitive Advantages	- Owner/Brewmaster Resume/Bio
- Trial Coupon	- Map of microbrewery location.
- Awards	- Business Hours

Sales Brochure Design

1. Speak in Terms of Our Prospects Wants and Interests.
2. Focus on all the Benefits, not Just Features.
3. Put the company logo and Unique Selling Proposition together to reinforce the fact that your company is different and better than the competition.
4. Include a special offer, such as a discount, a free report, a sample, or a free trial to increase the chances that the brochure will generate sales.

We will incorporate the following Brochure Design Guidelines:

1. Design the brochure to achieve a focused set of objectives (marketing of programs) with a target market segment (residential vs. commercial).
2. Tie the brochure design to our other marketing materials with colors, logo, fonts and formatting.
3. List capabilities and how they benefit clients.
4. Demonstrate what we do and how we do it differently.
5. Define the value proposition of our engineering installing services
6. Use a design template that reflects your market positioning strategy.
7. Identify your key message (unique selling proposition)
8. List our competitive advantages.
9. Express our understanding of client needs and wants.
10. Use easy to read (scan) headlines, subheadings, bullet points, pictures, etc.
11. Use a logo to create a visual branded identity.
12. The most common and accepted format for a brochure is a folded A3 (= 2 x A4), which gives 4 pages of information.
13. Use a quality of paper that reflects the image we want to project.
14. Consistently stick to the colors of our corporate style.
15. Consider that colors have associations, such as green colors are associated with the environment and enhance an environmental image.
16. Illustrations will be appropriate and of top quality and directly visualize the product assortment, product application and production facility.
17. The front page will contain the company name, logo, the main application of your product or service and positioning message or Unique Selling Proposition.
18. The back page will be used for testimonials or references, and contact details.

Sales Presentation Folder Contents

1. Resumes
2. Product Label Photos
3. Contract/Application
4. Frequently Asked Questions
5. Sales Brochure
6. Business Cards
7. Testimonials/References
8. Program Descriptions
9. Informative Articles
10. Referral Program
11. Company Overview
12. Operating Policies
13. Order Forms

Employee Personal Marketing

We will develop a training program and business cards to help employees to market themselves as sales agents and get new people interested in our microbrewery. Employee personal marketing is the ability to showcase employee talents and present them in a fashion that our customers and prospects will recognize them. This type of marketing will also be very important for the customers we already have. We will develop an employee certification program to make sure our customers are aware of all the ways our products and services can benefit them, and that every customer gets serviced properly.

Coupons

We will use coupons with limited time expirations to get prospects to try our products and service programs. We will also accept the coupons of our competitors to help establish new client relationships. We will run ads directing people to our Web site for a $____ coupon certificate. This will help to draw in new clients and collect e-mail addresses for the distribution of a monthly newsletter. Research indicates that we can use our coupons to spark online searches of our website and drive sales. This will help to draw in new clients and collect e-mail addresses for the distribution of a monthly newsletter. We will include a coupon with each sale or send them by mail to our mailing list.

We will leverage bargain-hunting services like FatWallet, RetailMeNot, and DealsPl.us to reach our most price-sensitive buyers.

Resources:
http://www.businessknowhow.com/marketing/couponing.htm
https://www.constantcontact.com/features/coupons

We will use the following discounts to benefit our brand and also show customer appreciation:
- first time buyer's discount
- volume discount
- member discount
- free shipping
- returning customer discount
- teacher, senior, military or student discounts
- donation receipt discount

Examples:
http://www.fatwallet.com/Craft-Beer-Club-coupons/
https://www.coupons.com/coupon-codes/craft-beer-club/

We will use coupons selectively to accomplish the following:
1. To introduce a new product or service.
2. To attract loyal customers away from the competition
3. To prevent customer defection to a new competitor.

4.   To help celebrate a special event.

Types of Coupons:
1.	Courtesy Coupons	Rewards for repeat business
2.	Cross-Marketing Coupons	Incentive to try other products/services.
3.	Companion Coupon	Bring a friend incentive.

Websites like Groupon.com, LivingSocial, Eversave, and BuyWithMe sell discount vouchers for services ranging from custom _____ to ____ consultations. Best known is Chicago-based Groupon. To consumers, discount vouchers promise substantial savings — often 50% or more. To merchants, discount vouchers offer possible opportunities for price discrimination, exposure to new customers, online marketing, and "buzz." Vouchers are more likely to be profitable for merchants with low marginal costs, who can better accommodate a large discount and for patient merchants, who place higher value on consumers' possible future return visits.
Examples:
https://www.groupon.com/coupons/stores/craftbeerclub.com

Cross-Promotions

We will develop and maintain partnerships with local businesses that cater to the needs of our customers, such as restaurants, fitness clubs and sporting goods stores, and conduct cross-promotional marketing campaigns. These cross-promotions will require the exchanging of customer mailing lists and endorsements.

Premium Giveaways

We will distribute logo-imprinted promotional products at events, also known as giveaway premiums, to foster top-of-mind awareness (www.promoideas.org). These items include logo-imprinted T-shirts, business cards with magnetic backs, mugs with contact phone number, cooking with beer recipe booklets and calendars that feature important beer festival date reminders.

Local Newspaper Ads

We will use these ads to announce the opening of our microbrewery and get our name established. We will adhere to the rule that frequency and consistency of message are essential. We will include a list of our top brand names and specialty services. We will include a coupon to track the response in zoned editions of 'Shopper' Papers, Theater Bills, and Community Newsletters and Newspapers. We will use the ad to announce any weekly or monthly price specials.

Our newspaper ads will utilize the following design tips:
1.   We will start by getting a media kit from the publisher to analyze their demographic information as well as their reach and distribution.
2.   Don't let the newspaper people have total control of our ad design, as we know how we want our company portrayed to the market.
3.   Make sure to have 1st class graphics since this will be the only visual distinction we can provide the reader about our business.

4.   Buy the biggest ad we can afford, with full-page ads being the best.
5.   Go with color if affordable, because consumers pick color ads over black 82% of the time.
6.   Ask the paper if they have specific days that more of our type of buyer reads their paper.
7.   If we have a hit ad on our hands, we will make it into a circular or door-hanger to extend the life of the offer.
8.   Don't change an ad because we are getting tired of looking at it.
9.   We will start our headline by telling our story to pull the reader into the ad.
10.   We will use "Act Now" to convey a sense of urgency to the reader.
11.   We will use our headline to tell the reader what to do.
12.   The headline is a great place to announce a free offer.
13.   We will write our headline as if we were speaking to one person and make it personal.
14.   We will use our headline to either relay a benefit or intrigue the reader into wanting more information.
15.   Use coupons giving a dollar amount off, not a percentage, as people hate doing the math.

Local Newspaper Classified Ads

We will use these ads to announce the opening of our microbrewery and get our name established. We will adhere to the rule that frequency and consistency of message are essential. We will include a list of our top brand names. We will include a coupon to track the response in zoned editions of 'Shopper' Papers, Theater Bills, and Community Newsletters and Newspapers. We will use the ad to announce any weekly or monthly price specials.

Local Publications

We will place low-cost classified ads in neighborhood publications to advertise our organic beers. We will also submit public relations and informative articles to improve our visibility and establish our expertise and trustworthiness. These publications include the following:
1.   Neighborhood Newsletters
2.   Local Restaurant Association Newsletter
3.   Local Chamber of Commerce Newsletter
4.   Realtor Magazines
5.   Homeowner Association Newsletters
Resources:
Hometown News   www.hometownnews.com
Pennysaver   www.pennysaverusa.com

Publication Type	Ad Size	Timing	Circulation	Section	Fee

Doorhangers

Our doorhangers will feature a calendar of 'Free Beer Tastings'. The doorhanger will include a list of all our beer brands and info about retail availability. We will also attach our business card to the doorhanger and distribute the doorhangers multiple times to the same subdivision.

Article Submissions

We will pitch articles to consumer magazines, local newspapers, business magazines and internet articles directories to help establish our specialized expertise and improve our visibility. Hyperlinks will be placed within written articles and can be clicked on to take the customer to another webpage within our website or to a totally different website. These clickable links or hyperlinks will be keywords or relevant words that have meaning to our Microbrewery. In fact, we will create a position whose primary function is to link our Microbrewery with opportunities to be published in local publications.

Publishing requires an understanding of the following publisher needs:

1.	Review of good work.	2.	Editor story needs.
3.	Article submission process rules	4.	Quality photo portfolio
5.	Exclusivity requirements.	6.	Target market interests

Our Article Submission Package will include the following:

1.	Well-written materials	2.	Good Drawings
3.	High-quality Photographs	4.	Well-organized outline.

Examples of General Publishing Opportunities:

1.	Document a new solution to old problem	2.	Publish a research study
3.	Addiction prevention advice	4.	Present a different viewpoint
5.	Introduce a local angle on a hot topic.	6.	Reveal a new trend.
7.	Share specialty niche expertise.	8.	Share beer health benefits

Examples of Specific Article Titles:

1. "Everything You Ever Wanted to Know About the Health Benefits of Beer"
2. "How to Evaluate and Compare Microbrews"
3. "Tips for Cooking with Beer"
4. "Why Drink Local Beer?".

Write Articles with a Closing Author Resource Box or Byline

1.	Author Name with credential titles.	2.	Explanation of area of expertise.
3.	Mention of a special offer.	4.	A specific call to action
5.	A Call to Action Motivator	6.	All possible contact information
7.	Helpful Links	8.	Link to Firm Website.

Article Objectives:

Article Topic	Target Audience	Target Date

Article Tracking Form

SubjectPublication	Target Audience	Business Development	Resources Needed	Target Date

Possible Magazines to submit articles include:

1. Gourmet Magazine
2. Food Magazine
3. InStyle Magazine
4. BYO
5. Zymurgy
6. All About Beer
7. Cigar Magazines
8. Beer Connoisseur Magazine
9. Zymurgy
10. Food Republic

Resources:

Writer's Market   www.writersmarket.com

Directory of Trade Magazines   www.techexpo.com/tech_mag.html

Internet article directories include:

http://ezinearticles.com/

http://www.articlecity.com

http://www.articledashboard.com

http://www.webarticles.com

http://www.article-buzz.com

www.articletogo.com

http://article-niche.com

www.internethomebusinessarticles.com

http://www.articlenexus.com

http://www.articlefinders.com

http://www.articlewarehouse.com

http://www.easyarticles.com

http://ideamarketers.com/

http://clearviewpublications.com/

http://www.goarticles.com/

http://www.webmasterslibrary.com/

http://www.connectionteam.com

http://www.MarketingArticleLibrary.com

http://www.dime-co.com

http://www.reprintarticles.com

http://www.articlestreet.com

http://www.articlepeak.com

http://www.simplysearch4it.com

http://www.valuablecontent.com

http://www.article99.com

http://www.mommyshelpercommunity.com

http://www.amazines.com

http://www.submityourarticle.com/articles

http://www.articlecube.com

http://www.free-articles-zone.com

http://www.content-articles.com

http://superpublisher.com

http://www.site-reference.com

www.articlebin.com

www.articlesfactory.com

www.buzzle.com

www.isnare.com

//groups.yahoo.com/group/article_announce

www.ebusiness-articles.com

www.authorconnection.com/

www.businesstoolchest.com

www.digital-women.com/submitarticle.htm

www.searchwarp.com

www.articleshaven.com

www.articles411.com

www.articleshelf.com

www.articlesbase.com

www.articlealley.com

www.articleavenue.com

www.virtual-professionals.com

Online Classified Ad Placement Opportunities

The following free classified ad sites will enable our Microbrewery to thoroughly describe the benefits of our consuming our beer brands:

1. **Craigslist.org**
2. Ebay Classifieds

3.	Classifieds.myspace.com	4.	KIJIJI.com
5.	//Lycos.oodle.com	6.	Webclassifieds.us
7.	USFreeAds.com	8.	www.oodle.com
9.	Backpage.com	10.	stumblehere.com
11.	Classifiedads.com	12.	gumtree.com
13.	Inetgiant.com	14.	www.sell.com
15.	Freeadvertisingforum.com	16.	Classifiedsforfree.com
17.	www.olx.com	18.	www.isell.com
19.	Base.google.com	20.	www.epage.com
21.	Chooseyouritem.com	22.	www.adpost.com
23.	Adjingo.com	24.	Kugli.com
25.	Bevindustry.com/classifieds		

Sample Classified Ad:
Looking for Specialty Beers with Distinctive Flavors? We have been serving the __area since __ (year). We have the largest selection of seasonal beers in the _____area. Free local delivery to commercial accounts. Come and Experience Our New Tasting Room. Give us a call at _____ for open hours or visit us at _____ (Website) for our beer tasting and facility tour schedules.

Two-Step Direct Response Classified Advertising
We will use 'two-step direct response advertising' to motivate readers to take a step or action that signals that we have their permission to begin marketing to them in step two. Our objective is to build a trusting relationship with our prospects by offering a free unbiased, educational report in exchange for permission to continue the marketing process. This method of advertising has the following benefits:

1.	Shorter sales cycle.	2.	Eliminates need for cold calling.
3.	Establishes expert reputation.	4.	Better qualifies prospects
5.	Process is very trackable.	6.	Able to run smaller ads.

Sample Two Step Lead Generating Classified Ad:
FREE Report Reveals "The Health Benefits of Moderate Beer Drinking!"
Or….. "How to Plan a Successful Beer Tasting Party".
Call 24 hour recorded message and leave your name and address.
Your report will be sent out immediately.
Note: The respondent has shown they have an interest in our product specialty.
We will also include a section in the report on our beer and cheese catering service and our complete contact information, along with a time limited discount coupon.

Yellow Page Ads
Research indicates that the use of the traditional Yellow Page Book is declining, but that new residents or people who don't have many personal acquaintances will look to the Yellow Pages to establish a list of potential businesses to call upon. Even a small 2" x 2" boxed ad can create awareness and attract the desired target client, above and beyond the ability of a simple listing. We will use the following design concepts:

1.   We will use a headline to sell people on what is unique about our microbrewery.
2.   We will include a service guarantee to improve our credibility.
3.   We will include a coupon offer and a tracking code to monitor the response rate and decide whether to increase or decrease our ad size in subsequent years.
4.   We will choose an ad size equal to that of our competitors and evaluate the response rate for future insertion commitments.
5.   We will include our hours of operation, motto or slogan and logo.
6.   We will include our key competitive advantages.
7.   We will list under the same categories as our competitors.
8.   We will use some bold lettering to make our ad standout.
9.   We will utilize yellow books that also offer an online dimension.

Resource: www.superpages.com   www.yellowpages.com
Example: http://www.yellowpages.com/rialto-ca/area-51-craft-brewery

Ad Information:

Book Title: _____	Coverage Area: _____
Yearly Fee: $_____	Ad Size: _____ page
Renewal date: _____	Contact: _____

Cable Television Advertising

Cable television will offer us more ability to target certain market niches or demographics with specialty programming. We will use our marketing research survey to determine which cable TV channels our customers are watching. It is expected that many watch the Home & Garden TV channel, and that people with surplus money watch the Golf Channel and the Food Network. Our plan is to choose the audience we want, and to hit them often enough to entice them to take action. We will also take advantage of the fact that we will be able to pick the specific areas we want our commercial to air in. Ad pricing will be dependent upon the number of households the network reaches, the ratings the particular show has earned, contract length and the supply and demand for a particular network.

Resources:
Spot Runner   www.spotrunner.com
Television Advertising   http://televisionadvertising.com/faq.htm

Comcast Spotlight   **www.comcastspotlight.com/**
An advertising sales company providing video solutions to local, regional and national businesses through television and digital advertising. Comcast Spotlight provides local market coverage across multiple platforms (cable TV, satellite, telco, online, VOD) and can target customers geographically, demographically and by message to more efficiently and effectively reach specific audience segments.

Ad Information:

Length of ad "spot": ____ seconds	Development costs: $_____ (onetime fee)
Length of campaign: ___ (#) mos.	Runs per month: Three times per day
Cost per month.: $_____	Total campaign cost: $_____.

Radio Advertising

We will use non-event-based radio advertising. This style of campaign is best suited for non-retail businesses, such as our Microbrewery. We will utilize a much smaller schedule of ads on a consistent long-range basis (48 to 52 weeks a year) with the objective of continuously maintaining top-of-mind-awareness. This will mean maintaining a sufficient level of awareness to be either the number one or number two choice when a triggering-event, such as a promotional event moves the consumer into the market for services and forces "a consumer choice" about which microbrewery in the consumer's perception might help them the most. This consistent approach will utilize only one ad each week day (260 days per year) and allow our company to cost-effectively keep our message in front of consumers once every week day. The ad copy for this non-event campaign, called a positioning message, will not be time-sensitive. It will define and differentiate our business' "unique market position" , and will be repeated for a year.
Note: On the average, listeners spend over 3.5 hours per day with radio.

Radio will give us the ability to target our audience, based on radio formats, such as news-talk, classic rock and the oldies. Radio will also be a good way to get repetition into our message, as listeners tend to be loyal to stations and parts of the day.

1. We will use radio advertising to direct prospects to our Web site, advertise a limited time promotion or call for an informational brochure.
2. We will provide coupons for the radio station to give as prizes for contest winners in exchange for free advertising and promotion.
3. We will use a limited-time offer to entice first-time customer trials.
4. We will explore the use of on-air community bulletin boards to play our public announcements about community sponsored events.
5. We will also make the radio station aware of our expertise in the beer beverage field and our availability for interviews.
6. Our choice of stations will be driven by the market research information we collect via our surveys.
7. We will capitalize on the fact that many stations now stream their programming on the internet and reach additional local and even national audiences, and if online listeners like what they hear in our streaming radio spot, they can click over to our website.
8. Our radio ads will use humor, sounds, compelling music or unusual voices to grab attention.
9. Our spots will tell stories or present situations our target audience can relate to.
10. We will make our call to action, a website address or vanity phone number, easy to remember and tie it in with our company name or message.
11. We will approach radio stations about buying their unsold advertising space for deep discounts. (Commonly known at radio stations' as "Run of Station")
    On radio, this might mean very early in the morning or late at night. We will talk to our advertising representatives and see what discounts they can offer when one of those empty spaces comes open.

Resources: Radio Advertising Bureau   www.RAB.com
             Radio Locator   www.radio-locator.com
             Radio Directory   www.radiodirectory.com

Ad Information:

Length of ad "spot": ___ seconds Development costs: $____ (onetime fee)
Length of campaign: __ (#) mos. Runs per month: Three times per day
Cost per month.: $_____ Total campaign cost: $_____ .

Resources:

www.lfmaudio.com/best-practises-for-creating-radio-ads-your-listeners-will-respond-to/
https://fitsmallbusiness.com/radio-advertising-ideas/

Script Resources:

https://voicebunny.com/blog/5-tips-make-radio-ads-grab-attention-sell/
www.voices.com/documents/secure/voices.com-commercial-scripts-for-radio-and-
        television-ads.pdf
http://smallbusiness.chron.com/say-30second-radio-advertising-spot-10065.html
https://voicebunny.com/blog/5-tips-make-radio-ads-grab-attention-sell/

Blog Talk Radio

National Public Radio (www.NPR.org) plays host to a radio program called _____.
The program features _____ (type of experts) who talk and blog about _____ tips.
This will help to establish our craft beer brewing expertise and build the trust factor with
potential clients. Even if we can't get our own nationally syndicated talk show, we will
try to make guest appearances and try our hand with podcasting by using apps like
Spreaker or joining podcasting communities like BlogTalkRadio.
Resources:
National Public Radio   www.npr.org
Spreaker   http://www.spreaker.com/
Blog Talk Radio   http://www.blogtalkradio.com/
With BlogTalkRadio, people can either host their own live talk radio show with any
phone and a computer or listen to thousands of new shows created daily.
Examples:
http://www.blogtalkradio.com/thebusinessofcraftbeer
http://www.blogtalkradio.com/dramafreecraftbeer

Resource:

CUTV News Radio (http://www.blogtalkradio.com/cutvnewsradio) with veteran award-
winning broadcast TV and radio hosts/media personalities Jim Masters and Doug
Llewelyn is an exciting, informative, entertaining, thought-provoking and empowering
broadcast series featuring several LIVE episodes daily and is a service of the Telly-award
winning CUTV News, a full-service media company that provides entrepreneurs,
business owners and extraordinary people a platform to share their story worldwide.
Their Facebook Fan Page is: www.facebook.com/cutvnewsradio.

Press Release Overview:

We will use market research surveys to determine the media outlets that our demographic
customers read and then target them with press releases. We will draft a cover letter for
our media kit that explains that we would like to have the newspaper print a story about

the start-up of our new local business or a milestone that we have accomplished. And, because news releases may be delivered by feeds or on news services and various websites, we will create links from our news releases to content on our website. These links which will point to more information or a special offer, will drive our clients into the sales process. They will also increase search engine ranking on our site. We will follow-up each faxed package to the media outlet with a phone call to the lifestyle and business section editors.

Media Kit
We will compile a media kit with the following items:
1. A pitch letter introducing our Microbrewery and relevant impact newsworthiness for their readership.
2. A press release with helpful newsworthy story facts.
3. Biographical fact sheet or sketches of key personnel.
4. Listing of product and service features and benefits to customers.
5. Photos and digital logo graphics
6. Copies of media coverage already received.
7. FAQ
8. Customer testimonials
9. Sales brochure
10. Media contact information
11. URL links to these online documents instead of email attachments.
12. Our blog URL address.

Green Public Relations
We will create a positive image for our _____ by creating newsworthy stories that tout our green qualities using the following tactics:
1. We will host an environmental film screening or a craft beer tasting featuring organic and locally-grown foods. We will also hold a fundraiser or a community gathering that focuses on the environment.
2. We will ask other business to join in initiating a recycling or composting program. We will also partner with another eco-friendly business by offering our customers coupons for that business and asking them to do the same for our _____.
3. We will help with community programs, such as the hosting of school field trips or environmental educational classes for kids. This kind of community involvement will not only encourage environmentally responsible behavior in the next generation, but it will also get the community interested in our business as an established green leader in the community.

Example:
Hopworks Urban Brewery   http://hopworksbeer.com/
It launched a new series of beers born from the goal to experiment with flavors while highlighting their strong relationships with businesses focused on sustainability. Each beer in this Win-Win Partnership Series of beers features ingredients from businesses that share HUB's commitment to protecting the environment. Craft beer fans and eco stewards can take part in this win-win scenario by picking up a new limited-edition partner beer each month throughout 2018.

Press Releases

We will use well-written press releases to not only catch a reader's attention, but also to clearly and concisely communicate our business mission, goals and capabilities.

The following represents a partial list of some of the reasons we will issue a free press release on a regular basis:

1.   Announce Grand Opening or Planned Open House Tasting Event
3   Addition of new beer brand or a special Holiday or Christmas Beer.
4.   Support for a Non-profit Cause or other local event, such as a Blood Drive.
5.   Presentation of a free seminar, facility tour or beer making workshop.
6.   Report Survey Results
7.   Publication of an article or book on microbrew industry trends.
8.   Receiving an Association or Competition Award.
9.   Additional training/certification/licensing received.

Examples:
https://www.samueladams.com/media/press-releases

We will use the following techniques to get our press releases into print:

1.   Find the right contact editor at a publication, that is, the editor who specializes in lifestyle and beverage issues.
2.   Understand the target publication's format, flavor and style and learn to think like its readers to better tailor our pitch.
3.   Ask up front if the journalist is on deadline.
4.   Request a copy of the editorial calendar--a listing of targeted articles or subjects broken down by month or issue date, to determine the issue best suited for the content of our news release or article.
5.   Make certain the press release appeals to a large audience by reading a couple of back issues of the publication we are targeting to familiarize ourselves with its various sections and departments.
6.   Customize the PR story to meet the magazine's particular style.
7.   Avoid creating releases that look like advertising or self-promotion.
8.   Make certain the release contains all the pertinent and accurate information the journalist will need to write the article and accurately answer the questions "who, what, when, why and where".
9.   Include a contact name and telephone number for the reporter to call for more information.

Resource:
http://www.ehow.com/how_2043935_write-press-release.html
https://blog.hubspot.com/marketing/press-release-template-ht

PR Distribution Checklist

We will send copies of our press releases to the following entities:
1.   Send it to clients to show accomplishments.
2.   Send to prospects to help prospects better know who you are and what you do.

3.   Send it to vendors to strengthen the relationship and to influence referrals.
4.   Send it to strategic partners to strengthen and enhance the commitment and support to our firm.
5.   Send it to employees to keep them in the loop.
6.   Send it to Employees' contacts to increase the firm's visibility exponentially.
7.   Send it to elected-officials who often provide direction for their constituents.
8.   Send it to trade associations for maximum exposure.
9.   Put copies in the lobby and waiting areas.
10.   Put it on our Web site, to enable visitors to find out who we are and what our firm is doing, with the appropriate links to more detailed information.
11.   Register the Web page with search engines to increase search engine optimization.
12.   Put it in our press kit to provide members of the media background information about our firm.
13.   Include it in our newsletter to enable easy access to details about company activities.
14.   Include it in our brochure to provide information that compels the reader to contact our firm when in need of legal counsel.
15.   Hand it out at trade shows and job fairs to share news with attendees and establish credibility.

Media List

Journalist	Interests	Organization	Contact Info

Distribution:
www.1888PressRelease.com
www.prweb.com
www.PR.com
www.24-7PressRelease.com
www.PRnewswire.com
www.PRLog.org
www.businesswire.com
www.primezone.com
www.xpresspress.com/
www.Mediapost.com

www.ecomwire.com
www.WiredPRnews.com
www.eReleases.com
www.NewsWireToday.com
www.onlinePRnews.com

www.marketwire.com
www.primewswire.com
www.ereleases.com/index.html
www.craftbeer.com

Journalist Lists: www.mastheads.org   www.easymedialist.com
www.helpareporter.com

Media Directories
Bacon's –   www.bacons.com/   AScribe –   www.ascribe.org/
Newspapers – www.newspapers.com/   Gebbie Press – www.gebbieinc.com/

Support Services
PR Web -   http://www.prweb.com
Yahoo News –   http://news.yahoo.com/
Google News –   http://news.google.com/

Examples:
www.craftbeer.com/news/beer-release/valiant-brewing-company-newest-socal-

microbrewery

Media Resource Expert

We will send email and mail to local media outlets, like our local TV news stations, Local Newspapers, and News Radio Stations, to advise them that we are a readily available resource for liquor store related new stories. We will include our areas of specialty, and how we can contribute to media stories about _____ and home tasting and cocktail parties in general. We will also indicate our willingness to share our knowledge on how the public can prevent from being scammed by unethical _____. We will always be on the look-out for opportunities to interview with local and national reporters. We will sign up for the following services that notify companies of reporters looking for interviews:

Reporter Connection	http://reporterconnection.com/
ProfNet Connection	http://www.profnetconnect.com/
Muck Rack	https://muckrack.com/benefits
News Wise	www.newswise.com/
Pitch Rate	http://pitchrate.com/
Experts	www.experts.com
News Basis	http://newsbasis.com/

Help A Reporter Out   **www.helpareporter.com/**
HARO is an online platform that provides journalists with a robust database of sources for upcoming stories. It also provides business owners and marketers with opportunities to serve as sources and secure valuable media coverage.

Resources:
http://www.thebuzzfactoree.com/journalists-seeking-sources/
http://ijnet.org/en/blog/5-ways-find-sources-online

Sample Letter Template:
http://locksmithprofits.com/locksmith-guest-expert-marketing/

Direct Mail Campaign

A direct mail package consisting of a tri-fold brochure, letter of introduction, and reply card will be sent to a list of new businesses in _____ County. This list can be obtained from International Business Lists, Inc. (Chicago, IL) and is compiled from Secretary of State incorporation registrations, business license applications, announcements from newspaper clippings, and tax records. The letter will introduce _____ (company name) and describe our competitive advantages. The package will also include a promotional offer—the opportunity to sample our beers. Approximately ten days after the mailing, a telephone follow-up will be conducted to make sure the brochure was received, whether the client has any questions, or would like to schedule an appointment.
Resource: www.melissadata.com

Our direct mail program will feature the following key components:
1. A call to action with business reply card.
2. Test marketing and tracking using a limited 100-piece coded mailing.
3. A defined set of target markets.
4. A follow up phone call.
5. A personalized cover letter.
7. A special trial coupon offer with an expiration date.

Postcards
1. We will use a monthly, personalized, newsletter styled postcard, that includes beer and food pairing suggestions to stay-in-touch with prospects and customers.
2. Postcards will offer cheaper mailing rates, staying power and attention-grabbing graphics, but require repetition, like most other advertising methods.
3. We will develop an in-house list of potential clients for routine communications from open house events, seminar registrations, direct response ads, etc.
4. We will use postcards to encourage users to visit our website and take advantage of a special offer.
5. We will grab attention and communicate a single-focus message in just a few words.
6. The visual elements of our postcard (color, picture, symbol) will be strong to help get attention and be directly supportive of the message.
7. We will facilitate a call to immediate action by prominently displaying our phone number and website address.
8. We will include a clear deadline, expiration date, limited quantity, or consequence of inaction that is connected to the offer to communicate immediacy and increase response.
Resource: www.Postcardmania.com

Flyers
We will clearly show off the products we offer by creating a collage-like flyer design with the different labels of the beer brands we want to feature.
1. We will seek permission to post flyers on the bulletin boards in local businesses, community centers, party supply stores and local colleges.
2. We will also insert flyers into our direct mailings and sales kits.
3. We will use our flyers as part of a handout package at open house tasting events.
4. The flyers will feature a discount coupon to track response rates.
5. The flyers will contain a description of our seasonal beers.
6. We will use flyers to announce special promotions.

Referral Program
We understand the importance of setting up a formal referral network through contacts with the following characteristics:
1. We will give a premium reward based simply on people giving referral names on the registration form or customer satisfaction survey.

2. Send an endorsed testimonial letter from a loyal patient to the referred prospect.
3. Include a separate referral form as a direct response device.
4. Provide a space on the response form for leaving positive comments that can be used to build a testimonial letter, that will be sent to each referral.
5. We will clearly state our incentive rewards, and terms and conditions.
6. We will distribute a newsletter to stay in touch with our clients and include articles about our referral program success stories.
7. We will encourage our staff at weekly meetings to seek referrals from their personal contacts.

Sources:
1. Referrals from other retailers, particularly those of other niche specialties.
2. Give speeches on a complicated niche area that other practitioners may feel is too narrow for them to handle, thus triggering referrals.
3. Structured Client Referral Program.
4. Newsletter Coupons.

Methods:
1. Always have ready a 30-second elevator speech that describes what you do and who you do it for.
2. Use a newsletter to keep our name in front of referrals sources.
3. Repeatedly demonstrate to referral sources that we are also thinking about their practice or business.
4. Regularly send referrals sources articles on unique yet important topics that might affect their businesses.
5. Use Microsoft Outlook to flag our contacts to remind us it is time to give them some form of personal attention.
6. Ask referral sources for referrals.
7. Get more work from a referral source by sending them work.
8. Immediately thank a referral source, even for the mere act of giving his name to a third party for consideration.
9. Remember referral sources with generous gift baskets and gift certificates.
10. Schedule regular lunches with former school classmates and new contacts.

We will offer an additional donation of $ _____ to any organization whose member use a referral coupon to become a client. The coupon will be paid for and printed in the organization's newsletter.

Referral Tracking Form

Referral Source Name	Presently Referring Yes/No	No. of Clients Referred	Anticipated Revenue	Actions to be Taken	Target Date

Sample Referral Program
We want to show our appreciation to established customers and business network

partners for their kind referrals to our business. ____ (company name) wants to reward our valued and loyal customers who support our _____ Programs by implementing a new referral program. Ask any of our team members for referral cards to share with your family and friends to begin saving towards your next ____ (product/service) purchase. We will credit your account $___ (?) for each new customer you refer to us as well as give them 10% off their first visit. When they come for their first visit, they should present the card upon arrival. We will automatically set you up a referral account.
Examples:
http://www.flyingbike.coop/membership-2/membership-referral-program/

The Referral Details are as Follows:

1. You will receive a $__ (?) credit for every customer that you refer for _____ (products/services). Credit will be applied to your referral account on their initial visit.
2. We will keep track of your accumulated reward dollars and at any time we can let you know the amount you have available for use in your reward account.
3. Each time you visit ____ (company name), you can use your referral dollars to pay up to 50% of your total charge that day
4. Referral dollars are not applicable towards the purchase of _____ products.
5. All referral rewards are for _____ services and cannot be used towards _____ services.

Seminars

Seminars present the following marketing and bonding opportunities:
1. Signage and branding as a presenting sponsor.
2. Opportunity to provide logo imprinted handouts.
3. Media exposure through advertising and public relations.
4. The opportunity for one-on-one interaction with a targeted group of consumers to demonstrate an understanding of their needs and our matching expert solutions.
5. Use of sign-in sheet to collect names and email addresses for database build.
6. Present opportunity to sell products, such as workbooks.

Possible seminar funding sources:
1. Small registration fee to cover the cost of hand-outs and refreshments.
2. Get sponsorship funding from partner/networking organizations.
3. Sponsorship classified ads in the program guide or handouts.

We will establish our expertise and trustworthiness by offering free seminars on the following topics:
1. How to Locate and Evaluate Craft Beers
2. How to Plan a Successful Craft Beer Party

Seminar target groups include the following:

1.	Corporations	2.	Beer Clubs
3.	Party Stores	4.	Colleges
5.	Private Individuals	6.	Realtors
7.	Event Planners	8.	Restaurant Owners

Seminar marketing approaches include:
1.   Posting to website and enabling online registrations.
2.   Email blast to in-house database using www.constantcontact.com
3.   Include seminar schedule in newsletter and flyer.
4.   Classified ads using craigslist.org

Seminar Objectives:

Seminar Topic	Target Audience	Handout	Target Date

Customer Reward Program

As a means of building business by word-of-mouth, customers will be encouraged and rewarded as repeat customers. This will be accomplished by offering a discounted keg of beer to those customers who sign-up for our frequent buyer card and purchase $___ of products and services within a ___ (#) month period.

Frequent Buyer Program Types:

1.	Punch Cards	Receive something for free after? Purchases.
2.	Dollar-for-point Systems	Accrue points toward a free product.
3.	Percentage of Purchase	Accrue points toward future purchases.

E-mail Marketing

We will use the following email marketing tips to build our mailing list database, improve communications, boost customer loyalty and attract new and repeat business.
1.   Define our objectives as the most effective email strategies are those that offer value to our subscribers: either in the form of educational content or promotions. To drive sales, a promotional campaign is the best format. To create brand recognition and reinforce our expertise in our industry we will use educational newsletters.
2.   A quality, permission-based email list will be a vital component of our email marketing campaign. We will ask customers and prospects for permission to add them to our list at every touch-point or use a sign-in sheet.
3.   We will listen to our customers by using easy-to-use online surveys to ask specific questions about customers' preferences, interests and satisfaction.
4.   We will send only relevant and targeted communications.
5.   We will reinforce our brand to ensure recognition of our brand by using a recognizable name in the "from" line of our emails and including our company name, logo and a consistent design and color scheme in every email.

Resources:
https://www.thebalance.com/growing-and-nurturing-your-email-list-1794610
https://cbtnews.com/8-tips-drive-successful-email-marketing-campaign/
https://www.inman.com/2017/06/05/4-tips-for-effective-email-marketing/

https://due.com/blog/ways-take-good-care-email-list/

Our Microbrewery will send a promotional e-mail about a beer tasting event to beer aficionados, as indicated in their preferred membership application, while beer lovers receive a different e-mail promoting 12-pack specials during football season. Each segment gets notified of new products, specials and offers based on past buying patterns and what they've clicked on in our previous e-newsletters or indicated on their surveys. The objective is to tap the right customer's passion and need at the right time, with a targeted subject line and targeted content. Our general e-newsletter may appeal to most customers, but targeted mailings that reach out to our various audience segments will build even deeper relationships and drive higher sales.

Resources:
http://www.verticalresponse.com/blog/10-retail-marketing-ideas-to-boost-sales/
www.constantcontact.com/pricing/email-marketing.jsp

Google Reviews
We will use our email marketing campaign to ask people for reviews. We will ask people what they thought of our microbrewery business and encourage them to write a Google Review if they were impressed. We will incorporate a call to action (CTA) on our email auto signature with a link to our Google My Review page.
Source:
https://superb.digital/how-to-ask-your-clients-for-google-reviews/

Resources:
https://support.google.com/business/answer/3474122?hl=en
https://support.google.com/maps/answer/6230175?co=GENIE.Platform
          %3DDesktop&hl=en
www.patientgain.com/how-to-get-positive-google-reviews

Example:
We will tell our customers to:
1.   Go to https://www.google.com/maps
2.   Type in your business name, select the listing
3.   There's a "card" (sidebar) on the left-hand side. At the bottom, they can click 'Be the First to Write a Review' **or** 'Write a Review' if you already have one review.
Source:
https://www.reviewjump.com/blog/how-do-i-get-google-reviews/

The Beer and Wine Zone   www.beerandwinezone.com/
This company assists in building audiences for breweries and wineries. The Beer and Wine Zone team has developed email lists and Facebook and Twitter followings that it can share and cross market with any brewery. The Beer and Wine team assists in sending out a variety of products, promotions and messages by email, such as new product releases, white papers, seminars, webinars, contests, catalogues, membership privileges, gift certificates, loyalty points, coupons, limited time offers, free trials and discounts to

maintain and build client's lists.

Voice Broadcasting

A web-based voice broadcast system will provide a powerful platform to generate thousands of calls to clients and customers or create customizable messages to be delivered to specific individuals. Voice broadcasting and voice mail broadcast will allow our company to instantly send interactive phone calls with ease while managing the entire process right from the Web. We will instantly send alerts, notifications, reminders, GOTV - messages, and interactive surveys with ease right from the Web. The free VoiceShot account will guide us through the process of recording and storing our messages, managing our call lists, scheduling delivery as well as viewing and downloading real-time call and caller key press results. The voice broadcasting interface will guide us through the entire process with a Campaign Checklist as well as tips from the Campaign Expert. Other advanced features include recipient targeting, call monitoring, scheduling, controlling the rate of call delivery and customized text to speech (TTS). Resource: http://www.voiceshot.com/public/outboundcalls.asp

Facebook.com

We will use Facebook to move our businesses forward and stay connected to our customers in this fast-paced world. Content will be the key to staying in touch with our customers and keeping them informed. The content will be a rich mix of information, before and after photos, interactive questions, current trends and events, industry facts, education, promotions and specials, humor and fun. We will use the following step system to get customers from Facebook.com:

1.   We will open a free Facebook account at Facebook.com.
2.   We will begin by adding Facebook friends. The fastest way to do this is to allow Facebook to import our email addresses and send an invite out to all our customers.
3.   We will post a video to get our customers involved with our Facebook page. We will post a video called "How to Plan a Successful Beer Party." The video will be first uploaded to YouTube.com and then simply be linked to our Facebook page. Video will be a great way to get people active and involved with our Facebook page.
4.   We will send an email to our customers base that encourages them to check out the new video and to post their feedback about it on our Facebook page. Then we will provide a link, driving customers to our Facebook page.
5.   We will respond quickly to feedback, engage in the dialogue and add links to our response that direct the author to a structured mini-survey.
6.   We will optimize our Facebook profile with our business keyword to make it an invaluable marketing tool and become the "go-to" expert in our industry
7.   On a monthly basis, we will send out a message to all Facebook fans with a special offer, as Fan pages are the best way to interact with customers and potential customers on Facebook,
8.   We will use Facebook as a tool for sharing success stories and relate the ways in which we have helped our customers.
9.   We will use Facebook Connect to integrate our Facebook efforts with our regular

website to share our Facebook Page activity. This will also give us statistics about our website visitors and add social interaction to our site.

Resources:
http://www.facebook.com/advertising/
http://www.socialmediaexaminer.com/how-to-set-up-a-facebook-page-for-business/
http://smallbizsurvival.com/2009/11/6-big-facebook-tips-for-small-business.html

Example:
http://www.facebook.com/sprecherbrewing

We will use Facebook in the following ways to market our Microbrewery:
1. Promote our blog posts on our Facebook page
2. Post a video of our service people in action.
3. Make time-sensitive offers during slow periods
4. Create a special landing page for coupons or promotional giveaways
5. Create a Welcome tab to display a video message from our owner.
    Resource: Pagemodo.
6. Support a local charity by posting a link to their website.
7. Thank our customers while promoting their businesses at the same time.
8. Describe milestone accomplishments and thank customers for their role.
9. Give thanks to corporate accounts.
10. Ask customers to contribute stories about special experiences.
11. Use the built-in Facebook polling application to solicit feedback.
12. Use the Facebook reviews page to feature positive comments from customers, and to respond to negative reviews.
13. Introduce customers to our staff with resume and video profiles.
14. Create a photo gallery of unusual requests to showcase our beer expertise.

Facebook Profiles represent individual users and are held under a person's name. Each profile should only be controlled by that person. Each user has a wall, information tab, likes, interests, photos, videos and each individual can create events.

Facebook Groups are pretty similar to Fan Pages but are usually created for a group of people with a similar interest and they are wanting to keep their discussions private. The members are not usually looking to find out more about a business - they want to discuss a certain topic.

Facebook Fan Pages are the most viral of your three options. When someone becomes a fan of your page or comments on one of your posts, photos or videos, that is spread to all of their personal friends. This can be a great way to get your information out to lots of people...and quickly! In addition, one of the most valuable features of a business page is that you can send "updates" about new products and content to fans and your home building brand becomes more visible.

Facebook Live lets people, public figures and Pages share live video with their followers and

friends on Facebook.
Source:
https://live.fb.com/about/
Resources:
https://www.facebook.com/business/a/Facebook-video-ads
http://smartphones.wonderhowto.com/news/facebook-is-going-all-live-video-streaming-your-phone-0170132/

Facebook Business Page
Resources:
https://www.facebook.com/business/learn/set-up-facebook-page
https://fitsmallbusiness.com/how-to-create-a-facebook-business-page/
https://blog.hootsuite.com/steps-to-create-a-facebook-business-page/
https://www.pcworld.com/article/240258/how_to_make_a_facebook_page_for_your_small_business.html
https://blog.hubspot.com/blog/tabid/6307/bid/5492/how-to-create-a-facebook-business-page-in-5-simple-steps-with-video.aspx

Small Business Promotions
This group allows members to post about their products and services and is a public group designated as a Buy and Sell Facebook group.
Source: https://www.facebook.com/groups/smallbusinesspronotions/
Resource:
https://www.facebook.com/business/a/local-business-promotion-ads
https://www.facebook.com/business/learn/facebook-create-ad-local-awareness
www.socialmediaexaminer.com/how-to-use-facebook-local-awareness-ads-to-target-customers/

Facebook Ad Builder
https://waymark.com/signup/db869ac4-7202-4e3b-93c3-80acc5988df9/?partner=fitsmallbusiness

Facebook Lead Ads   www.facebook.com/business/a/lead-ads
A type of sponsored ad that appears in your audience's timeline just like other Facebook ads. However, the goal with lead ads is literally to capture the lead's info without them leaving Facebook. These ads don't link to a website landing page, creating an additional step.

Facebook Local Reach Ads
www.facebook.com/business/learn/facebook-create-ad-reach-ads
www.facebook.com/business/help/906073466193087?ref=fbb_reach

We will also explore location-based platforms like the following:
- FourSquare
- GoWalla
- Facebook Places
- Google Latitude

As a microbrewery serving a local community, we will appreciate the potential for hyper-local platforms like these. Location-based applications are increasingly attracting young, urban influencers with disposable income, which is precisely the audience we are trying to attract. People connect to geo-location apps primarily to "get informed" about local happenings.

Foursquare.com

A web and mobile application that allows registered users to post their location at a venue ("check-in") and connect with friends. Check-in requires active user selection and points are awarded at check-in. Users can choose to have their check-ins posted on their accounts on Twitter, Facebook, or both. In version 1.3 of their iPhone application, foursquare enabled push-notification of friend updates, which they call "Pings". Users can also earn badges by checking in at locations with certain tags, for check-in frequency, or for other patterns such as time of check-in.]
Resource:
https://foursquare.com/business/
Examples:
https://foursquare.com/v/vine-street-pub--brewery/49dfe1d2f964a52024611fe3

Instagram

Instagram.com is an online photo-sharing, video-sharing and social networking service that enables its users to take pictures and videos, apply digital filters to them, and share them on a variety of social networking services, such as
Facebook, Twitter, Tumblr and Flickr. A distinctive feature is that it confines photos to a square shape, similar to Kodak Instamatic and Polaroid images, in contrast to the 16:9 aspect ratio now typically used by mobile device cameras. Users are also able to record and share short videos lasting for up to 15 seconds.

Resources:
http://firstwefeast.com/drink/best-beer-instagram-accounts/
http://drinkwiththewench.com/2013/01/1-must-follow-craftbeer-instagramers/
www.pastemagazine.com/articles/2014/06/14-breweries-and-craft-beer-personalities-to-
    follo.html
http://brobible.com/life/article/instagram-craft-beer-lovers-following/
https://buyourbottles.com/blog/craft-breweries-on-instagram/

We will use Instagram in the following ways to help amplify the story of our brand, get people to engage with our content when not at our store, and get people to visit our store or site:
1.   Let our customers and fans know about specific product availability.
2.   Tie into trends, events or holidays to drive awareness.
3.   Let people know we are open and our ambiance is spectacular.
4.   Run a monthly contest and pick the winning hash-tagged photograph
      to activate our customer base and increase our exposure.
5.   Encourage the posting and collection of happy onsite or offsite customer photos.

Examples:
https://vinepair.com/wine-blog/the-17-best-breweries-to-follow-on-instagram/
https://www.instagram.com/explore/tags/microbrewery/
https://www.instagram.com/minhasbrewery/?hl=en

Note: Commonly found in tweets, a hashtag is a word or connected phrase (no spaces) that begins with a hash symbol (#). They're so popular that other social media platforms including Facebook, Instagram and Google+ now support them. Using a hashtag turns a word or phrase into a clickable link that displays a feed (list) of other posts with that same hashtag. For example, if you click on #_____ in a tweet, or enter #_____ in the search box, you'll see a list of tweets all about _____.

LinkedIn.com

LinkedIn ranks high in search engines and will provide a great platform for sending event updates to business associates. To optimize our LinkedIn profile, we will select one core keyword. We will use it frequently, without sacrificing consumer experience, to get our profile to skyrocket in the search engines. LinkedIn provides options that will allow our detailed profile to be indexed by search engines, like Google. We will make use of these options, so our business will achieve greater visibility on the Web. We will use widgets to integrate other tools, such as importing your blog entries or Twitter stream into your profile and go market research and gain knowledge with Polls. We will answer questions to show our expertise and ask questions in Questions and Answers to get a feel for what customers and prospects want or think. We will publish our LinkedIn URL on all our marketing collateral, including business cards, email signature, newsletters, and web site. We will grow our network by joining industry and alumni groups related to our business. We will update our status examples of recent work and link our status updates with our other social media accounts. We will start and manage a group or fan page for our product, brand or business. We will share useful articles that will be of interest to customers, and request LinkedIn recommendations from customers willing to provide testimonials. We will post our presentations on our profile using a presentation application. We will ask our first-level contacts for introductions to their contacts and interact with LinkedIn on a regular basis to reach those who may not see us on other social media sites. We will link to articles posted elsewhere, with a summary of why it's valuable to add to our credibility and list our newsletter subscription information and archives. We will post discounts and package deals. We will buy a LinkedIn direct ad that our target market will see. We will find vendors and contractors through connections. Example: http://www.linkedin.com/company/biddy-early-brewery

Podcasting

We will first decide if we are going to engage audio or video podcasting. Then we will decide what outlets we will use to disseminate our podcasts. There can be found on the web a listing of podcast directories that we can submit our podcast to, the most popular one being iTunes! One of the better-known podcast directories for podcast distribution services is podcast alley. We will develop a podcast blog because people can read and hear the content right from our own blog and as such create a lot of traffic. We will also decide on a target audience. Our target will be women, between the ages of 25-50 who are involved in direct sales, direct selling, home party plans, or home-based business. The focus of our podcast will be sharing stories, interviews, tips, marketing lessons, how to and educational lessons. We will write a podcast outline that includes an introduction, body and conclusion. We will then proceed to produce our Podcast. Mac computers come with inbuilt software through Garage Band that makes it very easy to record and covert our mp3 podcasts. This the file format that makes it easy to download podcasts.

Podcasting is a way of publishing audio broadcasts via the internet through MP3 files, which users can listen to using PCs and i-Pods. Our podcasts will provide both information and advertising. Our podcasts will allow us to pull in a lot of customers. Our monthly podcasts will be heard by ___ (#) eventual subscribers. Podcasts can now be downloaded for mobile devices, such as an iPod. Podcasts will give our company a new way to provide information and an additional way to advertise. Podcasting will give our business another connection point with customers. We will use this medium to communicate on important issues, what is going on with a planned event, and other things of interest to our health-conscious customers. The programs will last about 10 minutes and can be downloaded for free on iTunes. The purpose is not to be a mass medium. It is directed at a niche market with an above-average educational background and very special interests. It will provide a very direct and a reasonably inexpensive way of reaching our targeted audience with relevant information about our alcoholic beverages, products and services.

Resources: www.apple.com/itunes/download/.
                www.cbc.ca/podcasting/gettingstarted.html

Examples:
http://microbeerpodcast.pbworks.com/w/page/20862129/WI%20Microbrews,
        %20Pubs,%20supplies

Resources:
http://www.thebrewingnetwork.com/
http://microbrewr.com/open-a-microbrewery/

Blogging

We will use our blog to keep customers and prospects informed about products, events and services that relate to our Microbrewery business, new releases, contests, and specials. Our blog will show readers that we are a good source of expert information that they can count on. With our blog, we can quickly update our customers anytime our company releases a new product, the holding of a contest or are placing items on special pricing. We will use our blog to share customer testimonials and meaningful product usage stories. We will use the blog to supply advice on creative recipes for our beverages. Our visitors will be able to subscribe to our RSS feeds and be instantly updated without any spam filters interfering. We will also use the blog to solicit product usage recommendations and future craft beer addition suggestions. Additionally, blogs are free and allow for constant ease of updating.

Our blog will give our company the following benefits:
1.   A cost-effective marketing tool.
2.   An expanded network.

3. A promotional platform for new services.
4. An introduction to people with similar interests.
5. Builds credibility and expertise recognition.

We will use our blog for the following purposes:
1. To share customer testimonials, experiences and meaningful success stories.
2. Update our clients anytime our clinic releases a new service.
3. Supply advice on promotional and party planning options.
4. Discuss research findings.
5. To publish helpful content.
6, To welcome feedback in multiple formats.
7. Link together other social networking sites, including Twitter.
8. To improve Google rankings.
9. Make use of automatic RSS feeds.

We will adhere to the following blog writing guidelines:
1. We will blog at least 2 or 3 times per week to maintain interest.
2. We will integrate our blog into the design of our website.
3. We will use our blog to convey useful information and not our advertisements.
4. We will make the content easy to understand.
5. We will focus our content on the needs of our targeted audience.

Our blog will feature the following on a regular basis:
1. Useful articles and assessment coupons.
2. Give away of a helpful free report in exchange for email addresses
3. Helpful information for our professional referral sources, as well as clients, and online and offline community members.
5. Use of a few social media outposts to educate, inform, engage and drive people back to our blog for more information and our free report.

To get visitors to our blog to take the next action step and contact our firm we will do the following:
1. Put a contact form on the upper-left hand corner of our blog, right below the header.
2. Put our complete contact information in the header itself.
3. Add a page to our blog and title it, "Become My Client.", giving the reader somewhere to go for the next sign-up steps.
4. At the end of each blog post, we will clearly tell the reader what to do next; such as subscribe to our RSS feed, or to sign up for our newsletter mailing list.

Resources: www.blogger.com   www.blogspot.com   www.wordpress.com
Examples: http://beermanmicrobrewery.blogspot.com/
             http://foodyummers.wordpress.com/tag/microbrewery/
             http://domesticcraftbeer.blogspot.com/

Guest Blogging
We will guest blog on other blogs largely related, or semi-related to our websites niche.

Opening other peoples' eyes to our name and our website will always be good promotion. Additionally, networking with other bloggers will be great for business as well.

Twitter

We will use 'Twitter.com' as a way to produce new business from existing clients and generate prospective clients online. Twitter is a free social networking and micro-blogging service that allows its users to send and read other users' updates (otherwise known as tweets), which are text-based posts of up to 140 characters in length. Updates are displayed on the user's profile page and delivered to other users who have signed up to receive them. The sender can restrict delivery to those in his or her circle of friends, with delivery to everyone being the default. Users can receive updates via the Twitter website, SMS text messaging, RSS feeds, or email. We will use our Twitter account to respond directly to questions, distribute news, solve problems, post updates, hold trivia question contests for a chance to win a gift certificate and offer special discounts on craft beers and services. Our posts on Twitter will include our URL (address), our new offers, beer cooking recipe tips and new service offerings. On a long-term basis, using Twitter consistently and efficiently will help push our website up the rankings on Google.

We will also add our website, company logo, personal photo and/or blog on our profile page.
We will provide the following instructions to register as a 'Follower' of _____ (company name) on Twitter:
1.   In your Twitter account, click on 'Find People' in the top right navigation bar, which will redirect to a new page.
2.   Click on 'Find on Twitter' which will open a search box that say: 'Who are you looking for?'
3.   Type '_____ (company name) / _____ (owner name)' and click 'search'. This will bring up the results page.
4.   Click the blue '_____' name to read the bio or select the 'Follow' button.
Examples:
http://twitter.com/#!/liverybrew

Beer Club

_____ (company name) will build up its customer base by promoting a Beer Club--a free customer loyalty program. Members will earn Beer Club reward points for every dollar spent at _____ (company name). In addition, members will receive a monthly newsletter, invitations to free beer tastings throughout the year and access to tickets for brewery events before the general public. The beer club will foster a community of interests with our customers and deepen the culture of beer. The club will feature themed events, a comparison with other enthusiasts, and the constant support of a master brewer. Registration for the beer club will be free and available online via our website. We will schedule monthly paid events.

We will assign a key staff member to handle the business operations of the club.
The benefits include:

First right of refusal on all ultra-exclusive new releases
Special priority access to top tasting events with luminaries.
Complimentary private tutorials on upscale beer themes
Extraordinary concierge service for special events.
Special discounts on purchases during non-publicized sales events
Personalized beer management service
Instant access to our beer experts through his cell phone during off hours
VIP password access to the highly restricted section of our website along with free
    access to all educational modules and recipes.

Microbrewery Tours

Once a month, ____ (company name) will offer free brewery tours at its ___ (city)
location. The tours will be designed to help educate customers about how their favorite
beers are brewed. It will also offer a place where people can come to learn more about
beer and the brewing process. It will offer a variety of tours and tasting events where
people can learn about the styles and the history of beer.

Demonstrations

We will hold regular monthly cooking demonstrations that feature lessons on cooking
with beer. We will use flyers to promote the events and publish the featured recipe of the
event. It is assumed that those who like to drink beer, will also enjoy cooking with quality
beer, and this will help to drive the sales of selected beers.

Testimonial Marketing

We will regularly ask for testimonials from our customers. We will have something
prepared that we would like the client to say that is specific to the beers we offer, or
anything relevant to advertising claims that we have put together. For the convenience of
the client we will assemble a testimonial letter that they can either modify or just sign off
on. Additionally, testimonials can also be in the form of audio or video and put on our
website or mailed to potential clients in the form of a DVD or Audio CD. A picture with
a testimonial will be preferred. We will put testimonials directly on a magazine ad, slick
sheet, brochure, or website, or assemble a complete page of testimonials for our sales
presentation folder.
Examples:
http://saintpatricksbrewing.com/testimonials

We will collect customer testimonials in the following ways:
1.   Our website – A page dedicated to testimonials (written and/or video).
2.   Social media accounts – Facebook fan pages offer a review tab, which makes it
       easy to receive and display customer testimonials.
3.   Google+ also offers a similar feature with Google+ Local.
4.   Local search directories – Ask customers to post more reviews on Yelp and
       Yahoo Local.
5.   Customer Satisfaction Survey Forms

We will pose the following questions to our customers to help them frame their

testimonials:
1. What was the obstacle that would have prevented you from buying this product?
2. "What was your main concern about buying this product?"
3. What did you find as a result of buying this product?
4. What specific feature did you like most about this product?
5. What would be three other benefits about this product?
6. Would you recommend this product? If so, why?
7. Is there anything you'd like to add?

Resource:
https://smallbiztrends.com/2016/06/use-customer-testimonials.html

Business Logo
Our logo will graphically represent who we are and what we do, and it will serve to help brand our image. It will also convey a sense of uniqueness and professionalism. The logo will represent our company image and the message we are trying to convey. Our business logo will reflect the philosophy and objectives of our Microbrewery business. Our logo will incorporate the following design guidelines:

1. It will relate to our industry, our name, a defining characteristic of our company or a competitive advantage we offer.
2. It will be a simple logo that can be recognized faster.
3. It will contain strong lines and letters which show up better than thin ones.
4. It will feature something unexpected or unique without being overdrawn.
5. It will work well in black and white (one-color printing).
6. It will be scalable and look pleasing in both small and large sizes.
7. It will be artistically balanced and make effective use of color, line density and shape.
8. It will be unique when compared to competitors.
9. It will use original, professionally rendered artwork.
10. It can be replicated across any media mix without losing quality.
11. It appeals to our target audience.
12. It will be easily recognizable from a distance if utilized in outdoor advertising.

Examples:
https://99designs.com/blog/creative-inspiration/brewery-beer-logos/
https://www.tailorbrands.com/business-logo-design/beer-logo-design

Resources: www.freelogoservices.com/   www.hatchwise.com
              www.logosnap.com   www.99designs.com
              www.fiverr.com   www.freelancer.com
              www.upwork.com

Logo Design Guide:
www.bestfreewebresources.com/logo-design-professional-guide
www.creativebloq.com/graphic-design/pro-guide-logo-design-21221

Fundraisers

Community outreach programs involving charitable fundraising and showing a strong interest in the local school system will serve to elevate our status in the community as a "good corporate citizen" while simultaneously increasing microbrewery traffic. We will execute a successful fundraising program for our Microbrewery and build goodwill in the community, by adhering to the following guidelines:

1. Keep It Local

    When looking for a worthy cause, we will make sure it is local so the whole neighborhood will support it.

2. Plan It

    We will make sure that we are organized and outline everything we want to accomplish before planning the fundraiser.

3. Contact Local Media

    We will contact the suburban newspapers to do stories on the event and send out press releases to the local TV and radio stations.

4. Contact Area Businesses

    We will contact other businesses and have them put up posters in their stores and pass out flyers to promote the event.

5. Get Recipient Support

    We will make sure the recipients of the fundraiser are really willing to participate and get out in the neighborhood to invite everyone into our store for the event, plus help pass out flyers and getting other businesses to put up the posters.

6. Give Out Bounce Backs

    We will give a "bounce-back" coupon that allows for both a discount and an additional donation in exchange for customer next purchase. (It will have an expiration date of two weeks to give a sense of urgency.)

7. Be Ready with plenty of product and labor on hand for the event.

Fundraiser Action Plan Checklist:
1. Choose a good local cause for your fundraiser.
2. Calculate donations as a percentage for normal sales.
3. Require the group to promote and support the event.
4. Contact local media to get exposure before and after the event.
5. Ask area businesses to put up flyers and donate printing of materials.
6. Use a bounce-back coupon to get new customers back.
7. Be prepared with sufficient labor and product.

Resource:
http://www.fundraiserhelp.com/craft-beer-fundraiser.htm
Example:
http://www.fundraisingalmanac.com/microbrewery-tastings.php

Online Directory Listings

The following directory listings use proprietary technology to match customers with industry professionals in their geographical area. The local search capabilities for specific niche markets offer an invaluable tool for the customer. These directories help member businesses connect with purchase-ready buyers, convert leads to sales, and maximize the value of customer relationships. Their online and offline communities provide a quick and easy low or no-cost solution for customers to find a Microbrewery quickly. We intend to sign-up with all no cost directories and evaluate the ones that charge a fee.

1. www.zymerica.com/
2. www.brewpubzone.com/
3. www.beer100.com
4. http://www.microbrewindex.com/
5. http://www.brewhopping.com/
6. http://www.gourmetsleuth.com/Directory/List/Beer-Micro-Breweries-316.aspx
7. http://www.craftbeer.com/pages/breweries/featured-brewery
8   www.brewersassociation.org/directories/breweries/?type=micro&term= United%20States&searchby=country
    www.brewersassociation.org/directories/breweries/

We will make certain that our listings contain the following information:

- Business Name
- Phone number
- Email address
- Contact Person: name, phone #, email
- Company logo
- Short Business description
- Specialties
- Twitter Business Page Link

- Address
- Days and Hours of operation
- Website URL
- Facility Photos
- Products/ Services offered
- Affiliations
- Facebook Business Page Link
- LinkedIn Business Page Link

Other General Directories Include:

Listings.local.yahoo.com
YellowPages.com
Bing.com/businessportal
Yelp.com
InfoUSA.com
Localeze.com
YellowBot.com
InsiderPages.com
CitySearch.com
Profiles.google.com/me
Jigsaw.com
Whitepages.com
Judysbook.com
Google.com
SuperPages.com
ExpressUpdate.com
MojoPages.com
BOTW

Switchboard Super Pages
MerchantCircle.com
Local.com
BrownBook.com
iBegin.com
Bestoftheweb.com
HotFrog.com
MatchPoint.com
YellowUSA.com
Manta.com
LinkedIn.com
PowerProfiles.com
Company.com
Yahoo.com
TrueLocal.com
Citysquares.com
DMOZ
Business.com

Get Listed   http://getlisted.org/enhanced-business-listings.aspx
Universal Business Listing   https://www.ubl.org/index.aspx
                                        www.UniversalBusinessListing.org

Universal Business Listing (UBL) is a local search industry service dedicated to acting as a central collection and distribution point for business information online. UBL provides business owners and their marketing representatives with a one-stop location for broad distribution of complete, accurate, and detailed listing information.

Restaurant Placemats

We will explore opportunities for a business card-like ad to be placed on the paper placemats used in area restaurants (shelf-life of the ad is about six months), or for special (holiday) events taking place at a restaurant (1-off opportunities). An example would be getting on the Pizza Hut placemats (about 9,000 in six months. Placemat advertising will reach area residents as well as seasonal tourists.

Billboards

We will use billboard advertising to create brand awareness and strong name recognition. Billboards will be placed along all major freeways passing through downtown ____ (city) to entice people coming home from work to stop at their local grocery store and pick up some of our product. We will design Billboards that are eye-catching and informative and use easy to read fonts like Verdana. We will include our business name, location, a graphic, standout border and no more than eight words. In designing the billboard, we will consider the fact that the eye typically moves from the upper left corner to the lower right corner of a billboard. We will use colors that can be viewed by color blind people, such as yellow, black and blue, and pictures to contrast with the sky and other surroundings. We will keep the layout uncluttered and the message simple and include a direct call to action. Depending on the billboards size and location, the cost will range from $1,000 to $5,000 per month. We will try to negotiate a discount on a long-term contract.

Example: Time for a Cold One?   Drink Responsibly
Resources: Outdoor Advertising Association of America   www.oaaa.org
                  EMC Outdoor, Inc.   www.emcoutdoor.com

Theater Advertising

Theater advertising is the method of promoting our business through in-theatre promotions. The objective of theater advertising is to expose the movie patron to our advertising message in various ways throughout the theater. Benefits include; an engaged audience that can't change the channel, an audience that is in a quiet environment, an audience that is in a good mood and receptive, advertising that is targeted to our local geographic area, full color video advertising on a 40-foot screen, and a moving and interactive ad with music and voiceover.

Resources: Velocity Cinema Advertising   www.movieadvertising.com/index.html
              NCM   www.nationalcinemedia.com/intheatreadvertising/
              ScreenVision   www.screenvision.com

AMC Theaters   www.amctheatres.com
Regal Entertainment Group   www.regmovies.com

Mobile Marketing

We will create a new mobile marketing strategy that spotlights our new flagship product, And the importance of targeting a younger segment to expand our customer base. We will use mobile advertising to tap into a younger tech-savvy segment of the market to grow our brand in the coming years.

First, consumers will opt-in by sending a text to our SMS platform and in return they will receive an offer for a free burrito via their mobile phones. Once a customer redeems the text message offer, the software will provide us with a report that details what radio station that customer was listening to, the daypart, and which program they were listening to, that prompted the customer to respond to the offer. Our trained staff will be the key in assisting customers with the promotion and up-selling. We will work with Opt It, Inc. to execute its first text messaging campaign. We want the portion of our customer base that does not typically clip coupons out of the Sunday paper to have easy access to the great deals we offer. We believe there will be a large number of people who opted-in on our Web site to receive mobile offers even before the promotion begins. Now, instead of promoting what's happening in a few weeks, we can have managers text local people to let them know about an event that's happening in a few hours.

In a texting component, customers will be able to text "_____" to _____ (#) and receive mobile coupons. The second part of the message asks customers if they would like to register their e-mail addresses to receive weekly communications from _____ (company name). The first mobile coupon will reward customers with $___ off any family cheese platter/beer package. Customers will continue to receive additional offers, including special offers on holiday gift items. This will purely be an opt in campaign and will let us create an ongoing conversation with our customers.

We will use the following to leverage our mobile marketing program:
1. We will offer customers the opportunity to join a mobile loyalty club and receive special rewards and offers for mobile club members only.
2. We will encourage customers to sign up for the mobile program at the reception counter, on the website and on social media platforms.
3. We will develop compelling up-sell and cross-sell mobile coupon offers, such as a discount on a product when purchasing a service, or up-selling through offering service packages.
4. We will use mobile loyalty programs to stay top of mind with existing customers and drive repeat sales.
5. Our mobile messages will include mobile coupons as well as announcements about new employees or new available services and treatments.
6. We will use mobile messaging on special occasions, such as Mother's Day, and to drive traffic during the slower season.

Article: www.craftbrewingbusiness.com/business-marketing/learn-use-mobile-marketing-grow-craft-brewery/

Resource:

Thinfilm   https://www.thinfilmnfc.com/
Offers end-to-end mobile marketing solutions that feature hardware, label/packaging integration services and a powerful cloud-based software platform. Collectively, these components deliver a serious one-to-one digital marketing platform through which brands of all sizes can connect.

Other Resources:
Mobile Marketing Association   www.mmaglobal.com
BxP Marketing visit   www.bxpmarketing.com.
VizConnect   www.myvizconnect.com/
Offers an easy and affordable way for small business to easily communicate with their mobile customer using HD video.

Google Maps
We will first make certain that our business is listed in Google Maps. We will do a search for our business in Google Maps. If we don't see our business listed, then we will add our business to Google Maps. Even if our business is listed in Google Maps, we will create a Local Business Center account and take control of our listing, by adding more relevant information. Consumers generally go to Google Maps for two reasons: Driving Directions and to find a business.
Resource: http://maps.google.com/
Example:
www.google.com/maps/place/Dragonmead+Microbrewery/@42.492684,-82.9774386,
17z/data=!3m1!4b1!4m2!3m1!1s0x8824d9e1d9a38d51:0xc6d01b00c035f7f0?hl=en

Bing Maps   www.bingplaces.com/
Makes it easy for customers to find our business.

Apple Maps
A web mapping service developed by Apple Inc. It is the default map system of iOS, macOS, and watchOS. It provides directions and estimated times of arrival for automobile, pedestrian, and public transportation navigation.
Resources:
ttps://mapsconnect.apple.com
 http://www.stallcupgroup.com/2012/09/19/three-ways-to-make-your-pawn-business-
        more-profitable-and-sellable/
http://www.apple.com/ios/maps/
https://en.wikipedia.org/wiki/Apple_Maps

Google Places
Google Places helps people make more informed decisions about where to go to locate microbreweries. Place Pages connect people to information from the best sources across the web, displaying photos, reviews and essential facts, as well as real-time updates and offers from business owners. We will make sure that our Google Places listing is up to date to increase our online visibility. Google Places is linked to our Google Maps listing and will help to get on the first page of Google search page results when people search

for a microbrewery in our area.
Resource: www.google/com/places

Yelp.com

We will use Yelp.com to help people find our local business. Visitors to Yelp write local reviews, over 85% of them rating a business 3 stars or higher In addition to reviews, visitors can use Yelp to find events, special offers, lists and to talk with other Yelpers. As business owners, we will setup a free account to post offers, photos and message our customers. We will also buy ads on Yelp, which will be clearly labeled "Sponsored Results". We will also use the Weekly Yelp, which is available in 42 city editions to bring news about the latest business openings and other happenings.
Example:
www.yelp.com/biz/triple-7-restaurant-and-microbrewery-las-vegas

Manta.com

Manta is the largest free source of information on small companies, with profiles of more than 64 million businesses and organizations. Business owners and sales professionals use Manta's vast database and custom search capabilities to quickly find companies, easily connect with prospective customers and promote their own services. Manta.com, founded in 2005, is based in Columbus, Ohio.
Example: http://www.manta.com/c/mttxyp7/the-beer-man-microbrewery

Tripadvisor.com

A website designed to share travel reviews.
Ex: www.tripadvisor.com/ShowUserReviews-g57402-d292786-r141050940-
           Magic_Hat_Brewing_Company-South_Burlington_Vermont.html

Zomato.com

Zomato is used by millions every day to decide where to eat in over 10,000 cities across 23 countries.
Example:
www.zomato.com/ncr/manhattan-craft-brewery-golf-course-road-gurgaon

Pay-Per-Click Advertising

Google AdWords, Yahoo! Search Marketing, and Microsoft adCenter are the three largest network operators, and all three operate under a bid-based model. Cost per click (CPC) varies depending on the search engine and the level of competition for a particular keyword. Google AdWords are small text ads that appear next to the search results on Google. In addition, these ads appear on many partner web sites, including NYTimes.com (The New York Times), Business.com, Weather.com, About.com, and many more. Google's text advertisements are short, consisting of one title line and two content text lines. Image ads can be one of several different Interactive Advertising Bureau (IAB) standard sizes. Through Google AdWords, we plan to buy placements (ads) for specific search terms through this "Pay-Per-Click" advertising program. This

PPC advertising campaign will allow our ad to appear when someone searches for a keyword related to our business, organization, or subject matter. More importantly, we will only pay when a potential customer clicks on our ad to visit our website. For instance, since we operate a Microbrewery in ___ (city), _____ (state), we will target people using search terms such as "Microbrewery, craft beers, suds, brewpub, hops, Pilsner, in ____ (city), ____ (state)". With an effective PPC campaign our ads will only be displayed when a user searches for one of these keywords. In short, PPC advertising will be the most cost-effective and measurable form of advertising for our Microbrewery.
Resources: http://adwords.google.com/support/aw/?hl=en
          www.wordtracker.com

Yahoo Local Listings

We will create our own local listing on Yahoo. To create our free listing, we will use our web browser and navigate to http://local.yahoo.com. We will first register for free with Yahoo and create a member ID and password to list our business. Once we have accessed http://local.yahoo.com, we will scroll down to the bottom and click on "Add/Edit a Business" to get onto the Yahoo Search Marketing Local Listings page. In the lower right of the screen we will see "Local Basic Listings FREE". We will click on the Get Started button and log in again with our new Yahoo ID and password. The form for our local business listing will now be displayed. When filling it out, we will be sure to include our full web address (http://www.companyname.com). We will include a description of our craft beers and services in the description section, but avoid hype or blatant advertising, to get the listing to pass Yahoo's editorial review. We will also be sure to select the appropriate business category and sub categories.
Examples:
https://local.yahoo.com/CA/Carlsbad/Food+Dining/Beverages/Breweries

Sales Reps/Account Executives

_____ (company name) will use independent commissioned sales reps to penetrate markets outside of _____ (city/state). Management will work to keep in constant communication with the sales reps to ensure that their service is professional and timely. Independent sales representatives will provide the best mode for distribution in order to maintain pricing controls and higher margins. Independent sales reps are not full-time employees thus benefits are not necessary. Independent sales reps receive a flat commission based on gross sales. Our sales reps are set at a commission rate of __ (15?) % of gross sales. The average sales rep can service up to __ (#) accounts with the average location generating around $____ per year. We expect to have ___(#) independent sales reps covering ___ (#) states in place to sell the company's product. Sales agents will also be hired to directly market our products for catered functions to event planners and caterers. In addition to field calls, sales reps will represent the product line at all regional tradeshows, with the marketing director attending all national tradeshows.
Resources:
www.brewersassociation.org/news/providing-boost-brewery-reps/
www.americancraftbeer.com/a-day-in-the-life-fuh-can-around-with-oskar-blues-sales-
    rep-brent-hodgson/

Point-of-Purchase Displays (POP)

The term point-of-purchase, or POP, typically refers to the promotional graphics focused on influencing consumer behavior at the moment of the purchasing decision. These graphics serve to impact a buying decision in favor of a specific brand or product in-microbrewery where the purchase is imminent. POP is increasingly becoming one of the more important aspects of advertising and promotion, because of its efficiency in targeting the consumer in the actual buying environment, the decline of network television viewership and newspaper readership, and the stark reality of recession-sized ad budgets. Because of its impact, we will work with our liquor distributor to secure the following types of items from craft beer manufacturers:

1. Banners
2. Ceiling danglers
3. Themed wall coverings
4. Directional posters
5. Floor Decals
6. Props
7. Display Units

Examples:
https://www.pinterest.com/howardadkins/beersoda-displays/
https://www.pinterest.com/trantuong_van/beer-posm/

Light-up Signs

We will create light-up signs for the bars/pubs/groceries, because this could remind people what our product tasted like and may get them to purchase more in the bar or from a store for consumption in their homes. Getting as much exposure as possible at the bars and pubs will be key to getting our product a reputable name.

Advertorials

An advertorial is an advertisement written in the form of an objective article and presented in a printed publication—usually designed to look like a legitimate and independent news story. We will use quotes as testimonials to back up certain claims throughout our copy and break-up copy with subheadings to make the material more reader-friendly. We will include the "call to action" and contact information with a 24/7 voicemail number and a discount coupon. The advertorial will have a short intro about a client's experience with our craft beers and include quotes, facts, and statistics. We will present helpful information about party planning.

Affiliate Marketing

We will create an affiliate marketing program to broaden our reach. We will first devise a commission structure, so affiliates have a reason to promote our business. We will give them ___ (10) % of whatever sales they generate. We will go after event planner bloggers or webmasters who get a lot of web traffic for our keywords. These companies would then promote our products/services, and they would earn commissions for the sales they generated. We will work with the following services to handle the technical aspects of our program.

ConnectCommerce	https://www.connectcommerce.com/
Commission Junction	https://members.cj.com

ShareASale	http://www.shareasale.com/
Share Results	
LinkShare	https://cli.linksynergy.com/cli/publisher/registration/
Affiliate Scout	http://affiliatescout.com/
Affiliate Seeking	http://www.affiliateseeking.com/
Clix Galore	http://www.clixgalore.com/

Media Relations

We will stay in contact with journalists at the following media outlets: CNN, Culture Magazine, Food & beer Magazine, FOX News, Men's Journal Magazine, Martha Stewart Living Radio (Sirius/XM), The Boston Globe, The Food Network, The Los Angeles Times, The Washington Post, U.S. News & World Report, National Public Radio, beer Enthusiast, and the Wall Street Journal.

Beer Sponsorships

We will work to exploit relationships on a grassroots level. We will develop relationships with places like the ____ (city) Academy of Music and the _____ (city) Art Museum. We will also seek to sponsor the _____ Concert Series in _____ (city).

Gift with Purchase (GWP)

A GWP is an item that is presented to our client when he or she spends above a specified amount on products or services. The Gift with purchase or free item could be anything from beer recipe booklets, company voucher, bottle opener, product samples, etc. We will attach our marketing logo and business card to the gift and use it as means to thank the customer for their patronage. We will also explore the dramatic impact of a surprise gift with purchase, because an unexpected bonus item is often very appreciated and remembered.

HotFrog.com

HotFrog is a fast-growing free online business directory listing over 6.6 million US businesses. HotFrog now has local versions in 34 countries worldwide.
Anyone can list their business in HotFrog for free, along with contact details, and products and services. Listing in HotFrog directs sales leads and enquiries to your business. Businesses are encouraged to add any latest news and information about their products and services to their listing. HotFrog is indexed by Google and other search engines, meaning that customers can find your HotFrog listing when they use Google, Yahoo! or other search engines.
Resource:
http://www.hotfrog.com/AddYourBusiness.aspx
Example:
http://www.hotfrog.com/business/ny/coop/lucky-mutt-brewing

Local.com

Local.com owns and operates a leading local search site and network in the United States.

Its mission is to be the leader at enabling local businesses and consumers to find each other and connect. To do so, the company uses patented and proprietary technologies to provide over 20 million consumers each month with relevant search results for local businesses, products and services on Local.com and more than 1,000 partner sites. Local.com powers more than 100,000 local websites. Tens of thousands of small business customers use Local.com products and services to reach consumers using a variety of subscription, performance and display advertising and website products.
Resource: http://corporate.local.com/mk/get/advertising-opportunities

Autoresponder

An autoresponder is an online tool that will automatically manage our mailing list and send out emails to our customers at preset intervals. We will write a short article that is helpful to potential microbrewery buyers. We will load this article into our autoresponder. We will let people know of the availability of our article by posting to newsgroups, forums, social networking sites etc. We will list our autoresponder email address at the end of the posting, so they can send a blank email to our autoresponder to receive our article and be added to our mailing list. We will then email them at the interval of our choosing with special offers. We will load the messages into our autoresponder and set a time interval for the messages to be mailed out.
Resource: www.aweber.com

Corporate Incentive/Employee Rewards Program

Our Employee Rewards Program will motivate and reward the key resources of local corporations – the people who make their business a success. We will use independent sales reps to market these programs to local corporations. It will be a versatile program, allowing the corporate client to customize it to best suit the following goals:

1.   Welcome New Hires
2.   Introduce an Employee Discount Program for our microbrews.
3.   Reward increases in sales or productivity with an Employee Incentive Program
4.   Thank Retirees for their service to the company
5.   Initiate a Loyalty Rewards Program geared towards the customers of our corporate clients or their employees.

Database Marketing

Database marketing is a form of direct marketing using databases of customers or potential customers to generate personalized communications in order to promote a product or service for marketing purposes. The method of communication can be any addressable medium, as in direct marketing. As marketers trained in the use of database marketing tools, we will be able to carry out customer nurturing, which is a tactic that attempts to communicate with each customer or prospect at the right time, using the right information to meet that customer's need to progress through the process of identifying a problem, learning options available to resolve it, selecting the right solution, and making the purchasing decision. As marketers we will use our databases to learn more about customers, select target markets for specific campaigns, through customer segmentation, compare customers' value to the company, and provide more specialized offerings for customers based on their transaction histories and surveyed needs and wants.

We will use sign-in sheets, coupons, surveys and newsletter subscriptions to collect the following information from our customer relationship management (CRM) system:

1. Name
2. Telephone Number
3. Email Address
4. Address
5. Birth Date
6. Preferred Style of Beer
7. Preferred Taste Profile
8. Preferred Price Range
9. Preferred Quantity Packaging
10. Preferred Container Type

Cause Marketing

Cause marketing or cause-related marketing refers to a type of marketing involving the cooperative efforts of a "for profit" business and a non-profit organization for mutual benefit. The possible benefits of cause marketing for business include positive public relations, improved customer relations, and additional marketing opportunities.

Cause marketing sponsorship by American businesses is rising at a dramatic rate, because customers, employees and stakeholders prefer to be associated with a company that is considered socially responsible. Our business objective will be to generate highly cost-effective public relations and media coverage for the launch of a marketing campaign focused on _____ (type of cause), with the help of the _____ (non-profit organization name) organization.

Resources:
www.causemarketingforum.com/
www.cancer.org/AboutUs/HowWeHelpYou/acs-cause-marketing

Courtesy Advertising

We will engage in courtesy advertising, which refers to a company or corporation "buying" an advertisement in a nonprofit dinner program, event brochure, and the like. Our company will gain visibility this way while the nonprofit organization may treat the advertisement revenue as a donation. We will specifically advertise in the following non-profit programs, newsletters, bulletins and event brochures: _____

_____

Meet-up Group

We will form a meet-up group to encourage people to participate in our beer tasting programs.

Resource: http://www.meetup.com/create/
Example: http://beer.meetup.com/

Sampling Program

We will giveaway kegs of our micro-brewed beer to _____ (25?) pubs across the city of _____ with strict orders that they only be unsealed at a precise time and date:_____.
We will issue a press release in anticipation of this coordinated product release event.
We will include customer satisfaction surveys and requests for testimonials that can be published. We will also include samples of our marketing materials for comment on.
We will ask our sales reps to follow-up with these potential accounts to collect feedback

and possible orders.

Continuity Program
Our Micro Continuity Program will be a continuity program that has a definitive start and finish date. It will be a program that offers 12 different product labeled cases of microbrews over a 12-month period and charges recipients on a recurring basis. On the other hand, a service that charges a monthly fee until the customer cancels isn't a Micro Continuity program, it's just considered a regular continuity program.
Resource: www.continuityprograms.com/

BBB Accreditation
We will apply for BBB Accreditation to improve our perceived trustworthiness. BBB determines that a company meets BBB accreditation standards, which include a commitment to make a good faith effort to resolve any consumer complaints. BBB Accredited Businesses pay a fee for accreditation review/monitoring and for support of BBB services to the public. BBB accreditation does not mean that the business' products or services have been evaluated or endorsed by BBB, or that BBB has made a determination as to the business' product quality or competency in performing services. We will place the BBB Accreditation Logo in all of our ads.
Ex: www.bbb.org/nebraska/business-reviews/wineries/schillingbridge-winery-and-
       microbrewery-in-pawnee-city-ne-300023891

Sponsor Events
The sponsoring of events, such as beer festivals and golf tournaments, will allow our company to engage in what is known as experiential marketing, which is the idea that the best way to deepen the emotional bond between a company and its customers is by creating a memorable and interactive experience. We will ask for the opportunity to prominently display our company signage and the set-up of a booth from which to handout sample products and sales literature. We will also seek to capitalize on networking, speech giving and workshop presenting opportunities.

Sponsorships
We will sponsor a local team, such as our child's little league baseball team, the local soccer club or a bowling group. We will then place our company name on the uniforms or shirts in exchange for providing the equipment and/or uniforms.

Patch.com
A community-specific news and information platform dedicated to providing comprehensive and trusted local coverage for individual towns and communities. Patch makes it easy to: Keep up with news and events, Look at photos and videos from around town, Learn about local businesses, Participate in discussions and Submit announcements, photos, and reviews.
Ex: http://brighton.patch.com/articles/brighton-planning-body-oks-microbrewery
       http://plymouth.patch.com/topics/Microbreweries

Mobile iPhone Apps

We will use new distribution tools like the iPhone App Store to give us unprecedented direct access to consumers, without the need to necessarily buy actual mobile *ads* to reach people. Thanks to Apple's iPhone and the App Store, we will be able to make cool mobile apps that may generate as much goodwill and purchase intent as a banner ad. We will research Mobile Application Development, which is the process by which application software is developed for small low-power handheld devices, such as personal digital assistants, enterprise digital assistants or mobile phones. These applications are either pre-installed on phones during manufacture, or downloaded by customers from various mobile software distribution platforms. iPhone apps make good marketing tools. The bottom line is iPhones and smartphones sales are continually growing, and people are going to their phones for information. Apps will definitely be a lead generation tool because it gives potential clients easy access to our contact and business information and the ability to call for more information while they are still "hot". Our apps will contain: directory of staffers, publications on relevant issues, office location, videos, etc.

We will especially focus on the development of apps that can accomplish the following:

1.   **Mobile Reservations:** Customers can use this app to access mobile reservations linked directly to your in-house calendar. They can browse open slots and book facility tour appointments easily, while on the go.

2.   **Appointment Reminders:** You can send current customers reminders of regular or special appointments through your mobile app to increase your yearly revenue per customer.

3.   **Style Libraries**
     Offer a style library in your app to help customers to pick out a label style.
     Using a simple photo gallery, you can collect photos of various styles, and have customers browse and select specific label designs.

4.   **Customer Photos**
     Your app can also have a feature that lets customers take photos and email them to you. This is great for creating a database of customer photos for testimonial purposes, advertising, or just easy reference.

5.   **Special Offers**
     Push notifications allow you to drive activity on special promotions, deals, events, and offers. If you ever need to generate revenue during a down time, push notifications allow you to generate interest easily and proactively.

6.   **Loyalty Programs**
     A mobile app allows you to offer a mobile loyalty program (buy ten ___, get one free, etc.). You won't need to print up cards or track anything manually – it's all done simply through users' mobile devices.

7.   **Referrals**
     A mobile app can make referrals easy. With a single click, a user can post to a social media account on Facebook or Twitter about their experience with your business. This allows you to earn new business organically through the networks of existing customers.

8. Product Sales

You can sell hair grooming products through your mobile app. Customers can browse products, submit orders, and make payments easily, helping you open up a new revenue stream.

Resources: http://www.apple.com/iphone/apps-for-iphone/
                                    http://iphoneapplicationlist.com/apps/business/
Software Development: http://www.mutualmobile.com/
                                    http://www.avenuesocial.com/mob-app.php#
Example:
https://itunes.apple.com/us/app/craft-crawler-local-brewery/id921822501?mt=8

Cash Mob

A gathering, similar to a flash mob, organized through social media, where a group meets near a small business and spends about $20 each. It is important to get together with the owner of the store and tell them about the mob's intentions to avoid all kinds of confusion by store owners and staff on the day the mob arrives. They are organized via social networking sites to support local, independent, small businesses. Chosen businesses have usually given back to the community in the past. Encourage others to participate in the cash mob by posting a message to the contact list on Facebook or Twitter. Create a Twitter handle just for the cash mob and place a "CM" in front of your city name to alert cash mobbers. You can also use Facebook to notify your list that a cash mob is coming up. Create an event and invite your entire contact list to participate. Talk with other local business and government organizations interested in helping the local community and getting the word out. Talk with city managers to secure the permits for the cash mob event. Distribute a press release to get plenty of exposure.

Forums

We will use the following types of foodie forums to get the word out about our microbrewery:

1.   http://chowhound.chow.com/boards
        Food-lovers worldwide gather here to swap and post expert tips about restaurants, foods, stores, and bars, as well as cooking, wine, beer, cookware, and more.
2.   http://www.dailycandy.com/all-cities/food-drink/
        A place to get the scoop on hot new RESTAURANTS, DESIGNERS, secret NOOKS, and charming DIVERSIONS in a favorite city.
        Ex: www.dailycandy.com/all-cities/article/21636/Kittichai-Restaurant-Opens

Transit Ads

According to the Metropolitan Transportation Authority, MTA subways, buses and railroads provide billions of trips each year to residents. Marketing our microbrewery in subway cars and on the walls of subway stations will be a great way to advertise our brews to a large, captive audience.

Tastings and Sampling

We will utilize sampling events, because research indicates that at product demonstrations, 51% of customers try products they normally would never try and 79% of the people who sampled a product bought it later when they perceived a need for it. We will offer free samples at local farmers' markets, food festivals and street fairs and distribute coupons. We will also send complimentary boxed lunches with our signature dishes to employees of targeted companies and local news, radio and TV reporters. We will also provide free menu items for radio call-in contests.

Meeting Place

We will set-up a private party room and offer to serve as a meeting place for local professional groups, such as SCORE and charitable organizations. This will help to convince customers that we appreciate their business, care about their community and expose more people to our location and brews.

Publish e-Book

Ebooks are electronic books which can be downloaded from any website or FTP site on the Internet. Ebooks are made using special software and can include a wide variety of media such as HTML, graphics, Flash animation and video. We will publish an e-book to establish our microbrewery expertise and reach people who are searching for ebooks on how to make better use our microbrewery products and/or services. Included in our ebook will be links back to our website, product or affiliate program. Because users will have permanent access to it, they will use our ebook again and again, constantly seeing a link or banner which directs them to our site. The real power behind ebook marketing will be the viral aspect of it and the free traffic it helps to build for our website. ebook directories include: www.e-booksdirectory.com/
            www.ebookfreeway.com/p-ebook-directory-list.html
            www.quantumseolabs.com/blog/seolinkbuilding/top-5-free-ebook-
                directories-subscribers/
Resource: www.free-ebooks.net/
Ex: www.washingtonpost.com/local/va-couple-creates-book-that-pairs-beer-with-
        food/2018/08/26/5c83bb52-2d59-11e4-be9e-60cc44c01e7f_story.html

e-books are available from the following sites:

Amazon.com	Createspace.com
Lulu.com	Kobobooks.com
BarnesandNoble.com	Scribd.com
AuthorHouse.com	www.e-junkie.com

Resource:
www.smartpassiveincome.com/ebooks-the-smart-way/

Business Card Exchanges

We will join our Chamber of Commerce or local retail merchants' association and volunteer to host a mixer or business card exchange at our store. We will take the opportunity to invite social and business groups to our facility to enjoy beer tastings, and market to local businesses that will be looking for employee and customer holiday gifts.

We will also build our email database by collecting the business cards of all attendees.

Storefront Banner Advertising

We will use banners as an affordable way to draw attention to our business. We will place one on the side or front of our building, or on a prominent building and have it point to ours. We will use colorful storefront banners with catchy phrases to grab the attention of local foot and vehicle traffic.

Resource: http://www.fastsigns.com/

Ex: "Beer, it's cheaper than gas. Drink, don't drive."
          "Free: Cooking with Beer Classes"

Hubpages.com

HubPages has easy-to-use publishing tools, a vibrant author community and underlying revenue-maximizing infrastructure. Hubbers (HubPages authors) earn money by publishing their Hubs (content-rich Internet pages) on topics they know and love and earn recognition among fellow Hubbers through the community-wide HubScore ranking system. The HubPages ecosystem provides a search-friendly infrastructure which drives traffic to Hubs from search engines such as Google and Yahoo and enables Hubbers to earn revenue from industry-standard advertising vehicles such as Google AdSense and the eBay and Amazon Affiliates program. All of this is provided free to Hubbers in an open online community.

Pinterest.com

The goal of this website is to connect everyone in the world through the 'things' they find interesting. They think that a favorite book, toy, or recipe can reveal a common link between two people. With millions of new pins added every week, Pinterest is connecting people all over the world based on shared tastes and interests. What's special about Pinterest is that the boards are all visual, which is a very important marketing plus. When users enter a URL, they select a picture from the site to pin to their board. People spend hours pinning their own content, and then finding content on other people's boards to "re-pin" to their own boards. We will use Pinterest for remote personal shopping appointments. When we have a customer with specific needs, we will create a board just for them with items we sell that would meet their needs, along with links to other tips and content. We will invite our customer to check out the board on Pinterest and let them know we created it just for them.

Resources:
www.copyblogger.com/pinterest-marketing/
www.shopify.com/infographics/pinterest
www.pinterest.com/entmagazine/retail-business/
www.pinterest.com/brettcarneiro/ecommerce/
www.pinterest.com/denniswortham/infographics-retail-online-shopping/
www.cio.com/article/3018852/e-commerce/how-to-use-pinterest-to-grow-your-
      business.html
Examples:
http://pinterest.com/fredak/breweries-i-ve-visited/

Pinterest usage recommendation include:

1. Conduct market research by showing photos of potential products or test launches,   asking the customer base for feedback.
2. Personalize the brand by showcasing style and what makes the brand different, highlighting new and exciting things through the use of imagery.
3. Add links from Pinterest photos to the company webstore, putting price banners on each photo and providing a link where users can buy the products directly.
1. Share high-quality pictures or property images and put links back to our blog/website.
2. Make Boards interesting with beer label photos.
3. Showcase beautiful pictures of homes listed and include a link back to our website or blog.
4. Focus on educating followers and sharing what they would like to see, like images from a label design company.
5. Ask happy clients to pin pictures of themselves in their favorite pub.
6. We will create a video and add a Call to Action in the description or use annotations, such as check my YouTube article, for the viewers to Pin videos or follow our Pins on Pinterest.
7. Encourage followers' engagement with a call to action, because 'likes', beer brewing questions, comments and 'repins' will help our pins get more authority and visibility.
8. Optimize descriptions with keywords that people might be looking for when searching Pinterest, as we can add as many hashtags as we want.
9. Be consistent by pinning regularly.
10. Let people know we are on Pinterest by adding "Pin it" and "follow" buttons to our blog and/or website.

Topix.com

Topix is the world's largest community news website. Users can read, talk about and edit the news on over 360,000 of our news pages. Topix is also a place for users to post their own news stories, or initiate a forum discussion or survey, as well as comment about stories they have seen on the Topix site. Each story and every Topix page comes with the ability to add your voice to the conversation.

Ex: www.topix.com/city/clinton-township-mi/2018/12/long-awaited-microbrewery-nears-opening

Ex: www.topix.com/forum/city/mountain-home-ar/T4AER5HDS0NVVENRC

Survey Marketing

We will conduct a door-to-door survey in our target area to illicit opinions to our proposed business. This will provide valuable feedback, lead to prospective clients and serve to introduce our microbrewery business, before we begin actual operations.

'Green' Marketing

We will target environmentally friendly customers to introduce new customers to our business and help spread the word about going "green". We will use the following 'green' marketing strategies to form an emotional bond with our customers:

1. We will use clearly labeled 'Recycled Paper' and Sustainable Packaging, such as receipts and storage containers.
2. We will use "green", non-toxic cleaning supplies.
3. We will install 'green' lighting and heating systems to be more eco-friendly.
4. We will use web-based Electronic Mail and Social Media instead of using paper advertisements.
5. We will find local suppliers to minimize the carbon footprint that it takes for deliveries.
6. We will use food products that are made with organic ingredients and supplies.
7. We will document our 'Green' Programs in our sales brochure and website.
8. We will be a Certified Energy Star Partner.
9. We will install new LED warehouse lighting, exit signs, and emergency signs.
10. We will install motion detectors in low-traffic areas both inside and outside of warehouses.
11. We will implement new electricity regulators on HVAC units and compressors to lower energy consumption.
12. We will mount highly supervised and highly respected recycling campaigns.
13. We will start a program for waste product to be converted into sustainable energy sources.
14. We will start new company-wide document shredding programs.
15. We will use of water-based paints during the finishing process to reduce V.O.C.'s to virtually zero.

Resource:
www.brewersassociation.org/best-practices/sustainability/sustainability-manuals/

Six breweries — Allagash Brewery, Brewery Vivant, Deschutes Brewery, Odell Brewing, Redhook and Widmer Brothers — boast that they use 100-percent renewable energy to meet their electricity needs. Sierra Nevada generates at least 50 percent of its energy with more than 10,000 on-site solar panels and hydrogen fuel cells. In fact, the array owned by the Chico, California-based brewery is one of the country's largest privately-owned photovoltaic systems.

Source: www.mintpressnews.com/craft-beer-industry-boldly-brews-with-sustainability-in-mind/203850/

USPS Every Door Direct Mail Program

Every Door Direct Mail from the U.S. Postal Service® is designed to reach every home, every address, every time at a very affordable delivery rate. Every business and resident living in the ____ zip code will receive an over-sized post card and coupon announcing the _____ (company name) grand opening 7-days before the grand opening:

Price – USPS Marketing Mail™ Flats up to 3.3 oz
EDDM Retail® USPS Marketing Flats $0.177 per piece
EDDM BMEU USPS Marketing Mail at $0.156 per piece

Resource:
https://www.usps.com/business/every-door-direct-mail.htm
https://eddm.usps.com/eddm/customer/routeSearch.action

ZoomInfo.com
Their vision is to be the sole provider of constantly verified information about companies and their employees, making our data indispensible — available anytime, anywhere and anyplace the customer needs it. Creates just-verified, detailed profiles of 65 million businesspeople and six million businesses. Makes data available through powerful tools for lead generation, prospecting and recruiting.
Examples:
http://www.zoominfo.com/c/Brooklyn-Brewery-Company/5669209

Zipslocal.com
Provides one of the most comprehensive ZIP Code-based local search services, allowing visitors to access information through our online business directories that cover all ZIP Codes in the United States. Interactive local yellow pages show listings and display relevant advertising through the medium of the Internet, making it easy for everyone to find local business information

BusinessVibes   www.businessvibes.com/about-businessvibes
A rapidly growing B2B networking platform for global trade professionals. BusinessVibes uses a social networking model for businesses to find and connect with international partner companies. With a network of over 5000+ trade associations, 20 million companies and 25,000+ business events across 100+ major industries and 175 countries, BusinessVibes is a decisive source to companies looking for international business partners, be they clients, suppliers, JV partners, or any other type of business contact.
Examples:
www.businessvibes.com/companyprofile/Brewerkz-Restaurant-And-Microbrewery

Product Cards
We will attach products cards to our products and displays, and hand them out to our sales reps, distributors and retailers. The product cards will describe how we make our craft beer. We will include information such as where we get our beer making inspiration, descriptions of our ingredients, and what distinguishes our craft beer line from mass produced beer. The cards will also feature the product brand name, contact information and our logo and slogan. We will also use a side of the card to solicit feedback and comments.

Brewery Tours
These _____ (Saturday?) morning and afternoon tours will give visitors an inside look at the brewery operation as well as the chance to ask questions and sample the beer. We will include the tour schedule on our Facebook page and website 'events calendar', and

enable people to sign-up for the tour. The tours will cost $_____ (5.00?) and customers will get a logo imprinted pint glass to take home and ____ (#) samples of beer along with the detailed tour. Our goal is to provide a tourist attraction for ale enthusiasts and real ale 'beginners' alike, with brewery tours and a brew day experience, and to help boost the local economy and to put _____ (city) 'on the map' in terms of real ale production.
Ex: http://gnarlybeer.com/visit.html

Sponsor Beer Recipe Contest
We will stimulate community interest in our local microbrewery by creating a festival for local home brewers to compete for a chance to have our microbrewery brew their award-winning recipe under a licensing agreement.

Google+
We will pay specific attention to Google+, which is already playing a more important role in Google's organic ranking algorithm. We will create a business page on Google+ to achieve improved local search visibility. Google+ will also be the best way to get access to Google Authorship, which will play a huge role in SEO.
Resources:
https://plus.google.com/pages/create
http://www.google.com/+/brands/
https://www.google.com/appserve/fb/forms/plusweekly/
https://plus.google.com/+GoogleBusiness/posts
http://marketingland.com/beyond-social-benefits-google-business-73460
Examples:
https://plus.google.com/+BreweryBeckerBrighton/posts

Inbound Marketing
Inbound marketing is about pulling people in by sharing relevant craft beer information, creating useful content, and generally being helpful. It involves writing everything from buyer's guides to blogs and newsletters that deliver useful content. The objective will be to nurture customers through the buying process with unbiased educational materials that turn consumers into informed buyers.
Resource:
www.Hubspot.com

Google My Business Profile   www.google.com/business/befound.html
We will have a complete and active Google My Business profile to give our microbrewery a tremendous advantage over the competition, and help potential customers easily find our company and provide relevant information about our business. This is a free listing that connects to Google Maps. It's the primary way that Google knows where our service area is located, so we can come up for local searches. We will optimize our descriptions with keywords and try to get customer reviews to increase our ranking.

Google My Business will let us:
- Manage business listing info for search, maps and Google+
- Upload photos and/or a virtual tour of our business
- Share content and interacting with followers on Google+
- See reviews from across the web and responding to Google+ reviews
- Integrate with AdWords Express to create and track campaigns
- Access Insights reports, the new social analytics tool for Google+
- See information about our integrated YouTube and Analytics accounts
- Resource:
- https://www.wordstream.com/blog/ws/2014/06/12/google-my-business

Sampling Program

We will give each sample craft beer with a mini-survey to enable customers to rate the product and supply constructive feedback.

Reddit.com

An online community where users vote on stories. The hottest stories rise to the top, while the cooler stories sink. Comments can be posted on every story, including stories about startup microbrewery companies.
Resources:
https://www.reddit.com/r/homebrewing
Examples:
https://www.reddit.com/r/beerreleases

Community Outreach

Example:
The spirit of inclusion that is supposed to mark the city's year-long party figures in the beer's marketing strategy, as 25 cents per every bottle sold is being donated to Promis, a Montreal-based organization that helps immigrants and refugees in Quebec.
Source:
http://montrealgazette.com/life/quebec-beer-labels-tap-into-politics-and-culture-chez-nous

Exterior Signage

We will make effective use of the following types of signage: (select)
1. **Channel Letter**
    Channel letters can be illuminated by LED or neon and come in a variety of colors and sizes. Front-lit signs are illuminated from the letter face, while reverse-lit signs are lit from behind the sign. Open-face channel letters lit by exposed neon work well to create a night presence.
2. **Monument Signs**
    Monument signs are usually placed at the entrance to a parking lot or a building. This sign can easily be installed on a median or lawn. The size for a monument

sign is typically based on city regulations for the specific location. These signs can be illuminated or non-illuminated, single- or double-sided.

3. **Pylon Signs**

   Also known as pole signs, they soar high above a business location to set the business apart from other businesses. They get attention from highway motorists who are still a distance away.

4. **Cabinet Signs**

   Commonly called "wall" or "box" signs, they are a traditional form of signage. They effectively use a large copy area and eye-popping graphics. This type of signage can highlight our business day or night because we have the option to add illumination. The background can be the element that lights up, and the copy can be lit or non-lit.

5. **Sandwich Signs**

   This sign will be placed on the sidewalk in front of our business to attract foot traffic.

6. **Vehicle Roof-top and Side-panel Signage**

6.4.1   Strategic Alliances

We will form strategic alliances to accomplish the following objectives:
1. To share marketing expenses.
2. To realize bulk buying power on wholesale purchases.
3. To engage in barter arrangements.
4. To collaborate with industry experts.
5. To set-up mutual referral relationships.

_____ (company name) will seek out opportunities to establish viable strategic alliances, such as co-marketing with gourmet food operations, beer and spirits distributors, importers, and producers. One such opportunity, is an alliance with an upscale gourmet food market. Packaging party catering and event food services with a complement of fine beers and spirits will help promote both businesses and provide an extra measure of service to our neighborhood customers. Coordinating gift baskets with beer orders in a single delivery package presents another compelling co-marketing opportunity. Information specific to pairing beers with food can be used to stimulate sales as well.

We will develop strategic alliances with the following service providers by conducting introductory 'cold calls' to their offices and making them aware of our capabilities by distributing our brochures and business cards:

1.	Party Supply Stores	2.	Pubs/Bars
3.	Dance Clubs	4.	Gourmet Food Stores
5.	Day Spas	6.	Boutiques
7.	Hotels	8.	Beauty Salons
9.	Nightclubs	10.	Bridal Centers

11.	Caterers	12.	Event Planners
13.	Corporate Offices	14.	Gift Basket Makers
15.	Cooking Schools	16.	Restaurants
17.	Casinos		

We will develop a program, complete with packing materials, that teaches businesses how to use our products as part of their employee rewards strategy.

We will assemble and present a sales presentation package that includes sales brochures, business cards, and a DVD presentation of basic party planning tips, and client testimonials. We will include coupons that offer a discount or other type of introductory deal. We will ask to set-up a take-one display for our sales brochures at the business registration counter.

We will promptly give the referring business any one or combination of the following agreed upon reward options:

1.	Referral fees	2.	Free services
3.	Mutual referral exchanges		

We will monitor referral sources to evaluate the mutual benefits of the alliance and make certain to clearly define and document our referral incentives prior to initiating our referral exchange program.

6.4.2   Monitoring Marketing Results

To monitor how well _____ (company name) is doing, we will measure how well the advertising campaign is working by taking customer surveys. What we would like to know is how they heard of us and how they like and dislike about our services. In order to get responses to the surveys, we will be give discounts as thank you rewards.

Response Tracking Methods
Coupons: ad-specific coupons that easily enable tracking
Landing Pages: unique web landing pages for each advertisement
800 Numbers: unique 1-800-# per advertisement
Email Service Provider: Instantly track email views, opens, and clicks
Address inclusion of dept # or suite #.

Our financial statements will offer excellent data to track all phases of sales. These are available for review on a daily basis. _____ (company name) will benchmark our objectives for sales promotion and advertising in order to evaluate our return on invested marketing dollars and determine where to concentrate our limited advertising dollars to realize the best return. We will also strive to stay within our marketing budget.

Key Marketing Metrics

We will use the following two marketing metrics to evaluate the cost-effectiveness of our marketing campaign:

1. The cost to acquire a new customer: The average dollar amount invested to get one new client. Example: If we invest $3,000 on marketing in a single month and end the month with 10 new customers, our cost of acquisition is $300 per new customer.
2. The lifetime value of the average active customer. The average dollar value of an average customer over the life of their business with you. To calculate this metric for a given period of time, we will take the total amount of revenue our business generated during the time period and divide it by the total number of customers we had from the beginning of the time period.
3. We will track the following set of statistics on a weekly basis to keep informed of the progress of our business:
    A. Number of total referrals.
    B. Percentage increase of total referrals (over baseline).
    C. Number of new referral sources.
    D. Number of new customers/month.
    E. Number of Leads

Key Marketing Metrics Table

We've listed some key metrics in the following table. We will need to keep a close eye on these, to see if we meet our own forecasted expectations. If our numbers are off in too many categories, we may, after proper analysis, have to make substantial changes to our marketing efforts.

Key Marketing Metrics	2018	2019	2020
Revenue			
Leads			
Leads Converted			
Avg. Transaction per Customer			
Avg. Dollars per Customer			
Number of Referrals			
Number of PR Appearances			
Number of Testimonials			
Number of New Club Members			
Number of Returns			
Number of BBB Complaints			
Number of Completed Surveys			
Number of blog readers			
Number of Twitter followers			
Number of Facebook Fans			

Metric Definitions

1. Leads: Individuals who step into the store to consider a purchase.
2. Leads Converted: Percent of individuals who actually make a purchase.
3. Average Transactions Per Customer: Number of purchases per customer per

month. Expected to rise significantly as customers return for more and more
_____ items per month

4. Average $ Per Customer: Average dollar amount of each transaction. Expected to rise along with average transactions.

5. Referrals: Includes customer and business referrals

6. PR Appearances: Online or print mentions of the business that are not paid advertising. Expected to be high upon opening, then drop off and rise again until achieving a steady level.

7. Testimonials: Will be sought from the best and most loyal customers. Our objective is ___ (#) per month) and they will be added to the website. Some will be sought as video testimonials.

8. New Loyalty Club Members: This number will rise significantly as more customers see the value in repeated visits and the benefits of club membership.

9. Number of Returns/BBB Complaints: Our goal is zero.

10. Number of Completed Surveys: We will provide incentives for customers to complete customer satisfaction surveys.

6.4.3   Word-of-Mouth Marketing

We plan to make use of the following techniques to promote word-of-mouth advertising:

1. Repetitive Image Advertising
2. Provide exceptional customer service.
3. Make effective use of loss leaders.
2. Schedule in-microbrewery activities, such as demonstrations or special events.
3. Make trial easy with a coupon or introductory discount.
4. Initiate web and magazine article submissions
5. Utilize a sampling program
6. Add a forward email feature to our website.
7. Share relevant and believable testimonial letters
8. Publish staff bios.
9. Make product/service upgrade announcements
10. Hold contests or sweepstakes
12. Have involvement with community events.
13. Pay suggestion box rewards
14. Distribute a monthly newsletter
15. Share easy-to-understand information (via an article or seminar).
16. Make personalized marketing communications.
17. Structure our referral program.
18. Sharing of Community Commonalities
19. Invitations to join our community of shared interests.
20. Publish Uncensored Customer Reviews
21. Enable Information Exchange Forums
22. Provide meaningful comparisons with competitors.
23. Clearly state our user benefits.

24. Make and honor ironclad guarantees
25. Provide superior post-sale support
26. Provide support in the pre-sale decision making process.
27. Host Free Informational Seminars or Workshops
28. Get involved with local business organizations.
29. Issue Press Release coverage of charitable involvements.
30. Hold traveling company demonstrations/exhibitions/competitions.

6.4.4   Customer Satisfaction Survey

We will design a customer satisfaction survey to measure the "satisfaction quotient" of our Microbrewery customers. By providing a detailed snapshot of our current customer base, we will be able to generate more repeat and referral business and enhance the profitability of our craft beer company.

Our Customer Satisfaction Survey will include the following basics:
1. How do our customers rate our microbrewery business?
2. How do our customers rate our competition?
3. How well do our customers rate the value of our products or services?
4. What new customer needs and trends are emerging?
5. How loyal are our customers?
6. What can be done to improve customer loyalty and repeat business?
7. How strongly do our customers recommend our business?
8. What is the best way to market our business?
9. What new value-added services would best differentiate our business from that of our competitors?
10. How can we encourage more referral business?
11. How can our pricing strategy be improved?

Our customer satisfaction survey will help to answer these questions and more. From the need for continual new products and services to improved customer service, our satisfaction surveys will allow our business to quickly identify problematic and underperforming areas, while enhancing our overall customer satisfaction.

Examples:
https://www.surveymonkey.com/blog/2014/05/01/what-kind-beer-people-like/
http://blog.surveymethods.com/customer-satisfaction-surveys-in-the-alcohol-industry/
http://www.barnstormerbrewing.com/survey

Resources:
https://www.survata.com/
https://www.google.com/insights/consumersurveys/use_cases
www.surveymonkey.com
http://www.smetoolkit.org/smetoolkit/en/content/en/6708/Customer-Satisfaction-Survey-
    Template-
http://smallbusiness.chron.com/common-questions-customer-service-survey-1121.html

Because consumer reviews are integral to the craft beer experience and since our craft brewery will be constantly experimenting and coming up with new recipes, the cycle of seeking consumer reviews will never stop. Consequently, we will develop and package a Sampler Pack in the spring or summer. This program will provide:

- The opportunity for consumers to try smaller batch brews that have previously had limited or no distribution outside of _____;
- A prompt to send direct feedback on the beer styles via our website or attached comment card.

Survey Results:
New research by Mintel revealed some insight into craft beer drinkers:
- 55% are willing to spend more money for craft beer
- 51% indicated the beer style was most important in their product selection: (IPA, wheat, stout, etc.)
- 47% say brand is not a factor in their choice (compared to 56% of non-craft drinkers)
- 13% select craft beer with packaging that "looks cool" when their brand of choice is unavailable
- 53% enjoy sharing information of craft beers with others
- Millennials aged 25-34 years old consume the most craft beers – and 70% believe that the brand of beer says a lot about them.

6.4.5   Marketing Training Program

Our Marketing Training Program will include both an initial orientation and training, as well as ongoing continuing education classes. Initial orientation will be run by the owner until an HR manager is hired. For one week, half of each day will be spent in training, and the other half shadowing the store's operation manager.

Training will include:
Learning the entire selection of microbrewery products and services.
Understanding our Mission Statement, Value Proposition, Position Statement and Unique Selling Proposition.
Appreciating our competitive advantages.
Understanding our core message and branding approach.
Learning our store's policies; returns processing, complaint handling, etc.
Learning our customer services standards of practice.
Learning our customer and business referral programs.
Learning our Membership Club procedures, rules and benefits.
Becoming familiar with our company website, and online ordering options.
Service procedures specific to the employee's role.

Ongoing workshops will be based on customer feedback and problem areas identified by mystery buyers, which will better train employees to educate customers. These ongoing workshops will be held _____ (once?) a month for _____ (three?) hours.

6.5   Sales Strategy

_____ (company name) Microbrews will be available in bars as well as retail outlets, such as local markets and corner stores. It will also aim to distribute through supermarkets, but it is envisioned that getting shelf space in national supermarkets will be more difficult and more expensive.

The development of our sales strategy will start by developing a better understanding of our customer needs. To accomplish this task, we will pursue the following research methods:
1.   Join the associations that our target customers belong to.
2.   Contact the membership director and establish a relationship to understand their member's needs, challenges and concerns.
3.   Identify non-competitive suppliers who sell to our customer to learn their challenges and look for partnering solutions.
4.   Work directly with our customer and ask them what their needs are and if our business may offer a possible solution.

The management of our microbrewery will focus on daily sales revenue goals and explaining any variances. Best value products will be identified to assist customers with smart purchase selections. Deliveries will be geared to the customer's convenience. The situation will be monitored to ensure that the company invests adequately in its own delivery operations.

Sales feedback will be elicited to stimulate ideas, approaches, relate success stories, instruct in new techniques, share news, and implement improvements. Major accounts will be solicited through networking, neighborhood solicitations via sales agents, and opportunistic encounters at any time by management. We will also make a point of getting out the grains and hops and other ingredients that go into the beer to explain how it is made and how the different ingredients can affect the taste.

_____ (company name) will keep its beverage prices competitive with other microbreweries in a ___ (#) mile radius of our microbrewery in order to attract commuters. Customers that purchase more than $___ (100) worth of product will be given ___ (10)% coupon on future purchases.

We will become a one-stop shop for beer and cheese catering services, and specialized program offerings. We will also be very active in the community, building a solid reputation with professionals and community leaders.

Our clients will be primarily obtained through word-of-mouth referrals, but we will also advertise introductory offers to introduce people to our frequent buyer and preferred club membership programs. The combination of the perception of higher quality, exceptional purchase guidance, innovative service and the recognition of superior value should turn referral leads into satisfied customers.

The company's sales strategy will be based on the following elements:
> Advertising in the Yellow Pages - two inch by three-inch ads describing our services will be placed in the local Yellow Pages.
> Placing classified advertisements in the regional editions of gourmet magazines.
> Word of mouth referrals - generating sales leads in the local community through customer referrals.

Our basic sales strategy is to:
> Develop a website for lead generation by _____ (date).
> Provide exceptional customer service.
> Accept payment by all major credit cards, cash, PayPal and check.
> Survey our customers regarding products and services they would like to see added.
> Sponsor charitable and other community events.
> Provide tours of the microbrewery so customers can learn how to become discriminating customers and build a trust bond with our operations.
> Motivate employees with a pay-for-performance component to their straight salary compensation package, based on profits and customer satisfaction rates.
> Build long-term customer relationships by putting the interests of customers first.
> Establish mutually beneficial relationship with local businesses serving the entertainment and socializing needs of local residents.

6.5.1   Customer Retention Strategy

We will use the following post-purchase techniques to improve customer retention, foster referrals and improve the profitability of our business:
1.   Keep the microbrewery sparkling clean and well-organized.
2.   Use only well-trained sales associates.
3.   Actively solicit customer feedback and promptly act upon their inputs.
4.   Tell customers how much you appreciate their business.
5.   Call regular customers by their first names.
6.   Send thank you notes.
7.   Offer free new product samples.
8.   Change displays and sales presentations on a regular basis.
9.   Practice good phone etiquette
10.   Respond to complaints promptly.
11.   Reward referrals.
12.   Publish a monthly opt-in direct response newsletter with customized content, dependent on recipient stated information preferences.

13.   Develop and publish a list of frequently asked questions.
14.   Issue Preferred Customer Membership Cards.
15.   Hold informational seminars and workshops.
16.   Provide an emergency hotline number.
17.   Publish code of ethics and our service guarantees.
18.   Help customers to make accurate competitor comparisons.
19.   Build a stay-in-touch (drip marketing) communications calendar.
20.   Keep marketing communications focused on our competitive advantages.
21.   Offer repeat user discounts and incentives.
22.   Be supportive and encouraging, and not judgmental.
23.   Measure customer retention and look at recurring revenue and customer surveys.
24.   Build a community of shared interests by offering a website forum or discussion group for professionals and patients to allow sharing of knowledge.
25.   Offer benefits above and beyond those of our competitors.
26.   Issue reminder emails and holiday gift cards.

We will also consider the following Customer Retention Programs:

Type of Program	Customer Rewards
Frequency Purchase Loyalty Program	Special Discounts
	Free Product or Services
'Best Customer' Program	Special Recognition/Treatment/Offers
Affinity Programs	Sharing of Common Interests
	Accumulate Credit Card Points
Customer Community Programs	Special Event Participation
Auto-Knowledge Building Programs	Purchase Recommendations based On Past Transaction History
Profile Building Programs	Recommendations Based on Stated Customer Profile Information.

6.5.2   Sales Forecast

Our sales projections are based on the following:
1.   Actual sales volumes of local competitors
2.   Interviews with Microbrewery owners and managers
3.   Observations of microbrewery sales and traffic at competitor establishments.
4.   Government and industry trade statistics
5.   Local population demographics and projections.

Regarding beer revenue potential, we are forecasting average sales of ___ bottles per capita per year for residents of _____, and an average retail price of $___ per bottle. Trade statistics show that, on a national basis, 10% of the population is responsible for 90% of alcoholic beverage consumption. The average _____ (community name) customer, representing ___ (10)% of the _____ (community name) population, therefore, would be expected to purchase ____ (#) bottles of beer per week from our microbrewery. With _____ (community name) growing from a base of ____ (#) to

_____ (#) residents, we see beer revenue potential from these residents in a range of $_____ to $_____ over the course of the next _____ (#) years.

The balance of our forecasted beer sales, representing some _____ (20)% of total beer sales, will come from sources external to _____ (community name), including catering services, corporate accounts, deliveries to consumers outside _____ (community name), and visitors to the _____ complex of residences, stores, and recreational sites in the city of _____ .

Our sales forecast is an estimated projection of expected sales over the next three years, based on our chosen marketing strategy, economic conditions and assumed competitive environment. _____ (company name) will focus on increasing brewpub food sales in order to meet total sales forecast goals.

Sales are expected to be below average during the first year, until a regular customer base has been established. It has been estimated that it takes the average Microbrewery a minimum of two years to establish a significant customer base. After the customer base is built, sales will grow at an accelerated rate from word-of-mouth referrals and continued networking efforts. We expect sales to steadily increase as our marketing campaign, employee training programs and contact management system are executed. By using advertising, especially discounted introductory coupons, as a catalyst for this prolonged process, _____(company name) plans to attract more customers sooner. Throughout the first year, it is forecasted that sales will incrementally grow until profitability is reached toward the end of year ___(one?). Year two reflects a conservative growth rate of_____ (20?) percent. Year three reflects a growth rate of _____ (25?) percent. We expect to be open for business on _____ (date), and start with an initial enrollment of _____ (#) patients. With our unique product and service offerings, along with our thorough and aggressive marketing strategies, we believe that sales forecasts are actually on the conservative side.

Table: Sales Forecast

	Annual Sales		
Sales	**2018**	**2019**	**2020**
Microbrews			
Logo Product Sales			
Party Supplies			
Gift Merchandise			
Gift Baskets			
Catering Services			
Consulting/Seminars			
Food Sales			
Misc.			
Total Unit Sales			
Direct Cost of Sales:			
Microbrews			
Logo Product Sales			
Party Supplies			
Gift Merchandise			

Gift Baskets	_____
Catering Services	_____
Consulting/Seminars	_____
Food Sales	_____
Misc.	_____
Subtotal Direct Cost of Sales	_____

6.6 Merchandising Strategy

Merchandising is that part of our marketing strategy that is involved with promoting the sales of our merchandise, as by consideration of the most effective means of selecting, pricing, displaying, and advertising items for sale in our convenience microbrewery business.
Through proper product placement, space allocation, and in-microbrewery promotion, sales space will be geared towards high profit margin products.

To be successful, our retail area must be impressive and compelling. It must have sufficient space, excellent inventory and beautiful display furnishings.
We will develop a merchandising strategy around the following design principles:

1. We will strive to feature merchandise that is not found in competitor stores.
2. Use proper and informative signage to help sell merchandise.
3. We plan to group similar types of merchandise together for maximum visual appeal.
4. Product presentation will be designed to lead the customers through the entire display area.
5. We will designate a specific in-microbrewery location for new product introductions.
6. We will reduce the clutter to increase customer convenience.
7. We will set up of special displays to coincide with a specific event, also known as occasion management.
8. Adjustable shelving will give us the ability to vary the depth of each individual shelf and adjust it to allow more light to fall toward the bottom.
9. We will cluster the best beers into approachable groupings.
10. We will use beer/food pairing charts and flyers to make people more comfortable with their beer selections and realize the power of suggestive selling.
11. We will make available beer publication ratings, because an educated consumer is our best customer.
12. We will prominently feature beer club specials to encourage membership.
13. We will use bottle neckers to identify items featured at beer tastings or club events.
14. We will allocate our best microbrewery real estate to a chilled beer cooler to facilitate impulse sales.
15. We will set-up a permanent booth within the microbrewery to conduct regular beer tasting events and beer club sign-ups.

The décor of the merchandising area is extremely important to sales. Display units are primary, but lighting, furniture, wall surfaces, window treatments, carpeting, accessories and countertops will all play important supporting roles. We will monitor our sales figures and data to confirm that products in demand are well-stocked and slow-moving products are phased-out. We will improve telephone skills of employees to boost phone orders.

6.7 Pricing Strategy

When setting prices, we will consider the following factors:
1.   Direct Costs: labor, time and supplies
2.   Indirect Costs: rent, utilities, taxes and expenses.
3.   Demand: economic conditions, demographics, consumer behavior, etc.
4.   Marketing Promotions
5.   Level of Competition
6.   Positioning Image
7.   Goals: profit objectives, return on investment, growth objectives.

Each of our products will have a different price; all will be similar but not the same. Our heavier and darker beers will cost more mainly because they cost us more to make. On the other hand, our seasonal and light beer may cost a little less because we want to get a lot of sales from these products, mainly the seasonal brews, while they are on the market to keep customer loyalty and interest at high level. Our midrange beers, which will consist of the wheat and brown ale, will be the median between our porter and our light beer. All of our beers will still remain at a high status and there will not even be a very big price discrepancy between the individual products, but we feel that there must be some difference in price from one beer to the next. We will also want to be very competitive, price wise, with the other microbreweries throughout _____ (city).

Product pricing will be based on competitive parity guidelines. Prices will be consistent with those of the retail stores in our area, with the exception of very high-volume operations who have more powerful pricing leverage. Pricing will be monitored continuously against neighborhood and other competitive sources who we can readily research. Our plan is to discount thematically, that is, tied to an event theme.

Our pricing strategy will take into view the following factors: (State Dependent)
1.   The brewer's price to the Board.
2.   Federal taxes: excise tax on all liquor & custom duty rates on imported liquor.
3.   Freight costs: From the suppliers to the Distribution Center and to the stores.
4.   Mark-up: As established by the State Board.
5.   State sales and liter taxes as established by the State Legislature.

We are not interested in being the low-price leader, as our pricing strategy plays a major role in whether we will be able to create and maintain customers for a profit. Our revenue structure must support our cost structure, so the salaries we pay to our staff are balanced by the revenue we collect.

The number of competitors in the area largely determines what type of pricing we will have. We don't want to be known as the highest price place in town, but it is equally important not to be the cheapest.

Profit margins will depend on the competition and how well we buy. In our particular area, we will aim for ____ (25)% profit margin on craft beer. We will pick some well-known items and make them cheap. People know these high-profile items and will think our microbrewery is pricy or cheap based on a few items. On lesser known ales we will be able to get away with charging a higher price because people don't necessarily know what the item should cost.

We will continuously try to expand our selection. If a customer asks for something that we don't have, we will write it down and work to get it for them. Friendliness, product knowledge and convenience are what will keep people coming to our Microbrewery.

Pricing Strategies
We will consider the following basic pricing strategies:
Quantity Discounts: Bulk purchase breaks to increase sales volume.
Bundling Discounts: Additive deal sweetners to differentiate product offering.
Version Pricing: Degree of functionality pricing, from Basic to Premium
Loss Leaders   Attract first-time customer deals
Competitive Pricing   Reference point for product positioning.

Price List Comparison

Competitor	Service/Product	Our Price	Competitor Price	B/(W) Competitor

We will adopt the following pricing guidelines:
1. We must insure that our price plus service equation is perceived to be an exceptional value proposition.
2. We must refrain from competing on price, but always be price competitive.
3. We must develop value-added services, and bundle those with our products to create offerings that cannot be easily price compared.
4. We must focus attention on our competitive advantages.
5. Development of a pricing strategy based on our market positioning strategy, which is ____ (mass market value leadership/exceptional premium niche value?)
6. Our pricing policy objective, which is to _____ (increase profit margins/   achieve revenue maximization to increase market share/lower unit costs).
7. We will use marketplace intelligence and gain insights from competitor pricing.

8.   We will solicit pricing feedback from customers using surveys and interviews.
9.   We will utilize limited time pricing incentives to penetrate niche markets
10.   We will conduct experiments at prices above and below the current price to determine the price elasticity of demand. (Inelastic demand or demand that does not decrease with a price increase, indicates that price increases may be feasible.)
11.   We will keep our offerings and prices simple to understand and competitive, based on market intelligence.
12.   We will consider a price for volume strategy on certain items and study the effects of price on volume and of volume on costs, as in a recession, trying to recover these costs through a price increase can be fatal.
13.   All prices must cover costs.
14.   The best and most effective way of lowering our sales prices is to lower costs.
15.   Our prices must reflect the dynamics of cost, demand, changes in the market, and response to our competition.
16.   Prices must be established to assure sales.
17.   We will not price against a competitive operation alone, but rather, price to sell.
18.   Product utility, longevity, maintenance, and end use must be judged continually, and target prices adjusted accordingly.
19.   Prices must be set to preserve order in the marketplace.

Determining the costs of servicing business is the most important part of covering our expenses and earning profits. We will factor in the following pricing formula: Product Cost + Materials + Overhead + Labor + Profit + Tax = Price
Materials are those items consumed in the delivering of the service.
Overhead costs are the variable and fixed expenses that must be covered to stay in business. Variable costs are those expenses that fluctuate including vehicle expenses, rental expenses, utility bills and supplies. Fixed costs include the purchase of equipment, service ware, marketing and advertising, and insurance. After overhead costs are determined, the total overhead costs are divided among the total number of transactions forecasted for the year.
Labor costs include the costs of performing the services. Also included are Social Security taxes (FICA), vacation time, retirement and other benefits such as health or life insurance. To determine labor costs per hour, keep a time log. When placing a value on our time, we will consider the following: 1) skill and reputation; 2) wages paid by employers for similar skills and 3) where we live. Other pricing factors include image, inflation, supply and demand, and competition.
Profit is a desired percentage added to our total costs. We will need to determine the percentage of profit added to each service. It will be important to cover all our costs to stay in business. We will investigate available computer software programs to help us price our services and keep financial data for decision-making purposes. Close contact with customers will allow our company to react quickly to changes in demand.

We will develop a pricing strategy that will reinforce the perception of value to the customer and manage profitability, especially in the face of rising inflation. To ensure our success, we will use periodic competitor and customer research to continuously evaluate our pricing strategy. We intend to review our profit margins every six months.

6.8 Differentiation Strategies

We will use differentiation strategies to develop and market unique products for different customer segments. To differentiate ourselves from the competition, we will focus on the assets, creative ideas and competencies that we have that none of our competitors has. The goal of our differentiation strategies is to be able to charge a premium price for our unique products and services and/or to promote loyalty and assist in retaining our customers.

We intend to use many innovative and clever ideas, such as, offering one of the first light and organic microbrews and introducing four seasonal beers to be rotated in and out of the market, to set our brewery above the rest and to generate a significant profit.

Differentiation in our microbrewery business will be achieved in the following types of ways, including:

Explanation

☐ Product features _____
☐ Complementary services _____
☐ Technology embodied in design _____
☐ Location _____
☐ Service innovations _____
☐ Superior service _____
☐ Creative advertising _____
☐ Better supplier relationships _____

Source:
http://scholarship.sha.cornell.edu/cgi/viewcontent.cgi?article=1295&context=articles

Differentiating will mean defining who our perfect target market is and then catering to their needs, wants and interests better than everyone else. It will be about using surveys to determine what's most important to our targeted market and giving it to them consistently. It will not be about being "everything to everybody"; but rather, "the absolute best to our chosen targeted group".

In developing our differentiation strategy will we use the following form to help define our differences:

1. Targeted customer segments _____
2. Customer characteristics _____
3. Customer demographics _____
4. Customer behavior _____
5. Geographic focus _____
6. Ways of working _____
7. Service delivery approach _____
8. Customer problems/pain points _____
9. Complexity of customers' problems _____
10. Range of services _____

We will use the following approaches to differentiate our products and services from those of our competitors to stand apart from standardised offerings:
1. Superior quality
2. Unusual or unique product features
3. More responsive customer service
4. Rapid product or service innovation
5. Advanced technological features
6. Engineering design or styling
7. Additional product features
8. An image of prestige or status

Specific Differentiators will include the following:
1. Being a Specialist in one procedure
2. Utilizing advanced/uncommon technology
3. Possessing extensive experience
4. Building an exceptional facility
5. Consistently achieving superior results
6. Having a caring and empathetic personality
7. Giving customer s WOW experience, including a professional customer welcome package.
8. Enabling convenience and 24/7 online accessibility
9. Calling customers to express interest in their challenges.
10. Keeping to the appointment schedule.
11. Remembering customer names and details like they were family
12. Assuring customer fears.
13. Building a visible reputation and recognition around our community
14. Acquiring special credentials or professional memberships
15. Providing added value services, such as taxi service, longer hours, financing plans, and post-sale services.

Primary Differentiation Strategies:
1. We will utilize software systems that will enable us to personalize each customer's buying experience, including easy access to customer transaction history, preference profile and information about all the products of interest to that client.
2. Wide aisles and the open floor design will make it easier not only to navigate the many offerings, but to see them from afar, a feature that will speed up service for customers looking to get in and out quickly.
4. We will offer a comfortable seating area for beer tasting events (if permitted?).
6. We will enable the online and fax ordering of our products and services.
7. We will offer private labeling services to certain wholesalers.
8. We will build an extensive profile on customers to capture information about their lifestyle, taste preferences and key occasion reminder dates.
9. We will develop a referral program that turns our clients into referral agents.
10. We will use regular client satisfaction surveys to collect feedback, improvement

ideas, referrals and testimonials.

11. We will promote our "green" practices, such as establishing a recycling program, purchasing recycled-content office goods and responsibly handling hazardous wastes.

12. We will customize our craft beers according to the language, cultural influences, customs, interests and taste preferences of our local market to create loyalty and increase sales.

13. We will develop the expertise to satisfy the needs of targeted market segments with customized and exceptional support services.

14. We will offer the first 'light' microbrews and four seasonal beers to be rotated in and out of the market to set our brewery above the rest.

6.9 Milestones   (select)

The Milestones Chart is a timeline that will guide our company in developing and growing our business. It will list chronologically the various critical actions and events that must occur to bring our business to life. We will make certain to assign real, attainable dates to each planned action or event.

_____ (company name) has identified several specific milestones which will function as goals for the company. The milestones will provide a target for achievement as well as a mechanism for tracking progress. The dates were chosen based on realistic delivery times and necessary construction times. All critical path milestones will be completed within their allotted time frames to ensure the success of contingent milestones. The following table will provide a timeframe for each milestone.

Table: Milestones

Milestones	Start Date	End Date	Budget	Responsibility
Business Plan Completion				
Secure Permits/Licenses				
Locate & Secure Space				
Obtain Insurance Coverage				
Secure Additional Financing				
Get Start-up Supplies Quotes				
Obtain County Certification				
Purchase Office Equipment				
Renovate Facilities				
Define Marketing Programs				
Install Equipment/Displays				
Technology Systems				
Set-up Accounting System				
Develop Office Policies				
Develop Procedures Manual				
Arrange Support Service Providers				

Finalize Media Plan _____

Create Facebook Brand Page _____

Open Twitter Account _____

Conduct Blogger Outreach _____

Develop Personnel Plan _____

Develop Staff Training Programs _____

Hire/Train Staff _____

Implement Marketing Plan _____

Get Website Live _____

Conduct SEO _____

Form Strategic Alliances _____

Purchase Start-up Inventory/Supplies _____

Press Release Announcements _____

Advertise Grand Opening _____

Kickoff Advertising Program _____

Join Community Orgs./Network _____

Conduct Satisfaction Surveys _____

Evaluate/Revise Plan _____

Devise Growth Strategy _____

Monitor Social Media Networks _____

Respond to Reviews _____

Measure Return on Marketing $$$ _____

Revenues Exceed $_____ _____

Reach Profitability _____

Totals: _____

7.0 Website Plan Summary

_____ (company name) is currently developing a website at the URL address www. (company name).com. We will primarily use the website to promote an understanding of the craft beers we offer by posting helpful articles, circulating information about coming events and to enable online product ordering. Supplying the visitors to our websites with this information will make a huge difference in turning our website visitors into new customers. Note: Make certain that by law you are permitted to ship alcoholic beverages to other states.

The website will be developed to offer customers a product catalog for online orders. The overriding design philosophy of the site will be ease of use. We want to make the process of placing an order as easy and fast as possible thereby encouraging increased sales. We will incorporate special features such as a section that is specific to each customer, so the customer can easily make purchases of repeat items. Instead of going through the website every month and locating their monthly needs, the site will capture regularly ordered items for that specific customer, significantly speeding up the ordering process. This ease-of-use feature will help increase sales as customers become more and more familiar with the site and appreciate how easy it is to place an order.

We will also provide multiple incentives to sign-up for various benefits, such as our newsletters and promotional sale notices. This will help us to build an email database, which will supply our automated customer follow-up system. We will create a personalized drip marketing campaign to stay in touch with our customers and prospects.

We will develop our website to be a resource for web visitors who are seeking knowledge and information about craft beers, with a goal to service the knowledge needs of our customers and generate leads. Our home page will be designed to be a "welcome mat" that clearly presents our service offerings and provides links through which visitors can gain easy access to the information they seek. We will use our website to match the problems our customers face with the solutions we offer.

We will use the free tool, Google Analytics (http://www.google.com/analytics), to generate a history and measure our return on investment.

To improve the readability of our website, we will organize our website content in the following ways.

1. Headlines
2. Bullet points
3. Callout text
4. Top of page summaries

To improve search engine optimization, we will maximize the utilization of the following;

1. Links
2. Headers
3. Bold text
4. Bullets
5. Keywords
6. Meta tags

This website will serve the following purposes:

About Us — How We Work/Our Philosophy
Contact Us — Customer service contact info
Our Beer Quiz — See below
Our Services — Event Planning Services/Consulting
Our Brewpub — Menu/Specials/Sample Program
Our Product Catalog — Online Ordering/Shopping Cart
— Logo Imprinted Items
Our Distribution Network — Find Our Beer
Gift Baskets — Gourmet Foods/beers
Buy Gift Certificates — Order Form/Manage Account
New Arrivals — New Releases/Pre-Sales
Food/Beer Pairings — Articles
Frequently Asked Questions — FAQs
Club Membership — Sign-up
Newsletter Sign-up — Join Mailing List
Newsletter Archives — Foot Care Articles
Upcoming Events — Beer Tasting Schedule
What's New — Beer Festival Participation
Cooking with Beer — Recipes
Customer Testimonials — Letters w/photos
Referral Program — Details
Directions — Location directions.
Customer Satisfaction Survey — Feedback
Hours of Operation
Press Releases — Community Involvement
Strategic Alliance Partners — Links
Resources — Professional Associations
Our Blog — Center diary/Accept comments
Refer-a-Friend — Viral marketing
YouTube Video Clips — Seminar Presentation/Testimonials
Guarantees
Code of Ethics
Career Opportunities
Classified Ads

Classified Ads

By joining and incorporating a classified ad affiliate program into our website, we will create the ultimate win-win-win. We will provide our guests with a free benefit, increase our rankings with the search engines by incorporating keyword hyperlinks into our site, attract additional markets to expose to our product, create an additional income source as they upgrade their ads, and provide our prospects a reason to return to our web site again and again.

Resources:

    App Themes   www.appthemes.com/themes/classipress/
    e-Classifieds   http://www.e-classifieds.net/

Noah's Classifieds   http://www.noahsclassifieds.org/
Joom Prod   http://www.joomprod.com/

Beer Quiz
We will post a 'Beer Quiz' on our website so that we can continually ascertain how our customers choose the beers that they purchase and what they want or are looking for. We will seek responses to the following types of selection criteria: taste profile, price, style of beer, brand name, bottles vs. cans, alcohol content, packaging size, label design, production location/distance, food pairing capabilities, etc.
Resource:
https://www.surveymonkey.com/curiosity/what-kind-beer-people-like/

7.1   Website Marketing Strategy

Our online marketing strategy will employ the following distinct mechanisms:

1.   Search Engine Submission
     This will be most useful to people who are unfamiliar with _____ (company name) but are looking for a local Microbrewery. There will also be searches from customers who may know about us, but who are seeking additional information.

     Search Engine Optimization (SEO)
     SEO is a very important digital marketing strategy because search engines are the primary method of finding information for most internet users. SEO is simply the practice of improving and promoting a website in order to increase the number of visitors a site receives from search engines. Basic SEO techniques will range from the naming of webpages to the way that other websites link to our website. We will also need to get our business listed on as many relevant online directories as possible, such as Google, Yelp, Kudzu and Yahoo Local, write a blog that solicit comments and be active on social media sites.
     We will also try to incorporate local terms potential clients would use, such as "_____ (city) microbrewery" or "craft beer manufacturer". This will make it more likely that local customers will find us close to the top of their search.
     Resource;
     https://www.semrush.com/
     www.officerreports.com/blog/wp-content/uploads/2014/11/SEOmoz-The-
          Beginners-Guide-To-SEO-2012.pdf

2.   Website Address (URL) on Marketing Materials
     Our URL will be printed on all marketing communications, business cards, letterheads, faxes, and invoices and product labels. This will encourage a visit to our website for additional information

3.   Online Directories Listings
     We will list our website on relevant, free and paid online directories and

manufacturer website product locators.

The good online directories possess the following features:

Free or paid listings that do not expire and do not require monthly renewal.

Ample space to get your advertising message across.

Navigation buttons that are easy for visitors to use.

Optimization for top placement in the search engines based on keywords that people typically use to find Microbreweries.

Direct links to your website, if available.

An ongoing directory promotion campaign to maintain high traffic volumes to the directory site.

4. Strategic Business Partners

We will use a Business Partners page to cross-link to prominent _____ (city) area dance web sites as well as the city Web sites and local recreational sites. We will also cross-link with brand name suppliers.

5.   YouTube Posting

We will produce a video of testimonials from several of our satisfied clients and educate viewers as to the range of our services and products. Our research indicates that the YouTube video will also serve to significantly improve our ranking with the Google Search Engine.

6.   Exchange of links with strategic marketing partners.

We will cross-link to non-profit businesses that accept our gift certificate donations as in-house run contest prize awards.

7.   E-Newsletter

Use the newsletter sign-up as a reason to collect email addresses and limited profiles and use embedded links in the newsletter to return readers to website.

8.   Create an account for your photos on flickr.com

Use the name of your site on flickr so you have the same keywords. To take full advantage of Flickr, we will use a JavaScript-enabled browser and install the latest version of the Macromedia Flash Player.

9.   Geo Target Pay Per Click (PPC) Campaign

Available through Google Adwords program. Example keywords include beer, Microbrewery, craft beer, beer tastings, brewpub, seasonal beers and _____ (city).

10.   Post messages on Internet user groups and forums.

Get involved with Microbrewery related discussion groups and forums and develop a descriptive signature paragraph.

Resources: www.reference.com   www.deja.com   www.tracerlock.com
www.microbrewforum.com/

www.probrewer.com/vbulletin/showthread.php?t=4111
http://forums.morebeer.com/

11. Write up your own LinkedIn.com and Facebook.com profiles.
     Highlight your background and professional interests.

12. Facebook.com Brand-Building Applications:
     As a Facebook member, we will create a specific Facebook page for our business
     through its "Facebook Pages" application. This page will be used to promote who
     we are and what we do. We will use this page to post alerts when we have new
     articles to distribute, news to announce, etc. Facebook members can then become
     fans of our page and receive these updates on their newsfeed as we post them.
     We will create our business page by going to the "Advertising" link on the bottom
     of our personal Facebook page. We will choose the "Pages" tab at the top of that
     page, and then choose "Create a Page." We will upload our logo, enter our
     company profile details, and establish our settings. Once completed, we will click
     the "publish your site" button to go live. We will also promote our Page
     everywhere we can. We will add a Facebook link to our website, our email
     signatures, and email newsletters. We will also add Facebook to the marketing
     mix by deploying pay-per-click ads through their advertising application. With
     Facebook advertising, we will target by specifying sex, age, relationship, location,
     education, as well as specific keywords. Once we specify our target criteria, the
     tool will tell us how many members in the network meet our target needs.

13. Blog to share our success stories and solicit comments
     Blogging will be a great way for us to share information, expertise, and news, and
     start a conversation with our customers, the media, suppliers, and any other target
     audiences. Blogging will be a great online marketing strategy because it keeps our
     content fresh, engages our audience to leave comments on specific posts,
     improves search engine rankings and attracts links. In the blog we will share fun
     drink recipes and party tips. We will also provide a link to our Facebook.com
     page.   Resources: www.blogger.com   www.wordpress.com

14. Other Embedded Links
     We will use social networking, article directory postings and press release web
     sites as promotional tools and to provide good inbound link opportunities.

15. Issue Press Releases
     We will create online press releases to share news about our new website.
     Resources: Sites that offer free press release services include:
              www.1888pressrelease.com and www.pr.com/press-releases.

7.2 Development Requirements

A full development plan will be generated as documented in the milestones. Costs that _____ (company name) will expect to incur with development of its new website include:

Development Costs

User interface design	$_____.
Site development and testing	$_____
Site Implementation	$._____

Ongoing Costs

Website name registration	$_____ per year.
Site Hosting	$_____ or less per month.

Site design changes, updates and maintenance are considered part of Marketing.

The site will be developed by _____ (company name), a local start-up company. The user interface designer will use our existing graphic art to come up with the website logo and graphics. We have already secured hosting with a local provider, _____ (business name). Additionally, they will prepare a monthly statistical usage report to analyze and improve web usage and return on investment.

The plan is for the website to be live by ____(date). Basic website maintenance, including update and data entry will be handled by our staff. Site content, such as images and text will be maintained by _____ (owner name). In the future, we may need to contract with a technical resource to build the trackable article download and newsletter capabilities.

Resources: www.webs.com   www.1and1.com
Model: http://mayflowerbrewing.com/

7.3   Sample Frequently Asked Questions

We will use the following guidelines when developing the frequently asked questions for the ecommerce section of the website:

1. Use a Table of Contents: Offer subject headers at the top of the FAQ page with a hyperlink to that related section further down on the page for quick access.
2. Group Questions in a Logical Way and group separate specific questions related to a subject together.
3. Be Precise with the Question: Don't use open-ended questions.
4. Avoid Too Many Questions: Publish only the popular questions and answers.
5. Answer the Question with a direct answer.
6. Link to Resources When Available: via hyperlinks so the customer can continue with self-service support.
7. Use Bullet Points to list step-by-step instructions.
8. Focus on Customer Support and Not Marketing.
9. Use Real and Relevant Frequently Asked Questions from actual customers.

10.   Update Your FAQ Page as customers continue to communicate questions.

The following frequently asked questions will enable us to convey a lot of important information to our clients in a condensed format. We will post these questions and answers on our website and create a hardcopy version to be included on our sales presentation folder.

Can you sell me some beer?
We sell beer only to our distributors (except for _____ (brand name)) available at the brewery for $____ / ___ oz. bottle).

Where can I buy your beer?
We are all over _____ (state) and _____ (state); the _____ (city), ___ (state) tri-city area; and ____ (city), _____ (state). We also distribute our beer in parts of ___ (state), and _____ (state). Please click on the distributor tab on this website for a detailed listing of our distributors and the territories they cover. Contact them for information on retail outlets that carry our brand. We are sold in all kinds of places - from fine dining restaurants to bowling allies.

Can I take a tour of your brewery?
Yes! We offer tours every weekday at 4 p.m. (We are closed on weekends and holidays.)

Where is your brewery located?
_____ (address)

How should I store your beer?
Beer should be stored in a cool place. In warmer climates this often means refrigeration and you get used to letting your beer warm a little before you drink it. Cooler climates often use cellars to store beer which works quite well. As long as temperatures are kept between 35F(2C) and 60F(15C) you're probably OK. Keep in mind that storing at the warmer end of this scale will increase any aging effects since any yeast remaining in the beer will be more active. This is a Good Thing if you're aging a barley but will cause lower gravity beers to go "stale" sooner.

Why does micro-brewed beer need to be kept refrigerated?
Like milk, microbrew is alive. As it sits around it changes. The changes can lead to off-tastes, bad flavors, cloudiness and color changes. If kept cold (below 40 degrees F), the changes are drastically slowed down. After you purchase your beer, be sure to put it in your refrigerator as soon as possible to preserve its fresh taste.

Do you offer gift cards?
Yes, we offer a variety of gift cards in our microbrewery.

Do you deliver or do mail orders?
Sorry, at this time we do not handle deliveries or mail orders.

Do you make suggestions on beer and food pairings?

Yes, we are trained to do beer and food pairings. We work closely with local chefs that offer catering and provide them with informed decisions on how to properly pair food and beer. We also handle beer tastings, and our staff includes former chefs with great insight on proper pairings.

Do you help with party and or/reception planning?
Yes, we offer a variety of event related services, please contact us for more information.

Do you offer beer gift baskets?
We make custom order gift baskets throughout the year. During the holidays we ask that you give at least 72-hours notice, due to the large quantity of baskets made during that time of year.

Is there a discount for bulk purchases of beer?
Yes, we offer a 10% discount on full cases of beer, excluding beers that are already offered at a discount price.

What does "microbrewed" mean?
Microbrewed beer is made in small quantities at small breweries and is usually only available from the local brewery where it was made. Almost all are all-natural without additives or preservatives.

What's the difference between lager and ale?
Technically the difference is in the yeasts used for fermentation, speed and temperature of fermentation, aging, and strength of the hops. Lager is more difficult, time consuming and expensive to produce than ale. Generally speaking, most lager is lighter, in body and alcoholic content, than ale. Some find it crispier, cleaner and more angular.

What makes your Lager special?
The source of the water for our Lager is an artesian well near the brewery. That spring water has chemical qualities similar to Austrian spring water and is considered perfect for the brewing of European style lager. In addition, our Brewmaster, _____ (name) has collected a treasury of traditional brewing know-how in his travels to small local producers in Germany and Austria.

What makes your process different from others?
There are many things we do differently. We use high quality German barley and whole flower German hops. Common brewing process is called infusion mashing, which is hydrating the malt at one temperature to convert starch to sugar. We employ a process called decoction. This is where the malt is hydrated at a certain temperature, then slowly raised during a series or temp rises and rests. We then transfer 3/4 of the mash to the Lauter tun and boil the remaining portion of mash. Then mix this boiled portion with the rest of the mash. This creates flavor compounds that are not able to be replicated in the single infusion method. This is very difficult, time consuming, and presents a wide array of variables which most brewers would rather avoid.

7.4 Website Performance Summary

We will use web analysis tools to monitor web traffic, such as identifying the number of site visits. We will analyze customer transactions and take actions to minimize problems, such as incomplete sales and abandoned shopping carts. We will use the following table to track the performance of our website:

Category	2018		2019		2020	
	Fcst	Act	Fcst	Act	Fcst	Act
No. of Customers						
New Subscribers						
Unique Visitors						
Total Page Views						
Bounce Rate						
Avg. Time on Site						
Page Views / Visit						
No. of Products						
Product Categories						
Number of Incomplete Sales						
Conversion Rate						
Affiliate Sales						
Customer Satisfaction Score						

7.5 Website Retargeting/Remarketing

Research indicates that for most websites, only 2% of web traffic converts readers on the first visit. Retargeting will keep track of people who have visited our website and displays our ads to them as they browse online. This will bring back 98% of users who don't convert right away by keeping our brand at the top of their mind. Setting up a remarketing tracking code on our website will allow us to target past visitors who did not convert or take the desired action on our site. After people have been to our website and are familiar with our brand, we will market more aggressively to this 'warm traffic.'

Resource:
www.marketing360.com/remarketing-software-retargeting-ads/

8.0   Operations Plan

Operations include the business aspects of running our business, such as conducting quality assessment and improvement activities, auditing functions, cost-management analysis, and customer service.

Operations Planning

We will use Microsoft Visio to develop visual maps, which will piece together the different activities in our organization and show how they contribute to the overall "value stream" of our business. We will rightfully treat operations as the lifeblood of our business. We will develop a combined sales and operations planning process where sales and operations managers will sit down every month to review sales, at the same time creating a forward-looking 12-month rolling plan to help guide the product development and manufacturing processes, which can become disconnected from sales. We will approach our operations planning using a three-step process that analyzes the company's current state, future state and the initiatives it will tackle next. For each initiative, such as launching a new product or service, the company will examine the related financials, talent and operational needs, as well as target customer profiles. Our management team will map out the cost of development and then calculate forecasted return on investment and revenue predictions.

Our operations plan will present an overview of the flow of the daily activities of the business and the strategies that support them. It will focus on the following critical operating factors that will make the business a success:

1.   We will enjoy the following advantages in the sourcing of our inventory:

        _____

2.   We will utilize the following technological innovations in the customer relationship management (CRM) process:

        _____

3.   We will make use of the following advantages in our distribution process:

        _____

4.   We will develop the following in-house training program to improve worker productivity: _____

5.   We will utilize the following system to better control inventory carrying costs.

        _____

6.   We will implement the following quality control plan:

        _____

Quality Control Plan

Quality Assurance of batches will be established with the following four QA departments:
1.   Microbiology
2.   Brewing Chemistry
3.   Sensory Evaluation
4.   Package Quality and Integrity

Our Quality Control Plan will include a review process that checks all factors involved in our operations. The main objectives of our quality control plan will be to uncover defects and bottlenecks, and reporting to management level to make the decisions on the improvement of the whole production process. Our review process will include the following activities:

Quality control checklist
Finished product review
Structured walkthroughs
Statistical sampling
Testing process

We will look at the following critical points in operational management during our microbrewery set up:

1. Manpower requirements, like operator, staff, brew master, etc.
2. Hiring, screening and training programs.
3. Performance and acceptance testing.
4. OSHA safety equipment, assessments, checks, audits and procedures.
5. Trial brew evaluations with limited production volumes.
6. Repeated product testing and re-formulating of recipes.
7. Performance evaluation of the entire brew process and report.
8. Trouble shooting, corrections, and modification processes.
9. Monitoring the operation of plant, process and production.
10. Facilities and equipment maintenance procedures, scheduling and checklists.
11. Inventory and production controls.
12. Operation accounting procedures.
13. Final acceptance standards and sign-offs.

Production will take place in the brewhouse of the microbrewery. Malt barley, hops, yeast, and water will be used to create most of the ales and lagers from scratch. The brewmaster will exercise strict standards of sanitation, quality production, and presentation or packaging over the brewery and service staff. The older way of beer making will apply to certain of our products, such as; brewing in smaller batches, forgoing filtration and pasteurization to produce beers that retain more of the flavor and character imparted by yeast during fermentation. Products will constantly be tested for our own high standards of purity. The business will produce less than 15,000 barrels per year in order to maintain its status as a microbrewery.

The beer will be produced in a ___ (15?) barrel brewhouse supplied by _____.
The various operations of the brewhouse are described as follows:

1. Mix the cracked malted barley with hot water in the mash/lauter tun, which produces "mash." The mash tun is a double-walled vessel crafted from polished stainless steel with fiberglass insulation and a top double door. A side manway makes grain removal easy. Standard features include a vee wire screen, complete drainage, a temperature well and sparging fittings.
2. A sweet, clear liquid called "wort" is filtered out of the mash and transferred to the brewkettle. The brewkettle is constructed similarly to the mash tun, featuring double-wall stainless steel with fiberglass insulation.

3. The wort in the kettle is brought to a rolling boil and some hops are added early to provide a mild bitterness. Other hops (finishing hops) are added later to give a fine aroma.

4. The hot wort is cooled to fermentation temperature through a heat exchanger. The heat removed from the wort is transferred to water, which is stored in a large tank called a hot liquor tank. This hot water is used constantly over and over again, either in cleaning, sterilization, or to fill the mash tun.

5. The cold wort is transferred to the fermenter.

6. Yeast is added, and fermentation begins. Fermenters are also known as uni-tanks. The fermenters we will use are double-wall stainless steel with dished heads and conical bottoms. The cooling jacket has automatic temperature control. The uni-tanks have sample ports as well as temperature controls, a pressure manifold, and adjustable legs.

7. During fermentation the brewers' yeast transforms the sweet wort into a flavorful solution containing alcohol and carbon dioxide.

8. After fermentation, the green beer is aged to develop its final smooth taste.

9. After the beer is aged properly, about ___ (14?) days, it is filtered to remove yeast and to clarify the beer.

10. After filtration the finished beer is stored in a bright beer tank (serving tank or tax tank) until it is ready to be served, bottled, or kegged. At this point the beer is at the height of its freshness and full of flavor.

Resource:
http://morebeer.com/brewingtechniques/index.html

Lagering/Cold Storage

The cold storage area will consist of single shell tanks contained in a walk-in cooler. The beer will be held here before moving on to the taps or the packaging area. These vessels need to maintain a temperature of 34 degrees F to 36 degrees F. The cold storage area will be located close to both the fermentation area and the bar area to allow for efficient transfer and dispense of product. In the case of brewpubs, the tanks will be connected directly to the tap (draft) lines by way of a beer python. This area will also require a CO_2 source, with an individual secondary regulator for each tank.

We will open accounts with liquor distributors in our state. Every state has liquor wholesalers who warehouse and sell alcohol to businesses that hold a liquor license. We will obtain a complete list of these companies from the Alcoholic Beverage Control Board or the equivalent office in our state.

Control Costs

We will implement the following cost of goods profit controls and manage them consistently to have a profound impact on the profitability of the business.

1. **Systematize Ordering** This means that the operation has an organized practice of procuring products each day. Components of that system include order guides, par levels, count sheets, inventory counts, a manager in charge of all procurement and a prime vendor relationship to reduce price and product fluctuations.

2. **Check It In.** We will assign a teammate to check in every product that comes through the door using an organized process of time and date specific delivery windows. We will not only check product count but also vigorously demand and inspect the consistency of product quality and product price.

3. **Store it well.** We will manage against profit erosion through theft, spoilage and other mishandling issues. We will ensure that each product has a specific home, that each product is labeled, that products are stored using the first-in, first-out storage method to ensure quality rotation and that products are locked and put away until they are needed.

4. **Standardize.** We will create process standards that can be duplicated through consistent training and management of staff members.

5. **Manage the Cash Flow**. We will follow a strict process whereby every item that is sold is accounted for and paid for by the end-user. We will carefully manage voided checks.

Recordkeeping

Our will engage in daily record keeping because not only does the TTB require a number of documents to be readily available at all times; state agencies expect the same. The following is a list of the records we will maintain for the TTB, because they could ask our business to produce them at a site visit:

1. Amounts and types of ingredients used.
2. Amount of beer produced.
3. Amount of beer transported for packaging or removed from brewery.
4. Beer used for laboratory samples.
5. Beer consumed at the brewery
6. Beer returned to the brewery
7. Beer received from other breweries
8. Beer lost due to breakage, theft, casualty, or otherwise
9. Ingredients sold or transferred to others as well as identification of others.
10. Record of tests of measuring devices
11. Flowmeter readings
12. Previously filed TTB & state reports
13. Beer purchased from or sold to other brewers

Source: http://www.dcbrewlaw.com/?p=245

The microbrewery will be run as a team, with each employee playing an integral part in the success or failure of the business. Employees will be given whatever tools and training is deemed necessary to carry out their assignments. An emphasis on process improvement will be instilled in each of the "teammates" by offering bonuses or special privileges. Teammates will be rewarded both monetarily and non-monetarily for jobs well done. Effective communication will be stressed in the business. This will cut down on misunderstandings and miscommunications among customers, employees, and managers. Weekly meetings will be held to discuss the weekly agenda, and to give a report of last week's happenings. Teammates will be given the opportunity to add input at these meetings in the form of suggestions, comments, and complaints. Teammates will have defined tasks but are to be open to doing whatever requests outside of their set guidelines need to be done to bring success to the business. Finally, we plan to offer perks to employees to keep them satisfied and willing to give the business 100 percent.

We will consolidate the number of suppliers we deal with to reduce the volume of paperwork and realize volume discounts. We will conduct a quality improvement plan, which consists of an ongoing process of improvement activities and includes periodic samplings of activities not initiated solely in response to an identified problem. Our plan will be evaluated annually and revised as necessary. Our client satisfaction survey goal is a ___ (98.0)% satisfaction rating.

We also plan to develop a list of specific interview questions and a worksheet to evaluate, compare and pre-screen potential suppliers. We will also check vendor references and their rating with the Hoovers.com.

We plan to write and maintain an Operations Manual and a Personnel Policies Handbook. The Operating Manual will be a comprehensive document outlining virtually every aspect of the business. The operating manual will include management and accounting procedures, hiring and personnel policies, and daily operations procedures, such as opening and closing the microbrewery, and how to _____. The manual will cover the following topics:

- Community Relations
- Media Relations
- Vendor Relations
- Competition Relations
- Environmental Concerns
- Intra Company Procedures
- Banking and Credit Cards
- Computer Procedures
- Quality Assurance Controls
- Microbrewery Open/Close Procedures
- Software Documentation
- Beer Recipes

- Customer Relations
- Employee Relations
- Government Relations
- Equipment Maintenance Checklist
- Water Purification
- Accounting and Billing
- Financing
- Scheduling Tips
- Safety Procedures
- Security Procedures
- Sanitation Procedures

We will also develop a personnel manual. Its purpose is to set fair and equal guidelines in print for all to abide. It's the playbook detailing specific policies, as well as enforcement, thereby preventing any misinterpretation, miscommunication or ill feelings. This manual will reflect only the concerns that affect our personnel. A companion policy and procedure manual will cover everything else. We plan to develop and install a computerized customer tracking system that will enable us to target customers who are likely to have an interest in a particular type of microbrewery promotional event.

Resource:

POS Solutions Plus	www.possolutionsplus.com
Performance POS	www.performancepos.com/
Brew Soft	www.brewsoft.net/
Quickbooks	www.intuit.com
Master Brewer's Toolbox	http://interactive.mbaa.com

9.0 Management Summary

The Management Plan will reveal who will be responsible for the various management functions to keep the business running efficiently. It will further demonstrate how that individual has the experience and/or training to accomplish each function. It will address who will do the planning function, the organizing function, the directing function, and the controlling function.

At the present time ____ (owner name) will run all operations for _____ (company name). _____ (His/Her) background in _____ (business management?) indicates an understanding of the importance of financial control systems. The microbrewery will be managed by _____ (name). ____ (He/She) will be in charge of production planning, purchasing, inventory control, quality control and accounts payable. _____ (name) has experience in all of the above areas through her working background in business. ____ (He/She) will be assisted by _____ (name). Sales will be handled by _____ (name), who has extensive management experience. ____ (name) has a B.S. degree in _____ from _____ University as well as a Masters Degree in Business Administration from _____ University. He is also a member of the Institute for Brewing Studies. The I.B.S. is an educational association for micro- and pub-brewers. He has attended the Siebel Institute of Technology's "Microbrewery and Pub Brewery Operations Course" This class was given in a working brewery for an entire week. Operations will be handled jointly by management and the brewmaster. The brewmaster will be hired in the near future. The person for the job will be a graduate from one of the nation's brewing schools who has worked under a Master Brewmaster for 2-4 years. Candidates are always available, as there are more brewers looking for work than there are openings. _____ (company name) will have the luxury of being very selective to identify the perfect candidate for the job. The brewhouse supplier has offered to assist in the interviewing process. Candidates are available through a resume service offered by the Institute for Brewing Studies and through trade journal advertising.

_____ (owner name) will be the owner and operations manager of _____ (company name). His/her general duties will include the following:
1.   Oversee the daily operations
2.   Ordering inventory and supplies.
3.   Develop and implementing the marketing strategy
4.   Purchasing equipment.
5.   Arranging for the routine maintenance and upkeep of the facility.
6.   Hiring, training and supervision of new assistants.
7.   Scheduling and planning of seminars and other special events.
8.   Creating and pricing products and services.
9.   Managing the accounting/financial aspect of the business.
10.   Contract negotiation/vendor relations.

9.1 Owner Personal History
The owner has been working in the _____ industry for over ____ (#) years, gaining

personal knowledge and experience in all phases of the industry. _____
(owner name) is the founder and operations manager of _____ (company name). The
owner holds a degree from the University of _____ at _____ (city).
He/she began his/her career as a _____ .

Over the last _ (#) years, ___ (owner name) became quite proficient in a wide range of
management activities and responsibilities, becoming an operations manager for ___
(former employer name) from __to _ (dates). There he/she was able to achieve _____.
For ____ years he/she has managed a business similar to _____ (company name).
_____ (His/her) duties included ____. Specifically, the owner brings _____ (#) years
of experience as a _____ , as well as certification as a _____ from the _____
(National _____ Association). He/she is an experienced entrepreneur with ____ years of
small business accounting, finance, marketing and management experience. Education
includes college course work in business administration, banking and finance,
investments, and commercial credit management. The owner will draw an annual salary
of $___ from the business although most of this goes to repay loans to finance business
start-up costs. These loans will be paid-in-full by _____ (month) of _____ (year).

9.2   Management Team Gaps

Despite the owner's and manager's experience in the _____ (?) industry, the company
will also retain the consulting services of _____ (consultant company name).
This company has over _____ (#) years of experience in the _____ industry and has
successfully opened dozens of Microbreweries across the country. The Consultants will
be primarily used for certification approval, market research, customer satisfaction
surveys and to provide additional input in the evaluation of new business opportunities.
The company also expects to retain the services of a local CPA to help the owner manage
cash flow. Additionally, the business will make use of the following advisory board to
provide support for strategic planning and human resource related issues.

The Board of Advisors will provide continuous mentoring support on business matters.
Expertise gaps in legal, tax, marketing and personnel will be covered by the Board of
Advisors. Most of the invitations will be extended in phone conversations, followed by a
letter and information about the company. None of the board members will be offered
compensation. In addition to listing the name of the advisory-board members on any
publication's masthead, we will include their names and quotes in advertising brochures
and direct-mail packages. Advisers will also assist in the editorial process by contributing
ideas for articles, suggesting writers and commenting on manuscripts.

The owner will also actively seek free business advice from SCORE, a national non-
profit organization with a local office. This is a group of retired executives and business
owners who donate their time to serve as business counselors to new business owners.

Advisory Resources Available to the Business Include:

	Name	Address	Phone
CPA/Accountant			

Attorney   _____

Insurance Broker   _____

Banker   _____

Business Consultant   _____

Wholesale Suppliers   _____

Trade Association   _____

Realtor   _____

SCORE.org   _____

Board of Directors   _____

Other   _____

9.2.1   Management Matrix

Name	Title	Credentials	Functions	Responsibilities

Management Team

The strength of the following management team derives from the combined expertise in both management and technical areas.

Name of Person	Position	Educational Background	Past Industry Experience	Other Companies Served

9.2.2   Outsourcing Matrix

Company Name	Functions	Responsibilities	Cost

9.3.0   Employee Requirements

1. **Recruitment**

   Experience suggests that personal referrals from contractors and distributor reps are an excellent source for experienced associates We will also place newspaper ads and use our Yellow Page Ad to indicate what types of staff we use and what types of customers we serve. We will also make effective use of our newsletter to post positions available and contact local trade schools for possible job candidates. We will give a referral bonus to existing employees.
   Resource:
   www.craftbeveragejobs.com/new-belgium-brewery-tips-for-craft-beer-job-seekers/
   www.brewbound.com/jobs
   www.brewersassociation.org/forums/forum/jobs/

2. **Training and Supervision**

Training will be given to new personnel in order to familiarize them with the beer brands in the microbrewery. In addition, sales opportunities will be lost unless the employees in the specialty microbrewery really do have superior knowledge about the products sold than those that work at discount houses. Employees will be trained, not only in their specific operational duties, including proper sanitation methods, but also in the philosophy and applications of our concept. They will receive extensive information from the brew master and be kept informed of the latest information on microbrewing. Training will largely be accomplished through hands-on experience and by supplier reps offering supplemental instruction. Additional knowledge will be gained through our Policy and Operations Manuals and attending trade association seminars. We will foster professional development and independence in all phases of our business. To help them succeed and confidently handle customer questions, employees will receive assistance with our internal certification program. They will participate in our written training modules and receive beer samples to evaluate.

3.   **Salaries and Benefits**
Staff will be basically paid a salary plus commission basis on product sales. Good training and incentives, such as cash bonuses handed out monthly to everyone for reaching goals, will serve to retain good employees. An employee discount of __ percent on personal sales is offered. As business warrants, we hope to put together a benefit package that includes insurance, and paid vacations. The personnel plan also assumes a 5% annual increase in salaries.

4.   **Employment Contacts**
We will h**ave our Brewer and Other Key Employees Sign Employment Agreements.** Key employees, who are integral to our success, will have written employment agreements that provide for a fixed term of employment. A covenant not to compete will also be included to deter a key employee from leaving to work for a competitor. Absent this type of agreement, the key employee can leave at any time. The master brewer employment agreement will include a covenant not to compete and provisions that clearly state that the beer formulas are "trade secrets" and thus the property of the brewery.
Source: http://growlermag.com/so-you-want-to-start-your-own-brewery/

9.4.0   Job Descriptions

Job Description -- Brewmaster
The amount of work required of a brewmaster mainly hinges on the work environment and amount of beer production required. In a large production facility, such as a commercial brewery, the position may involve more of a managerial role that involves overseeing those who do most of the hands-on work. At microbreweries, where the beer is produced in much smaller quantities, a brewmaster will usually have a much greater hands-on role throughout the process of making beer. The primary duty of the brewmaster is to ensure the quality of the beer brewed, which includes making sure

batches of the same beer are consistent. There are several steps to the process that must be followed to strict specifications. These begin with gathering the necessary ingredients, some of which must be handpicked by the brewer depending on the uniqueness of the beer. Unique ingredient possibilities are practically endless, but include malted grains, hops, yeast, woods, and fruits. What follows is a complicated process of mixing, boiling, cooling, storing and bottling all of the ingredients of the beer. A more involved brewmaster is present during most, if not all, of these steps. He or she must ensure that exact specifications are met regarding temperatures of mixtures and the various times they must be treated and left to rest. In a worst-case scenario, failure to follow proper protocol can lead to beer that is not good for consumption; this product must be disposed of, and the whole process must be started over from scratch. The most important consideration for a brewmaster is the cleanliness of the brewing equipment. Contamination, especially when the beer is cooled, will disrupt proper fermentation, rendering the batch useless. Improperly or impatiently brewed concoctions can also cause dangerous conditions, even leading to exploding beer bottles and other hazardous conditions. After brewing a batch of beer, a brewmaster must taste it. This is where their expertise really comes into play; they must be able to taste the smallest variation between batches, and ensure a unique brew has the flavors, colors, and other qualities that he or she had in mind. Beer tasting also may consist of garnering outside opinions of a product by allowing customers to test it. Brewmasters also network with other beer professionals for new ideas and business advice. Others are trainers and teachers in charge of showing beginners how to brew beer in both casual and professional atmospheres. Requirements to become a brewmaster vary by brewery, but generally involve years of experience. Some schools offer certifications that may help an aspiring brewer gain employment under an experienced brewmaster where he or she can start gaining the necessary experience to work independently.

Job Description -- Brewer

Responsibilities: Brewers select and check the malted barley or grain used in making a particular kind of beer, adding yeast, hops, water, and other ingredients. They monitor the fermentation process, operate a milling machine, and clean and repair tanks.

Education: A professional brewer's certificate earned after several months of training at one of the major training programs: Siebel Institute of Technology in Chicago; University of California, Davis; and the American Brewers Guild in Vermont, which offers distance learning.

Preferred background: An entry-level position on the bottling line can lead to a job as an assistant brewer.

Job Description— Microbrewery Manager

This position plans, organizes, and directs the operations of a Microbrewery. Incumbents monitor sales and inventory trends to forecast sales and maintain adequate stock levels. They order supplies, monitor and evaluate cost effectiveness and efficiency of microbrewery operations, prepare and balance daily reports and maintain and balance inventory records on a computerized point-of-sale system. Incumbents provide customer service and specialized information regarding beer products and laws, policies, and procedures governing liquor related issues. Incumbents utilize effective public relations to provide services to customers, respond to inquiries, handle complaints or resolve problems. This position is responsible for the efficient operations of the microbrewery. Incumbents determine staffing needs, prepare work schedules, establish and implement work procedures and priorities, and recommend changes to policies. They supervise staff including hiring and training employees, assigning work, preparing and conducting performance evaluations, and handling employee problem solving issues. The microbrewery manager must possess proven management skills, and the ability to drive sales in the microbrewery. Must have a passion for people development and delivering excellent customer service. Must be capable of delivering performance through their teams and drive customer service through high retail standards, availability and presentation.

Key Accountabilities:
Exceptional customer focus.
Excellent Interpersonal skills.
Effective planning and organizational skills.
Influencing and negotiation skills.
Budget management
Supportive and persuasive management style.
Tactical and strategic planning and implementation skills are a must.
Clear vision and a determination to succeed.

Job Description -- Assistant Manager
Assists in management of Microbrewery by performing the following duties:
1. Assist in planning and preparing work schedules and assignments of employees to specific duties.
2. Assists and supervises employees engaged in sales work, taking of inventories, reconciling cash with sales receipts, keeping operating records and preparing daily record of transactions or performs work of subordinates, as needed.
3. Ensures compliance of employees with established security, sales, and record keeping procedures and practices.
4. Orders merchandise or prepares requisitions to replenish merchandise on hand.
5. Ensures all reports, such as purchase, inventory and sales, are accurate and timely.
6. Monitors and verifies vendor activity in microbrewery.
7. Monitors and maintains proper microbrewery cleanliness, appearance and maintenance as per company guidelines.
8. Ensures all microbrewery employees are trained properly.
9. Coordinates sales promotion activities and prepares, or directs workers preparing, merchandise displays and advertising copy.
10. Maintains a customer service-oriented operation.
11. Performs all shift duties as required.
12. Able to perform daily duties of Microbrewery Manager in his/her absence.
13. Assists with overall operations improvement such as increasing customer base.
14. Assists in pricing adjustments, if necessary.

Job Description -- Marketing Director

Daily Duties, Functions, and Responsibilities:

1. Create authentic and original designs for retail, print, digital and brewery channels including but not limited to: point-of-sale materials, print and digital advertisements, brewery signs, beer labels and packaging, merchandise and social media content.
2. Collaborate with key stakeholders to brainstorm ideas and concepts that push our thinking and creative deliverables to new heights.
3. Ensure ideas and concepts align with marketing objectives and the our style guide.
4. Compile creative concepts for quarterly marketing campaigns and support kick-off meetings.
5. Design and illustration of approximately 6 new Beer labels annually.
6. Assist in the production of stylized photography and video assets to support storytelling.
7. Architect and implement the art gallery updates.
8. Participate in merchandise development meetings and contribute new ideas quarterly as well as assist with existing needs.
9. Contribute interior design, graphic and styling ideas to ongoing brewery projects and experiential ventures.
10. Find new sales opportunities by keeping a finger on the pulse of the craft beer industry as well as relevant lifestyle and design trends.

Job Description -- Sales Associate

Provides quality customer service to our customers. Must be able to fulfill all responsibilities listed below when necessary. Maximizes sales through excellent customer service. Requirements: Provides friendly, courteous, and prompt customer service. Completes proper packaging of all special orders. Conducts proper and safe use of all equipment. Proper stocking, pricing/labeling, and rotation of food items. Maintains proper case merchandising and allocation. Ability to safely operate all equipment. Ability to reach, stoop, bend, and lift as needed to stock or pull product for processing. Ability to withstand a cold working environment (45° F or less) for long periods of time. Ability to weigh, price, label, organize, rotate and identify all varieties of products carried by microbrewery. Other duties and responsibilities may be added to meet business demands.

Job Description -- Stocking Clerk

Processes sales of Microbrewery items. Maintains appearance of microbrewery and shelf stock for optimal retail and assists management with the maintenance of inventory. Works cooperatively with others and accepts direction from supervisors.
Requirements:
1. Stocks shelves and coolers/merchandise for optimal retail.
2. Processes sales of grocery and like items.
3. Cheerfully greets and interacts with customers and vendors.
4. Cleans and maintains microbrewery area before, during and at the end of shift (includes sweeping and mopping).
5. Effectively interacts with Manager, fellow employees, and student staff.
6. Monitors customer flow to lessen the potential of theft.

7. Helps count microbrewery inventory and enters arriving stock into POS system.
8. Assists in maintaining product database, updating product information such as new items, UPC codes, product costs and other data from vendor invoices.

Job Description -- Taproom Manager
Pour beers and uses people skills to develop relationships with end-consumers who visit the taproom and works to increase brand awareness.

Job Description -- Events Producer
An experienced event planner to help create and run an national events program, focused on highlighting The Brewery's leading portfolio and its place in the marketplace.
DUTIES
Plan & Execute original, recurring events throughout Brewery's distribution territory.
Make pre-event market visits
Work closely with Brewery's reps, distributors and customers
Work with Marketing Director to create new programming & identify production partners
Maintain partner relationships
On-site management during each event
Deliver reports and recaps following each event
Ability to travel throughout the year
REQUIREMENTS
3 years of event planning experience
Wide knowledge of the food and beverage industry
Passion for beer and food
Appreciation for our brand and its place in the industry
Ability to maintain a budget
Can work independently with the needs of the brand and individual markets in mind
Good food and beverage contacts and relationships
Ability to generate original event concepts

9.4.1   Job Description Format
Our job descriptions will adhere to the following format guidelines:

1.	Job Title	2.	Reports to:
3.	Pay Rate	4.	Job Responsibilities
5.	Travel Requirements	5.	Supervisory Responsibilities
6.	Qualifications	7.	Work Experience
8.	Required Skills	10.	Salary Range
11.	Benefits	12.	Opportunities

9.5   Personnel Plan
1. We will develop a system for recruiting, screening and interviewing employees.
2. Background checks will be performed as well as reference checks and drug tests.
3. We will develop an assistant training course.

4. We will keep track of staff scheduling.
5. We will develop client satisfaction surveys to provide feedback and ideas.
6. We will develop and perform semi-annual employee evaluations.
7. We will "coach" all our employees to improve their abilities and range of skills.
8. We will employ temporary employees via a local staffing agency to assist with one-time special projects.
9. Each employee will be provided an Employee Handbook, which will include detailed job descriptions and list of business policies, and be asked to sign these documents as a form of employment contract.
10. Incentives will be offered for reaching quarterly financial and enrollment goals, completing the probationary period and passing county inspections.
11. Customer service awards will be presented to those employees who best exemplify our stated mission and exceed customer expectations.

Our Employee Handbook will include the following sections:
1. Overview
2. Introduction to the Company
3. Organizational Structure
4. Employment and Hiring Policies
5. Performance Evaluation and Promotion Policies
6. Compensation Policies
7. Time Off Policies
8. Training Programs and Reimbursement Policies
9. General Rules and Policies
10. Termination Policies.

9.6 Staffing Plan

The following table summarizes our personnel expenditures for the first three years, with compensation costs increasing from $_____ in the first year to about $_____ in the third year, based on ____ (5?) % payroll increases each year. The payroll includes tuition reimbursement, pay increases, vacation pay, bonuses and state required certifications.
Resource: www.salary.com

Table: Personnel Plan

	Number of Employees	Hourly Rate	Annual Salaries 2018	2019	2020
Owner/Director					
General Manager					
Brewmaster					
Taproom Manager					
Operations Manager					
Assistant Managers					
Sales Associates					

Bottling Staff _____
Bottling & Shipping Manager _____
Shipping Staff _____
Marketing Director _____
Sales Manager _____
Bookkeeper _____
Janitor _____
Other _____

Total People: Headcount _____
Total Annual Payroll _____
Payroll Burden (Fringe Benefits)   (+) _____
Total Payroll Expense   (=) _____

Note: The typical brewmaster salary ranges from $25,000 at a local brew pub to more than $100,000 at a larger national brewery, says a source at a national brewers trade association. The average is in the $40,000 to $50,000 range with benefits.

10.0 Risk Factors

Risk management is the identification, assessment, and prioritization of risks, followed by the coordinated and economical application of resources to minimize, monitor, and control the probability and/or impact of unfortunate events or to maximize the realization of opportunities. For the most part, our risk management methods will consist of the following elements, performed, more or less, in the following order.

1. Identify, characterize, and assess threats
2. Assess the vulnerability of critical assets to specific threats
3. Determine the risk (i.e. the expected consequences of specific types of attacks on specific assets)
4. Identify ways to reduce those risks
5. Prioritize risk reduction measures based on a strategy

Types of Risks:

_____ (company name) faces the following kinds of risks:

1. **Financial Risks**

   Our quarterly revenues and operating results are difficult to predict and may fluctuate significantly from quarter to quarter as a result of a variety of factors. Among these factors are:
   - Changes in our own or competitors' pricing policies.
   - Recession pressures.
   - Fluctuations in expected revenues from advertisers, sponsors and strategic relationships.
   - Timing of costs related to acquisitions or payments.

2. **Legislative / Legal Landscape.**

   Our participation in the brewery arena presents unique risks:
   - Product and other related liability.
   - Federal and State regulations on licensing, privacy and insurance.

3. **Operational Risks**

   Deals with whether the business can set up internally to deliver goods to customers effectively. For product-related companies, this will include manufacturing and assembly of goods, which is often difficult to set up in terms of cost and quality control. Operational risk will also include logistical issues with delivery and returns and effective use of service staff.

   To attract and retain client to the _____ (company name) community, we must continue to provide differentiated and quality products. This confers certain risks including the failure to:
   - Anticipate and respond to changing consumer preferences and tastes.
   - Attract, excite and retain a large audience of customers to our community.
   - Create and maintain successful strategic alliances with quality partners.
   - Deliver high quality, customer service.
   - Build our brand rapidly and cost-effectively.
   - Compete effectively against better-established microbreweries.

4. **Market Risk**

A result of many factors, including whether the market is large enough to support our business, whether the market is growing, what trends exist in the industry, how the competition is structured, and how distribution works. If industry trends are moving away from our product or if potential customers are already locked up by competitors, it will be difficult to gain customer momentum.

5.   **Human Resource Risks**

The most serious human resource risk to our business, at least in the initial stages, would be my inability to operate the business due to illness or disability. The owner is currently in exceptional health and would eventually seek to replace himself on a day-to-day level by developing systems to support the growth of the business.

6.   **Marketing Risks**

Advertising is our most expensive form of promotion and there will be a period of testing headlines and offers to find the one that works the best. The risk, of course, is that we will exhaust our advertising budget before we find an ad that works. Placing greater emphases on sunk-cost marketing, such as our storefront and on existing relationships through direct selling will minimize our initial reliance on advertising to bring in a large percentage of business in the first year.

6.   **Business Risks**

A major risk to microbrewery businesses is the performance of the economy and the small business sector. Since economists are predicting this as the fastest growing sector of the economy, our risk of a downturn in the short-term is minimized. The entrance of one of the major breweries into our marketplace is a risk. They offer more of the latest equipment, provide a wider array of products and services, competitive prices and 24-hour service. This situation would force us to lower our prices in the short-term until we could develop an offering of higher margin, value-added services not provided by the large players. It does not seem likely that the relative size of our market today could support the overhead of one of those operations. Projections indicate that this will not be the case in the future and that leaves a window of opportunity for ___ (company name) to aggressively build a loyal client base. We will also not pursue big-leap, radical change misadventures, but rather strive to hit stepwise performance benchmarks, with a planned consistency over a long period of time.

We will also consider safety considerations involved in exposing the brewery to the public. In the case of the brewhouse it will be important that this room be under positive pressure to allow for proper evaporation during the boil as well as the need for makeup air in the case of direct fired kettles. From a visual standpoint, the brewing vessels will be orientated so that the front of the vessels and the stairs of the platform face the public. The back of the vessels will be aligned along a wall to allow the mechanical supplies to be supported. The equipment will be placed so that there is enough room to access all sides of the vessels for daily sanitation and occasional maintenance.

We will develop contingency plans to address the following types of problems:
1.   Equipment breakdowns
2.   Bacterial infections

3. Spoiled beer
4. Under-carbonated beer
5. Over-carbonated beer
6. Customer dirty beer lines
7. Theft of kegs
8. Inadequate production capacity.

To combat the usual start-up risks we will do the following:
1. Utilize our industry experience to quickly establish desired strategic relationships.
2. Pursue business outside of our immediate market area.
3. Diversify our range of product and service offerings.
4. Develop multiple distribution channels.
5. Monitor our competitor actions.
6. Stay in touch with our customers and suppliers.
7. Watch for trends which could potentially impact our business.
8. Continuously optimize and scrutinize all business processes.
9. Institute daily financial controls using Business Ratio Analysis.
10. Create pay-for-performance compensation and training programs to reduce employee turnover.

Further, to attract and retain customers the Company will need to continue to expand its market offerings, utilizing third party strategic relationships. This could lead to difficulties in the management of relationships, competition for specific services and products, and/or adverse market conditions affecting a particular partner.

The Company will take active steps to mitigate risks. In preparation of the Company's pricing, many factors will be considered. The Company will closely track the activities of all third parties and will hold monthly review meetings to resolve issues and review and update the terms associated with strategic alliances. Additionally, we will develop the following kinds of contingency plans:

Disaster Recovery Plan   Business Continuity Plan
Business Impact and Gap Analysis   Testing & Maintenance
Resource: http://www.preparemybusiness.org/

The Company will utilize marketing and advertising campaigns to promote brand identity and will coordinate all expectations with internal and third-party resources prior to release. This strategy should maximize customer satisfaction while minimizing potential costs associated with unplanned expenditures and quality control issues.

10.1   Business Risk Reduction Strategy

We plan to implement the following strategies to reduce our start-up business risk:
1. Implement our business plan based on go, no-go stage criteria.
2. Develop employee cross-training programs.
3. Regularly back-up all computer files/Install ant-virus software.
4. Arrange adequate insurance coverage with higher deductibles.

5. Develop a limited number of prototype samples.
6. Test market offerings to determine level of market demand and appropriate pricing strategy.
7. Thoroughly investigate and benchmark to competitor offerings.
8. Research similar franchised businesses for insights into successful prototype business/operations models.
9. Reduce operation risks and costs by flowcharting all structured systems & standardized manual processes.
10. Use market surveys to listen to customer needs and priorities.
11. Purchase used equipment to reduce capital outlays.
12. Use leasing to reduce financial risk.
13. Outsource manufacturing to job shops to reduce capital at risk.
14. Use subcontractors to limit fixed overhead salary expenses.
15. Ask manufacturers about profit sharing arrangements.
16. Pay advertisers with a percent of revenues generated.
17. Develop contingency plans for identified risks.
18. Set-up procedures to control employee theft.
19. Do criminal background checks on potential employees.
20. Take immediate action on delinquent accounts.
21. Only extend credit to established account with D&B rating
22. Get regular competitive bids from alternative suppliers.
23. Check that operating costs as a percent of rising sales are lower as a result of productivity improvements.
24. Request bulk rate pricing on fast moving supplies.
25. Don't tie up cash in slow moving inventory to qualify for bigger discounts.
26. Reduce financial risk by practicing cash flow policies.
27. Reduce hazard risk by installing safety procedures.
28. Use financial management ratios to monitor business vitals.
29. Make business decisions after brainstorming sessions.
30. Focus on the products with biggest return on investment.
31. Where possible, purchase off-the-shelf components.
32. Request manufacturer samples and assistance to build prototypes.
33. Design production facilities to be flexible and easy to change.
34. Develop a network of suppliers with outsourcing capabilities.
35. Analyze and shorten every cycle time, including product development.
36. Develop multiple sources for every important input.
37. Treat the business plan as a living document and update it frequently.
38. Conduct a SWOT analysis and use determined strengths to pursue opportunities.
39. Conduct regular customer satisfaction surveys to evaluate performance.

10.2   Reduce Customer Perceived Risk Tactics

We will utilize the following tactics to help reduce the new customer's perceived risk of starting to do business with our company.

Status

1. Publish a page of testimonials.

___

2. Secure Opinion Leader written endorsements. _____
3. Offer an Unconditional Satisfaction Money Back Guarantee. _____
4. Long-term Performance Guarantee (Financial Risk). _____
5. Guaranteed Buy Back (Obsolete time risk) _____
6. Offer free trials and samples. _____
7. Brand Image (consistent marketing image and performance) _____
8. Patents/Trademarks/Copyrights _____
9. Publish case studies _____
10. Share your expertise (Articles, Seminars, etc.) _____
11. Get recognized Certification _____
12. Conduct responsive customer service _____
13. Accept Installment Payments _____
14. Display product materials composition or ingredients. _____
15. Publish product test results. _____
16. Publish sales record milestones. _____
17. Foster word-of-mouth by offering an unexpected extra. _____
18. Distribute factual, pre-purchase info. _____
19. Reduce consumer search costs with online directories. _____
20. Reduce customer transaction costs. _____
21. Facilitate in-depth comparisons to alternative services. _____
22. Make available prior customer ratings and comments. _____
23. Provide customized info based on prior transactions. _____
24. Become a Better Business Bureau member. _____
25. Publish overall customer satisfaction survey results. _____
26. Offer plan options that match niche segment needs. _____
27. Require client sign-off before proceeding to next phase. _____
28. Document procedures for dispute resolution. _____
29. Offer the equivalent of open source code. _____
30. Stress your compatibility features (avoid lock-in fear). _____
31. Create detailed checklists & flowcharts to show processes _____
32. Publish a list of frequently asked questions/answers. _____
33. Create a community that enables clients to connect with
    each other and share common interests. _____
34. Inform customers as to your stay-in-touch methods. _____
35. Conduct and handover a detailed needs analysis worksheet. _____
36. Offer to pay all return shipping charges and/or refund all
    original shipping and handling fees. _____
37. Describe your product testing procedures prior to shipping. _____
38. Highlight your competitive advantages in all marketing materials. _____

11.0   Financial Plan

The over-all financial plan for growth allows for use of the significant cash flow generated by operations. We are basing projected sales on the market research, industry analysis and competitive environment. ___ (company name) expects a profit margin of over __ % starting with year one. By year two, that number should slowly increase as the law of diminishing costs takes hold, and the day-to-day activities of the business become less expensive. Sales are expected to grow at __% per year, and level off by year _____. Our financial statements will show consistent growth in earnings, which provides notice of the durability of our company's competitive advantage.

The initial investment in _____ (company name) will be provided by _____ (owner name) in the amount of $ _____. The owner will also seek a ___ (#) year bank loan in the amount of $ _____ to provide the remainder of the required initial funding. The funds will be used to renovate the space and to cover initial operating expenses. The owner financing will become a return on equity, paid in the form of dividends to the owner. We expect to finance steady growth through cash flow. The owners do not intend to take any profits out of the business until the long-term debt has been satisfied.

Our financial plan includes:
   Moderate growth rate with a steady cash flow.
   Investing residual profits into company expansion.
   Company expansion will be an option if sales projections are met.
   Marketing costs will remain below ___ (5?) % of sales.
   Repayment of our loan calculated at a high A.P.R. of ___ (10?) percent and at a
         5-year-payback on our $_____ loan.

11.1   Important Assumptions

Since this is a start-up operation, a steady increase in sales is forecast over three years, as consumer awareness and regular repeat business grows with a strong and consistent increase in the local population, from an initial _____ residents to about _____ residents upon completion. A solid business plan and the management skills and experience of the managing partners should be sufficient to orchestrate the necessary growth to make this a successful launch with steady increases in sales over the first three years.
Operating expenses are based on an assessment of operational needs for a microbrewery of this size. Observations of ____ (city) retail beer shop staffing, direct experience at _____ beer stores, and interviews with microbrewery owners and suppliers are the basis for these projections. Rent is based on negotiated lease agreement with the landlord. Other estimates are based on experience in operating a ___ (#) square foot _____ (city) storefront business, and on vendor quotes and estimates. Collection days should remain fairly short, given the substantial cash revenues, and standard credit card collection periods.

Financial Plan Assumptions

1. All operating costs are based on the management's research of similar operating companies.
2. Automated informational systems will reduce the staff requirements.
3. Developmental start-up costs are amortized over a five-year period.
4. Home office or other apartment expenses are not included.
5. Overhead and operations costs are calculated on an annual basis.
6. The founders' salary is based on a fixed monthly salary expense basis.
7. All fixed and variable labor costs are scheduled to rise annually at ___ (5?) percent.
8. All revenues are figured to rise annually at ____ (10?) percent.
9. Administrative and office expenses rise at an annual rate of 2.5 percent.
10. Operating costs increase at ____ (5) percent annually.
11. Loan amount interest rate at _____(10) percent.

Other Assumptions:

1. The economy will grow at a steady slow pace, without another major recession.
2. There will be no major changes in the industry, other than those discussed in the trends section of this document.
3. The State will not enact 'impact' legislation on our industry.
4. Sales are estimated at minimum to average values, while expenses are estimated at above average to maximum values.
5. Staffing and payroll expansions will be driven by increased sales.
6. Materials expenses will not increase dramatically over the next several years, but will grow at a rate that matches increasing consumption.
7. We assume access to equity capital and financing sufficient to maintain our financial plan as shown in the tables.
8. The amount of the financing needed from the bank will be approximately $_____ and this will be repaid over the next 10 years at $_____ per month.
9. We assume that the area will continue to grow at present rate of ___ % per year.
10. Interest rates and tax rates are based on conservative assumptions.

Revenue Assumptions:

	Year	Sales/Month	Growth Rate
1.			
2.			
3.			

Resource:
www.score.org/resources/business-plans-financial-statements-template-gallery

11.2   Break-even Analysis

Break-Even Analysis will be performed to determine the point at which revenue received equals the costs associated with generating the revenue. Break-even analysis calculates what is known as a margin of safety, the amount that revenues exceed the break-even point. This is the amount that revenues can fall while still staying above the break-even point. The two main purposes of using the break-even analysis for marketing is to (1) determine the minimum number of sales that is required to avoid a loss at a designated sales price and (2) it is an exercise tool so that you can tweak the sales price to determine the minimum volume of sales you can reasonably expect to sell in order to avoid a loss.

Definition: Break-Even Is the Volume Where All Fixed Expenses Are Covered.

Three important definitions used in break-even analysis are:
· **Variable Costs** (Expenses) are costs that change directly in proportion to changes in activity (volume), such as raw materials, labor and packaging.

· **Fixed Costs** (Expenses) are costs that remain constant (fixed) for a given time period despite wide fluctuations in activity (volume), such as rent, loan payments, insurance, payroll and utilities.

· **Unit Contribution Margin** is the difference between your product's unit selling price and its unit variable cost.
Unit Contribution Margin = Unit Sales Price - Unit Variable Cost

For the purposes of this breakeven analysis, the assumed fixed operating costs will be approximately $ _____ per month, as shown in the following table.

Averaged Monthly Fixed Costs:

Fixed Costs		Variable Costs	
Payroll	_____	Cost of Inventory Sold	_____
Rent	_____	Labor	_____
Insurance	_____	Supplies	_____
Utilities	_____	Direct Costs per Patient	_____
Security.	_____	Other	_____
Legal/Technical Help	_____		
Other	_____		
Total:	_____	Total	_____

A break-even analysis table has been completed on the basis of average costs/prices. With monthly fixed costs averaging $_____ , $_____ in average sales and $_____ in average variable costs, we need approximately $_____ in sales per month to break-even.

Based on our assumed ____ % variable cost, we estimate our breakeven sales volume at around $ _____ per month. We expect to reach that sales volume by our _____ month of operations. Our break-even analysis is shown in further detail in the following table.

Breakeven Formulas:

Break Even Units = Total Fixed Costs / (Unit Selling Price - Variable Unit Cost)

_____ = _____ / (_____ - _____)

BE Dollars = (Total Fixed Costs / (Unit Price – Variable Unit Costs))/ Unit Price

_____ = (_____ / (_____ - _____)) / _____

BE Sales = Annual Fixed Costs / (1- Unit Variable costs / Unit Sales Price)

_____ = _____ / (1 - _____ / _____)

Table: Break-even Analysis

Monthly Units Break-even	_____
Monthly Revenue Break-even	$ _____
Assumptions:	
Average Per-Unit Revenue	$ _____
Average Per-Unit Variable Cost	$ _____
Estimated monthly Fixed Cost	$ _____

Ways to Improve Breakeven Point:

1. Reduce Fixed Costs via Cost Controls
2. Raise unit sales prices.
3. Lower Variable Costs by improving employee productivity or getting lower competitive bids from suppliers.
4. Broaden product/service line to generate multiple revenue streams.

11.3　　Projected Profit and Loss

Pro forma income statements are an important tool for planning our future business operations. If the projections predict a downturn in profitability, we can make operational changes such as increasing prices or decreasing costs before these projections become reality.

Our monthly profit for the first year varies significantly, as we aggressively seek improvements and begin to implement our marketing plan. However, after the first ___ months, profitability should be established.
We predict advertising costs will go down in the next three years as word-of-mouth about our microbrewery gets out to the public and we are able to find what has worked well for us and concentrate on those advertising methods, and corporate affiliations generate sales without the need for extra advertising.

Our net profit/sales ratio will be low the first year. We expect this ratio to rise at least _____ (15?) percent the second year. Normally, a startup concern will operate with negative profits through the first two years. We will avoid that kind of operating loss on our second year by knowing our competitors and having a full understanding of our target markets.

Our projected profit and loss is indicated in the following table. From our research of the brewing industry, our annual projections are quite realistic and conservative, and we prefer this approach so that we can ensure an adequate cash flow.

Key P & L Formulas:
Gross Profit Margin = Total Sales Revenue - Cost of Goods Sold

Gross Margin % = (Total Sales Revenue - Cost of Goods Sold) / Total Sales Revenue
This number represents the proportion of each dollar of revenue that the company retains as gross profit.

EBITDA =Revenue - Expenses (exclude interest, taxes, depreciation & amortization)

PBIT = Profit (Earnings) Before Interest and Taxes = EBIT
A profitability measure that looks at a company's profits before the company has to pay corporate income tax and interest expenses. This measure deducts all operating expenses from revenue, but it leaves out the payment of interest and tax. Also referred to as "earnings before interest and tax ".

Net Profit = Total Sales Revenues - Total Expenses

Pro Forma Profit and Loss

	Formula	2018	2019	2020
Gross Revenue:				
Microbrew Sales				
Logo Product Sales				
Catering Services				
Consulting/Seminars				
Other Revenue				
Total Revenue	A			
Cost of Sales				
Cost of Goods Sold				
Other				
Total Costs of Sales	D			
Gross Margin	A-D=E			
Gross Margin %	E / A			
Operating Expenses:				
Payroll				
Payroll Taxes				
Sales & Marketing				
Conventions/Trade Shows				
Depreciation				
License/Permit Fees				
Dues and Subscriptions				
Rent				
Utilities				
Deposits				
Repairs and Maintenance				
Janitorial Supplies				
Office Supplies				
Leased Equipment				
Buildout Costs				
Insurance				
Van Expenses				
Professional Development				
Resource Library				
Merchant Fees				
Bad Debts				
Miscellaneous				
Total Operating Expenses	F			
Profit Before Int. & Taxes	E - F = G			
Interest Expenses	H			
Taxes Incurred	I			
Net Profit	G - H - I = J			
Net Profit / Sales	J / A = K			

11.4　Projected Cash Flow

The Cash Flow Statement shows how the company is paying for its operations and future growth, by detailing the "flow" of cash between the company and the outside world. Positive numbers represent cash flowing in, negative numbers represent cash flowing out. We are positioning ourselves in the market as a medium-risk concern with steady cash flows. Accounts payable is paid at the end of each month while sales are in cash and short-term credit card collectibles. Cash balances will be used to reduce outstanding line of credit balances or will be invested in a low-risk liquid money market fund to decrease the opportunity cost of cash held. Surplus cash balances during the critical first year of operations will function as protection against unforeseen changes in the timing of disbursements required to fund operations.

The first year's monthly cash flows are will vary significantly, but we do expect a solid cash balance from day one. We expect that the majority of our sales will be done in cash or by credit card and that will be good for our cash flow position. Additionally, we will stock only slightly more than one month's inventory at any time. Consequently, we do not anticipate any problems with cash flow, once we have obtained sufficient start-up funds.

A __ year commercial loan in the amount of $_____, sought by the owner will be used to cover our working capital requirement.   Our projected cash flow is summarized in the following table and is expected to meet our needs. In the following years, excess cash will be used to finance our growth plans.

Cash Flow Management:
We will use the following practices to improve our cash flow position:
1. Perform credit checks and become more selective when granting credit.
2. Seek deposits or multiple stage payments.
3. Reduce the amount/time of credit given to clients.
4. Reduce direct and indirect costs and overhead expenses.
5. Use the 80/20 rule to manage inventories, receivables and payables.
6. Invoice as soon as the project has been completed.
7. Generate regular reports on receivable ratios and aging.
8. Establish and adhere to sound credit practices.
9. Use more pro-active collection techniques.
10. Add late payment fees where possible.
11. Increase the credit taken from suppliers.
12. Negotiate purchase prices and extended credit terms from vendors.
13. Use some barter arrangements to acquire goods and service.
14. Use leasing to gain access to the use of productive assets.
15. Covert debt into equity.
16. Regularly update cash flow forecasts.
17. Defer projects which cannot achieve acceptable cash paybacks.
18. Require a 50% deposit upon the signing of the contract and the balance in full, due five days before the event.
19. Speed-up the completion of projects to get paid faster.

20. Ask for extended credit terms from major suppliers.
21. Put ideal bank balances into interest-bearing (sweep) accounts.
22. Charge interest on client installment payments.
23. Check the accuracy of invoices to avoid unnecessary rework delays.
24. Include stop-work clauses in contracts to address delinquent payments.
25. Speed up collection on receivables, either with incentives for early payment or by improving collections and invoicing earlier in the month.
26. Increase (speed up) your inventory turns per year.
27. Keep inventory at the minimum level necessary to sustain a given level of sales.
28. Reduce reliance on short-term borrowing to cover cash shortages will yield lower interest expense and increased profits.

Cash Flow Formulas:

Net Cash Flow = Incoming Cash Receipts - Outgoing Cash Payments

Equivalently, net profit plus amounts charged off for depreciation, depletion, and amortization. (also called cash flow).

Cash Balance = Opening Cash Balance + Net Cash Flow

We are positioning ourselves in the market as a medium risk concern with steady cash flows. Accounts payable is paid at the end of each month, while sales are in cash, giving our company an excellent cash structure.

Pro Forma Cash Flow

	Formula	2018	2019	2020
Cash Received				
Cash from Operations				
Cash Sales	A			
Cash from Receivables	B			
Subtotal Cash from Operations	A + B = C			
Additional Cash Received				
Non-Operating (Other) Income				
Sales Tax, VAT, HST/GST Received				
New Current Borrowing				
New Other Liabilities (interest fee)				
New Long-term Liabilities				
Sales of Other Current Assets				
Sales of Long-term Assets				
New Investment Received				
Total Additional Cash Received	D			
Subtotal Cash Received	C + D = E			
Expenditures				
Expenditures from Operations				
Cash Spending	F			
Payment of Accounts Payable	G			
Subtotal Spent on Operations	F+G = H			
Additional Cash Spent				
Non-Operating (Other) Expenses				
Sales Tax, VAT, HST/GST Paid Out				
Principal Repayment Current Borrowing				
Other Liabilities Principal Repayment				
Long-term Liabilities Principal Repayment				
Purchase Other Current Assets				
Dividends				
Total Additional Cash Spent	I			
Subtotal Cash Spent	H + I = J			
Net Cash Flow	**E - J = K**			
Cash Balance				

11.5   Projected Balance Sheet

Pro forma Balance Sheets are used to project how the business will be managing its assets in the future. As a pure start-up business, the opening balance sheet may contain no values.

As the business grows, our investment in inventory increases. This reflects sales volume increases and the commensurate ability to secure favorable volume discount terms with our distributors.

The projected accounts receivable position is relatively low and steady due to the nature of the business, in which up to 50% of our sales are cash, and the balance are consumer credit card purchases. No other consumer credit terms are envisioned or necessary for the operation of this business.

Capital assets of $_____ are comprised of a quoted $_____ for the build-out of the microbrewery (depreciating straight line over the 15-year term of the lease), $_____ for start-up costs (amortized over five years), and $_____ for the landlord's security deposit (about eight months rent).

Long-term liabilities are projected to decrease steadily, reflecting re-payment of the original seven-year term loan required to finance the business. It is important to note that part of the retained earnings may become a distribution of capital to the owners, while the balance would be reinvested in the business to replenish depreciated assets and to support further growth.

Note: The projected balance sheets must link back into the projected income statements and cash flow projections.

_____ (company name) does not project any real trouble meeting its debt obligations, provided the revenue predictions are met. We are very confident that we will meet or exceed all of our objectives in the Business Plan and produce a slow but steady increase in net worth.

All of our tables will be updated monthly to reflect past performance and future assumptions. Future assumptions will not be based on past performance but rather on economic cycle activity, regional industry strength, and future cash flow possibilities. We expect a solid growth in net worth by the year _____.

The Balance Sheet table for fiscal years 2018, 2019, and 2020 follows. It shows managed but sufficient growth of net worth, and a sufficiently healthy financial position.

Key Formulas:

Paid-in Capital = Capital contributed to the corporation by investors on top of the par value of the capital stock.

Retained Earnings = The portion of net income which is retained by the corporation and used to grow its net worth, rather than distributed to the owners as dividends.

Retained Earnings = After-tax net earnings - (Dividends + Stock Buybacks)

Earnings = Revenues - (Cost of Sales + Operating Expenses + Taxes)

Net Worth = Total Assets - Total Liabilities
Also known as 'Owner's Equity'.

Pro Forma Balance Sheet

	Formulas	2018	2019	2020
Assets				
Current Assets				
Cash				
Accounts Receivable				
Inventory				
Other Current Assets				
Total Current Assets	A			
Long-term Assets				
Long-term Assets	B			
Accumulated Depreciation	C			
Total Long-term Assets	B - C = D			
Total Assets	**A + D = E**			

Liabilities and Capital

	Formulas	2018	2019	2020
Current Liabilities				
Accounts Payable				
Current Borrowing				
Other Current Liabilities				
Subtotal Current Liabilities	**F**			
Long-term Liabilities				
Notes Payable				
Other Long-term Liabilities				
Subtotal Long-term Liabilities	**G**			
Total Liabilities	**F + G = H**			
Capital				
Paid-in Capital	I			
Retained Earnings	J			
Earnings	K			
Total Capital	I - J + K = L			
Total Liabilities and Capital	**H + L = M**			
Net Worth	**E - H = N**			

11.6 Business Ratios

The following financial ratios will be used to assist in determining the actual meaning of our financial statements and comparing the performance of similar businesses. The below table provides significant ratios for the brewing industry. Our comparisons to the SIC Industry profile are very favorable and we expect to maintain healthy ratios for profitability, risk and return. Use Business Ratio Formulas provided to assist in calculations.

Key Business Ratio Formulas:

EBIT = Earnings Before Interest and Taxes
EBITA = Earnings Before Interest, Taxes & Amortization. (Operating Profit Margin)

Sales Growth Rate =((Current Year Sales - Last Year Sales)/(Last Year Sales)) x 100
Ex: Percent of Sales = (Advertising Expense / Sales) x 100

Net Worth = Total Assets - Total Liabilities

Acid Test Ratio = Liquid Assets / Current Liabilities
Measures how much money business has immediately available. A ratio of 2:1 is good.

Net Profit Margin = Net Profit / Net Revenues
The higher the net profit margin is, the more effective the company is at converting revenue into actual profit.

Return on Equity (ROE) = Net Income / Shareholder's Equity
The ROE is useful for comparing the profitability of a company to that of other firms in the same industry. Also known as "return on net worth" (RONW).

Debt to Shareholder's Equity = Total Liabilities / Shareholder's Equity
A ratio below 0.80 indicates there is a good chance the company has a durable competitive advantage, with the exception of financial institutions, which are highly leveraged institutions.

Current Ratio = Current Assets / Current Liabilities
The higher the current ratio, the more capable the company is of paying its obligations. A ratio under 1 suggests that the company would be unable to pay off its obligations if they came due at that point.

Quick Ratio = Current Assets - Inventories / Current Liabilities
The quick ratio is more conservative than the current ratio, because it excludes inventory from current assets.

Pre-Tax Return on Net Worth = Pre-Tax Income / Net Worth
Indicates stockholders' earnings before taxes for each dollar of investment.

Pre-Tax Return on Assets = (EBIT / Assets) x 100
Indicates much profit the firm is generating from the use of its assets.

Accounts Receivable Turnover = Net Credit Sales / Average Accounts Receivable
A low ratio implies the company should re-assess its credit policies in order to ensure the timely collection of imparted credit that is not earning interest for the firm.

Net Working Capital = Current Assets - Current Liabilities
Positive working capital means that the company is able to pay off its short-term liabilities. Negative working capital means that a company currently is unable to meet its short-term liabilities with its current assets (cash, accounts receivable and inventory).

Interest Coverage Ratio = Earnings Before Interest & Taxes /Total Interest Expense
The lower the ratio, the more the company is burdened by debt expense. When a company's interest coverage ratio is 1.5 or lower, its ability to meet interest expenses may be questionable. An interest coverage ratio below 1 indicates the company is not generating sufficient revenues to satisfy interest expenses.

Collection Days = Accounts Receivables / (Revenues/365)
A high ratio indicates that the company is having problems getting paid for services.

Accounts Payable Turnover = Total Supplier Purchases/Average Accounts Payable
If the turnover ratio is falling from one period to another, this is a sign that the company is taking longer to pay off its suppliers than previously. The opposite is true when the turnover ratio is increasing, which means the firm is paying of suppliers at a faster rate.

Payment Days = (Accounts Payable Balance x 360) / (No. of Accounts Payable x 12)
The average number of days between receiving an invoice and paying it off.

Total Asset Turnover = Revenue / Assets
Asset turnover measures a firm's efficiency at using its assets in generating sales or revenue - the higher the number the better.

Sales / Net Worth = Total Sales / Net Worth

Dividend Payout = Dividends / Net Profit

Assets to Sales = Assets / Sales

Current Debt / Totals Assets = Current Liabilities / Total Assets

Current Liabilities to Liabilities = Current Liabilities / Total Liabilities

Business Ratio Analysis

	2018	2019	2020

Sales Growth

Percent of Total Assets
Accounts Receivable
Inventory
Other Current Assets
Total Current Assets
Long-term Assets
Total Assets

Current Liabilities
Long-term Liabilities
Total Liabilities
Net Worth

Percent of Sales
Sales
Gross Margin
Selling G& A Expenses
Advertising Expenses
Profit Before Interest & Taxes

Solvency (Main) Ratios
Current Ratio
Quick Ratio
Total Debt to Total Assets

Profitability Ratios
Pre-tax Return on Net Worth
Pre-tax Return on Assets
Net Profit Margin
Return on Equity

Efficiency (Activity) Ratios
Accounts Receivable Turnover
Collection Days
Inventory Turnover
Accounts Payable Turnover
Payment Days
Total Asset Turnover
Inventory Productivity
Sales per sq/ft.
Gross Margin Return on Inventory (GMROI)

Leverage (Debt) Ratios
Debt to Net Worth   _____
Current Liabilities to Liabilities   _____

Liquidity Ratios
Net Working Capital   _____
Interest Coverage   _____

Additional Ratios
Assets to Sales   _____
Current Debt / Total Assets   _____
Acid Test   _____
Sales / Net Worth   _____
Dividend Payout   _____

Business Vitality Profile
Sales per Employee   _____
Survival Rate   _____

12.0   Summary

_____ (company name) will be successful. This business plan has documented that the establishment of _____ (company name) is feasible. All of the critical factors, such as industry trends, marketing analysis, competitive analysis, management expertise and financial analysis support this conclusion.

Project Description: (Give a brief summary of the product, service or program.)
_____

Description of Favorable Industry and Market Conditions.
(Summarize why this business is viable.)
_____

Summary of Earnings Projections and Potential Return to Investors:
_____

Summary of Capital Requirements:
_____

Security for Investors & Loaning Institutions:
_____

Summary of expected benefits for people in the community beyond the immediate business concern:
_____

Means of Financing:
A. Loan Requirements: $_____
B. Owner's Contribution: $ $_____

C. Other Sources of Income: $_____
Total Funds Available: $_____

13.0   Potential Exit Scenarios

Two potential exit strategies exist for the investor:

1. **Initial Public Offering. (IPO)**
    We seek to go public within ____ (#) years of operations. The funds used will both help create liquidity for investors as well as allow for additional capital to develop our _____ (international/national?) roll out strategy.

2. **Acquisition Merger with Private or Public Company.**
    Our most desirable option for exit is a merger or buyout by a large corporation. We believe with substantial cash flows and a loyal customer base our company will be attractive to potential corporate investors within five years. Real value has been created through the novel combination of home health care services as well as partnering with key referral groups.

3. **Sale of the Business to a third party.**
    Microbreweries usually sell for approximately one to three times earnings given the financial strength of the business. In this event, the business would be sold by a business broker and the business loan sought in this plan would be repaid according to the covenants of the business loan agreement.

    Brew pubs are usually priced by taking 30% of gross revenues and averaging that with three times adjusted income. Example: The microbrewery, based on $_____ (60,000?) in expected ____ (year) earnings divided by a 35% industry risk factor, should sell for $_____ (171,000?).

APPENDIX

Purpose: Supporting documents used to enhance your business proposal.

Tax returns of principals for the last three years, if the plan is for new business

A personal financial statement, which should include life insurance and endowment policies, if applicable

A copy of the proposed lease or purchase agreement for building space, or zoning information for in-home businesses, with layouts, maps, and blueprints

A copy of licenses and other legal documents including partnership, association, or shareholders' agreements and copyrights, trademarks, and patents applications

A copy of résumés of all principals in a consistent format, if possible

Copies of letters of intent from suppliers, contracts, orders, and miscellaneous.

In the case of a franchised business, a copy of the franchise contract and all supporting documents provided by the franchisor

Newspaper clippings that support the business or the owner, including something about you, your achievements, business idea, or region

Promotional literature for your company or your competitors

Product/Service Brochures of your company or competitors

Photographs of your product. equipment, facilities, etc.

Market research to support the marketing section of the plan

Trade and industry publications when they support your intentions

Quotations or pro-forma invoices for capital items to be purchased, including a list of fixed assets, company vehicles, and proposed renovations

References/Letters of Recommendation

All insurance policies in place, both business and personal

Operation Schedules

Organizational Charts

Job Descriptions

Additional Financial Projections by Month

Customer Needs Analysis Worksheet

Sample Sales Letters

Copies of Software Management Reports

Copies of Standard Business Forms

Equipment List

Personal Survival Budget

Personal Financial Statement

With bank financing, every person who will have a 20% or more ownership position will need to provide a personal financial statement to show how effective they are at managing money. This statement will show assets (checking & savings accounts, IRA, 401K, valuables, home, vehicle, etc) as well as assets (mortgages, credit card bills, installment accounts, etc)

Helpful Resources:

Associations:

The Brewers Association — www.brewersassociation.org/

Professional organizations provide resources, consulting, and education to their members.

American Society of Brewing Chemists	612-454-7250
The Society of Independent Brewers (SIBA)	http://siba.co.uk/
Beer Institute	202-737-2337
Brewers Association of America	908-280-9153
Institute for Brewing Studies	303-447-0816
Master Brewers Association of the Americas	414-774-8558
The Distilled Spirits Council of the United States	http://www.discus.org
International Centre for Spirits and Liquors	http://www.ciedv.org
National Retail Federation	http://www.nrf.org
National Association of C-Stores	www.nacsonline.com
Alcohol and Tobacco Tax & Trade Bureau	www.ttb.gov/wine/control_board.shtml

Brewing Systems and Brewery Equipment

AAA Metal Fabrication	The Dalles, OR 97058	541-298-8313
Bavarian Brewing Technologies	Culver City, CA 90230	310-391-1091
Century Manufacturing	West Alexandria, OH 45381	513-839-4397
Criveller BrewTech	Lewiston, NY 14092	905-357-2930
DME Brewing Services	Charlottetown, PE	(902) 628-6900
Elliott Bay Fabricating, Inc.	Monroe, WA 98272	206-788-5297
IDD Process & Package, Inc.	Simi Valley, CA 93065	800-621-4144
JV NorthWest, Inc.	Wilsonville, OR 97070	503-682-2596
Newlands Services, Inc.	Sumas, WA 98295	604-855-4890
The Pub Brewing Co.	Mahwah, NJ 07430	201-512-0387
Specific Mechanical Systems	Saanichton, B.C. V8M 2A3	604-652-2111
VaFaC, Inc.	Fredericksburg, VA 22408	540-898-5425

Bottling Lines

Criveller Co.	Lewiston, NY 14092	905-357-2930
Krones, Inc.	Franklin, WI 53132	414-421-5650
Meheen Manufacturing	Pasco, WA 99301	509-547-7029
Prospero Equipment Co.	Pleasantville, NY	800-332-2219

Filtering Equipment

The Beverage Machine Co.	Arnold, MO 63010	800-292-4841
Criveller Co.	Lewiston, NY 14092	905-357-2930
Scott Laboratories, Inc.	Petaluma, CA 94975	707-765-6666
Schenk Filter Systems	Arold, MD 21012	410-647-4948

Chillers & Heat Exchangers

Laffranchi Wholesale	Ferndale, CA 95536	707-786-4853
Remcor Products	Glendale Heights, IL 60139	800-423-3477

Miscellaneous Equipment

Gamajet Cleaning Systems	Malvern, PA 19355	
Mettler Toledo, Inc.	Worthington, Ohio 43085	800-786-0038

Process Engineers	Hayward, CA 94545	510-782-5122
Sussman Electric Boilers	Long Island City, NY 11101	800-238-3535
Zahm & Nagel, Inc.	Buffalo, NY 14214	716-833-1532

Schools
Siebel Institute of Technology & World Brewing Academy

Malt

Briess Malting Co.	Chilton, WI 53014	414-849-7711
Brewmaster	San Leandro, CA 94577	800-288-8922
Crosby & Baker	Westport, MA 02790	800-999-2440
Great Western Malting Co.	Vancouver, WA 98668	206-693-3661
Liberty Malt Supply	Seattle, WA 98101	206-622-1880

Hops

Fromm, Mayer-Bass, Inc.	Yakima, WA 98907	800-FMB-HOPS
Hopsteiner	New York, NY 10021	212-838-8900
HopUnion	Yakima, WA 98909	509-457-3200
Morris Hanbury USA	Yakima, WA 98907	509-457-6699

Yeast

Scott Laboratories, Inc.	Petaluma, CA 94955	707-765-6666
Wyeast	Mt. Hood, OR 97041	503-354-1335
Yeast Culture Kit Co.	Ann Arbor, MI	800-742-2110

Bottles

Anchor Glass Container	Tampa. FL 33634	813-882-7756
Bavaria South	Manteo, NC 27954	800-896-5403
Owens-Brockway Glass	Toledo, OH 43666	708-933-4005

Kegs -

Sabco Industries	Toledo, OH 43615	419-531-5347
Spartanburg Stainless Products	Spartanburg, SC 29304	888.974.7500
Theilmann Container Systems	Alexandria, VA 22314	703-836-4003

Labels & Packaging

Inland Printing Co.	La Crosse, WI 54602	800-657-4413
Precision Printing & Packaging	Paris, TX 75460	800-450-1199
Standard Paper Box Corp.	Medina, WA 98039	206-454-6100
C.W. Zumbiel	Cincinatti, OH 45212	513-351-7050

Made in the USA
Lexington, KY
28 December 2018